JESUS CHRIST IN OUR WORLD

Religious Experience Series

Edward J. Malatesta, S.J., General Editor

Religious Experience Series
Volume 12

Jesus Christ
in Our World

by
Jacques Guillet, S.J.

Translated by Matthew J. O'Connell

ABBEY PRESS
St. Meinrad, Indiana 47577
1977

Jesus Christ in Our World is the English translation of *Jésus Christ dans notre monde,* which appeared in the collection Christus, Number 33, originally published by Desclée De Brouwer, Paris, France, and Bellarmin, Montreal, 1974.

Library of Congress Cataloging in Publication Data
Guillet, Jacques.
    Jesus Christ in our world.
    (Religious experience series; v. 12)
    Translation of Jésus-Christ dans notre monde.
    Includes bibliographical references.
    1. Jesus Christ—Person and offices. I. Title.
BT202.G8213   232   76-44371
ISBN 0-87029-129-7

© 1977 by Edward Malatesta, S.J.
Printed in the United States of America
Abbey Press
St. Meinrad, Indiana 47577

Preface

Eleven years ago the *Christus* series published a number of my articles as a book entitled *Jésus Christ hier et aujourd'hui* [*Jesus Christ Yesterday and Today*]. Almost all the articles had appeared in the periodical *Christus*. Their aim was to focus attention on some important characteristics of Jesus in the area of what might be called His spiritual outlook, and to discover in these characteristics the source and pattern of the Christian's experience. Not only is Jesus still today what He always was; the Christian too now is what Jesus once was and always is.

The present volume is a sequel to the earlier. It too reprints a series of articles, many of which appeared in *Christus*. The new series adopts the same general viewpoint as the old, and it seemed simple and logical to repeat the title of the earlier book, merely adding "New Series."

A different title has been adopted, however, and the choice of *Jesus Christ in Our World* has not been an arbitrary one. I can see as I reread pages written and published over the course of eleven years that my viewpoint has in fact shifted somewhat and that these essays are not quite like the earlier ones. Even those which are closest in character to the first series (they are grouped here in Part One, under the title "The Attitudes of Jesus") are more concerned with Jesus' relation to people and things. They deal less with Jesus living His life before the Father's eyes and more with Jesus living in our world, using its resources, engaged in its conflicts, exposed to the enmity of men, opening His heart to them in friendship and love, confronting suffering and death, and entering with men into the depths of pain. The reader may perhaps feel that my new focus of interest reflects the secularization that was so fashionable for a while. My horizons have, admittedly, broadened, but I hope I have not lost sight of the center.

This center is the subject of the second part of the book: "Who Is Jesus?" The encounter between Jesus and men necessarily forces us to ask some essential questions: Who is Jesus? How do we know Him? How does God reveal himself in Him? The questions are basic; indeed, they are at the very heart of the faith. They are questions that demand much thought for their answer, for, though faith is first and foremost life and action, it cannot do without understanding. The chapters of this second part are more theological than those of the first since the attempt is being made to understand as well as to see. At the same time, however, I have tried never to forget that the understanding of Christ and the commitment of faith require meditation on the Gospels.

In the third part, "Abiding Realities," we seem to move away from the Gospels. At least we are less close to the words and stories of the Gospel—though not less close, I hope, to their permanent center which is the person and ever-present reality of Jesus. Jesus is not only a personage upon Whom we gaze; He speaks today and draws men to follow Him. To gaze on Him is necessarily to listen to His word and to be open to His Spirit. Today as in the past, gazing on Jesus is a barren activity if it does not produce disciples who are able to bear witness in every age that the risen Lord is present in the world. Today, in our world.

I am grateful to the editors of *Christus* who have granted me permission to reprint texts published in the review, to Mr. Jacques Deschamel, who has accepted the book for publication by Desclée De Brouwer, and to Father Dominique Bertrand, S.J., who suggested the book and saw it through to its final form.

Jacques Guillet
Paris
October, 1974

Translator's Note

For Scriptural quotations, the New American Bible has been used, except for a few passages from the Jerusalem Bible. In the latter instances, JB has been added to the reference.

Matthew J. O'Connell

Contents

x

Part One
The Attitudes of Jesus

Chapter 1

Jesus Christ, True Man

Should a Christian make God or man the focus of his life? We must admit that he often has trouble these days in answering the question. Unbelievers urge him to abandon the hypocritical state his idea of God forces upon him by preventing him from dedicating himself to the service of man. As if that were not bad enough, many Christians and even priests in the pulpit were also telling him that the important thing is to struggle for the success of the human enterprise; only there will he find God, while he will be deluding himself as long as he looks for God elsewhere. The defenders of God's cause are outraged: "a betrayal of Christianity; a failure to acknowledge God's sovereign primacy!" Their sense of scandal is legitimate, even if not completely untainted and even if their aggressive attitude seems often to hint at a fear of losing the spiritual world that is their shelter. In order to rise superior to his instinctive reactions, whether rightist or leftist, in order to bring to light the passions or illusions that motivate him and to find not only a state of balance but, first and foremost, the truth of the matter, the Christian need only put his question to the Gospel. What answer will it give him?

The answer of the Gospel is not a completely simple one; it

is decisive, but it is also complex, sufficiently so, one might think, to provide justification for both sides in the argument. Even the Sermon on the Mount contains statements that seem at first sight not easily reconcilable: "Blest shall you be when men hate you" (Lk 6:22), since anything you do in order to attract men's notice will have no claim to a reward from God (Mt 6:1.5.7). Yet at the same time we are told that it is impossible to win pardon from God unless we pardon men (Mt 6:15), while the supreme norm, the one that sums up the Law and the Prophets, supposes that one very definitely adopts the viewpoint of men: "Treat others the way you would have them treat you" (Mt 7:12). Deliberately to pay no attention to men is to reject the Gospel; yet to want to please men is to renounce the service of Christ (Gal 1:10; cf. Jn 12:43)!

It is true enough, of course, that these various statements are not really irreconcilable, for it is one thing to dedicate one's life to the service of men and to try always to do what they may rightly expect of us, but another to seek their favor and the happiness they can offer. It must therefore be possible to live as one always dedicated to mankind, and yet to seek God alone. That is indeed the final word of the Gospel on the subject, as expressed in the indissoluble bond between the two great commandments which prescribe that we are to love men without reserve and yet love God above all else. But if this principle is easily expressed, it acquires its true significance and its full, exact meaning only as lived by Jesus Christ. If we are to give God and men their true place, and the full place that belongs to them, we must see precisely how Jesus Christ acted.

Jesus Christ is God and man: true God and true man. He is not alternately occupied with the Father and with men, sharing His attention between them; rather He is equally committed to both and offers the sacrifice of His life both for His friends (cf. Jn 15:13) and because "the world must know that I love the Father" (Jn 14:30). We cannot distinguish two parallel series of actions in Him, one proper to the man, the other to God. In each and every action, Jesus is present in His entirety, wholly God and wholly man. Whether He is raising a dead man or crying out that He is thirsty, whether He is forgiving sins or voicing His distress at being abandoned by His Father, it is always God who speaks and acts, but He does so at every point with the reactions of a fleshly human being and a human heart. But how, while existing as a man and possessing a consciousness like ours, did Jesus experience His twofold belonging and twofold consecration, to the Father and to mankind, to God and to man? What kind of man was God's only Son?

True Man

He was truly a man, a creature of flesh and blood. From the first disciples, those chosen witnesses who were aware that they must pass on to the rest of mankind what they themselves had heard and seen and touched (1 Jn 1:1), down to Pascal or Bernanos who saw "all human suffering . . . divinized . . . in the Garden of Gethsemani,"[1] the generations of Christians have never ceased contemplating the Saviour's manhood and the glory of the only Son as made visible in His flesh. From the first pictures of the Good Shepherd in the catacombs down to Georges Rouault's *Holy Face,* the Christian people has kept its eyes on the human face of its Saviour.

It is true enough that this gaze of Christians at Christ has not always been wholly objective. Some Christians, overly sentimental or their attention excessively concentrated on action, see in Him hardly anything more than the incomparable friend and superb master. But when Christ is stripped of His divine depth, or what St. John calls His "glory," He no longer elicits genuine adoration and loses His reality and coherence as a person. "Christ is my love for others," some will tell you; but that is not saying much for Him!

Deviations and blind spots such as these have always existed. Ever since He came on earth, Jesus has met with misunderstanding from men. Fear of being caught, disillusionment at the minimal visible results achieved, the deep-seated resistance of the hardened heart, the myopia of the specialist who cannot lift his eyes to broader horizons—all these prevent us from simply

looking at Jesus and seeing Him as He is. Yet if we concentrate on Him even briefly, we will see how strikingly real and
convincing is the picture of Him that every page of the Gospels
offers. It is the picture of a man who is extraordinary both for
His unparalleled actions and for His perfect naturalness. He is
very close to us yet always beyond us; ahead of us yet never
distant; overwhelmed by human suffering and spending His
life in receiving the sick and the weak, the physical and mental
outcast; sensitive to the least reserve shown Him and deeply
attached to disciples who were sometimes second-rate and always limited; serene and utterly lacking in self-deception;
strong for others, but, at the moment of His own suffering, almost paralyzed by fears and anxieties. His words and actions
are almost always unexpected, yet they come through to us as
the only proper response to the situation and as permanently
valid for similar situations. The person we see in the Gospels
cannot be explained away as a composite portrait painted by a
genius or as a legend which made a revered memory the focus
for the dreams and desires of the early Christians. He has the
coherence and individuality of a living man, a man of our own
race: one who is a continual surprise to us, yet whose every
trait is intelligible to us and bears the stamp of our humanity.

Some people nonetheless distrust the artificial psychologizing
which, in their view, is inseparable from excessive attention to
the humanity of Jesus. Unfortunately, we do have too many
presentations of Jesus that justify such distrust. At the very
least, we must grant that every century shows its limitations as
well as its insights in the way it thinks of the Lord. But the
limitations do not warrant our refusing in principle to attend
to the humanity of Jesus. Faith in Christ, after all, does not
mean simply confessing that He was and is a man; it also
means learning what manner of man He was, for His manhood
is the very face of God for us. The man Jesus, with His temperament and reactions, His way of looking at the world, and
His way of living among men, is the man whom God had been
foretelling for centuries, the man whom God had been preparing as a gift for His people and the whole human race. This

man is the Messiah of Israel and the Saviour of the world.

As Christians separated from Judaism, we tend to think that Jesus' role as Messiah is irrelevant to us and of importance only to the children of Israel. But such an attitude is seriously mistaken, since for us no less than for the Jews Jesus is the Messiah, that is, the man God had promised to His people. His very name tells us so, inasmuch as "Christ" is the Greek equivalent of the Hebrew "Messiah." To call Him Jesus Christ is to profess a faith that He is the one who is to come and for whom mankind is waiting, the man through whom God has decided to save the human race. If it is essential to our faith that Jesus be the Son of God, it is no less essential that He be the Christ, that is, not just one man among millions of others, but the man God gives us, the man whose every characteristic God shapes and whose every gesture God inspires.

Messiah of Israel and Son of Man

When Jesus makes Himself known in Israel, the decisive question is whether or not He is the Christ. All the Gospels are in explicit agreement on this point. Thus, His disciples follow Him because they recognize in Him the Messiah (Jn 1:41.45; Mk 8:29; Mt 16:16); men accept or reject Him according as they do or do not acknowledge Him to be the Messiah (Jn 4:26.28; 7:26.31; 10:24); the decisive question which the high priest asks Him as a way of deciding His fate is: "Are you the Messiah?" (Mt 26:63).

It is true enough that Jesus never answers this question with a formal and unqualified "Yes"; that He never accepts this title without careful reservations; and that when He does claim it before the Sanhedrin when His death is imminent, He adds a clarification, so that He is condemned for claiming to be a Christ who is both Son of Man and Son of God. The title "Christ," then, does not say fully what He is. But His reservations and qualifications do not mean that He rejects the title; and in fact He never simply refuses it. On the contrary, His care about the title shows that it is highly important to Him, so much so that men must be quite clear about what He and they are accepting when they use the title. Misunderstanding is possible, and if He does not clear it up, He will betray His mission.

What, then, is He telling them? He tells them that He is the Christ: that He must be acknowledged as such if He is to save his people, and that men must accept Him as the one God is sending them, the one through whom God will put an end to the rule of sin. But He also tells them that while He is the Christ whom God gives His people, He is hardly the kind of Christ they expected. Indeed, that is why He eventually dies: because He persists in claiming to be the Christ, the one sent by God, but refuses to act as they wanted Him to act. If He had agreed to multiply the loaves every day and put an end to death, the whole of His own people would have flocked to Him. If He had come down from the cross when death was imminent, his judges would have been ready to do a turnabout and applaud this magnificent feat, this proof that He was a mighty Messiah. Even if He had shown Himself publicly, after His resurrection, and proved Himself to be alive beyond a doubt, all Jerusalem with one voice would have acclaimed Him as its Messiah.

But such a turnabout would not have meant a real change in the world or any man's heart. The world is always ready to follow the stronger party. On Good Friday, the Sanhedrin was the stronger party; on Palm Sunday, it was Jesus—but a Jesus who was Jerusalem's idol and not the Messiah of God. To acknowledge Jesus as Messiah means to accept the face God chooses to show us; it means to be converted and to model our lives on the life of Jesus. That is the very first thing the new Church tells the world on Pentecost Sunday: "You must reform and be baptized, each one of you, in the name of Jesus Christ" (Acts 2:38).

The face the Messiah shows us is also the face both of the Son of Man and of the only Son of God. The qualifications and corrections which Jesus adds when He accepts the title of Messiah before the high priest and which the three synoptic Gos-

pels record, each in its own way, are extremely important.[2]
When Jesus says that He is the Son of Man foretold in Daniel
(7), He is bringing out two points: that, while He is the Son
of David and belongs to the royal Jewish line, His origin is in
fact higher and more mysterious; and that the name "Son of
Man" relates Him to the whole of mankind and establishes
Him as judge of man. When He claims to be the only Son,
He is telling us the secret of His being and His mission: that He
is the Christ of Israel because God was unable to touch His
people's heart through the servants He had sent them (namely,
the prophets) and therefore determined to send all that was
left to Him, that is, His beloved Son (Mk 12:6).

As long as we have not seen in Jesus the only Son of the
Father, equal to the Father and coming forth from Him, we
have not known Jesus, nor have we known the Father or the
Son. But neither do we know Jesus truly if we do not see in
this condemned man who is reduced to impotent silence the
king of Israel, the man for whom God created our race, and the
model for us as human beings. The one man who is fully and
authentically a man is the one Pilate brings out to the yelling
mob, before sending Him off to his death: "Look at the man!"
(Jn 19:5). To focus our attention on this man, to enter into
a genuinely human relationship with Him, and to become deeply attached to Him as a man—this is not an infantile or distorted form of Christianity. It is simply to accept the face
through which God reveals Himself; it is to accept Him as the
model of our lives; it is to be converted and be a Christian.

Son of Man

Jesus requires that we accept His humanness as normative
for ours. In so doing, does He intend as it were to do violence
to us and to save, even despite us, the image He has of us and
our human nature? By no means! Before being an ideal which
Jesus seeks to fulfill, our humanity is a value that already exists
before He comes into the world. Not only does He acknowledge
and accept it; He is Himself its fruit and its offspring. In Him,

as in every man, there are certain basic attitudes, convictions, and reactions which spring from the very depths of man's being and which no one thinks of justifying because they are so self-evident. These profound, elemental reactions reveal the personality.

In Jesus, the deepest and most spontaneous of these reactions is His attitude to His Father. Without His Father, existence itself is unthinkable to Him. A further reaction—less explicit because He does not have to call attention to it and because He inevitably shares it with us—is the interest and value mankind has for Him. The basic human reactions are not only legitimate in His eyes; they are also really basic, to the point that they are more important than the letter of the Law, and give us an understanding of the very reactions of God Himself. "Who among you, if he has a hundred sheep and loses one of them, does not leave the ninety-nine in the wasteland and follow the lost one until he finds it? And when he finds it, he puts it on his shoulders in jubilation" (Lk 15:4-5). "If one of you has a son or an ox and he falls into a pit, will he not immediately rescue him on the sabbath day?" (Lk 14:5). God is that way too; His reactions can be no different from those which arise spontaneously in any man, however evil the latter may be (Lk 11:13). It is perfectly right in Jesus' estimation that a vine-grower should worry about his crop, that a sick man should want to be cured, that a mother should weep over her son; it is right that a host whose guests have insulted him should be indignant and that a master should require service (Lk 17:7-10). None of these things are just cause for scandal.

These simply human reactions are not the whole of the Gospel, of course. The Gospel goes so far as to show us the Master kneeling before His disciples in order to wash their feet. This action inevitably stops us short, and we must make an effort to accept it. But far from separating Jesus from the rest of us men, it shows in a striking way the high value He sets on men. Even in its most startling paradoxes, the Gospel remains in profound continuity with the natural reactions of men. If a Christian is not to worry about what he is to eat or wear, the reason is not that food and clothing are unimportant or that a disciple of Christ is to condemn them. The reason is that, on the contrary, these things, important in men's eyes, are infinitely more important in God's sight. If God is concerned with such things when dealing with the birds or the flowers of the field, how much more when He turns to his children! This "how much more," which runs like a refrain through Jesus' discourses and is one of His favorite arguments (Mt 6:30; 7:11; 10:25; 12:12), is based on a truth that is immediately evident for Him: "How much more important man is!" The whole of His preaching and all the parables He uses to make us realize the reality of God's kingdom—the sower, the pearl merchant, the powerful prince, the unfortunate widow—show us that the humanity of Christ is not simply a set of exceptional endowments but first and foremost a direct and spontaneous sensitivity to all human problems and an infallible sense of the human condition.

It is true, then, that Jesus enters the human condition because He comes from on high and the whole of His life is traced out for Him by the Father and the Holy Spirit. It would be wrong, however, to think that this entry into our flesh is artificial on His part or that He feels out of His element in it. No, He comes "to his own,"[3] and if He is at home among us, the reason is not simply that everything belongs to Him because He created it. The reason is also that, being truly and fully a man, He does not take on His humanity at the last moment, as an actor might don his makeup just before going on stage and playing his part; He is, instead, truly born of our race. This means that He is heir to the slow ascent of the generations through the millennia of prehistory, fruit too of the encounter of civilizations at the crossroads where the East, Egypt, and Greece met, and supreme flower of the Jewish race, which the Spirit of God had fashioned.

His relationship to our humanity is twofold and, as it were, reciprocal. Without Him mankind has no coherence; its history is meaningless; it is destined to failure. Conversely, the human nature He takes to Himself has its own inherent value in His eyes before He unites it to Himself—it is worthy of God's respect and attention, and He becomes incarnate so that this value may not be lost. Without Jesus Christ, mankind has literally no value in God's sight; yet the value Christ confers upon mankind is truly ours and belongs to our flesh, our fields, our cities, our sufferings and successes. Péguy, who had such a profound grasp of the mystery of the Incarnation, has sung magnificently of this twofold aspect, this give-and-take between Jesus and mankind: "He was to be heir of the earth and of Rome, of the wine-dark sea and Zion's bitter taste. . . . . He was to inherit a world ready-made, and yet to remake it wholly new," for He has "primacy . . . in everything" (Col 1:18).

His attachment to His inheritance is, however, not that of a proprietor or a conqueror. It is that of a son who comes to save His mother. It is to Eve, His mother and ours that Jesus addresses His greeting of compassion and gratitude (in Péguy's *Eve*): "I love you so deeply, mother of our mother. . . . I greet you, first of women . . . ancestress with the long hair, mother of Our Lady." The poet's intuition here expresses the purest Catholic faith, for in defining the Incarnation the Catholic faith turns to the mystery of the Virgin Mary, the woman who truly gave God His human nature and whose virginal, sinless flesh was wholly penetrated by the Holy Spirit.

In confronting mankind which is His mother, the filial tender love of Jesus instinctively singles out the most profound and vulnerable area: simple, everyday life, with its suffering. He does not disdain our successes and says not a word of contempt for our masterpieces; but He is sensitive chiefly to their fragility. In the "enormous buildings" of the Jerusalem temple He sees hardly more than the pile of stones that will mark the place when catastrophe has struck (Mk 13:1-2). We might say that He sees chiefly the ridiculous limitations of human greatness: "Earthly kings lord it over their people" and "are called their benefactors" (Lk 22:25). But this clear-sighted irony does not spring from contempt, and He is the first to bear the burden of the disasters that strike us: "Coming within sight of the city [Jerusalem], he wept over it" (Lk 19:41). He knew the capital of His people was doomed, and the thought was ever before His mind. Yet, when He saw the proud city before Him, feelings were roused and the tears flowed.

Bernanos has written with great simplicity and an almost evangelical spirit of the Lord's love for our humanity:

> He has loved like a man, humanly, man's humble heritage, his poor fireside, his table, his bread, his wine—the gray roads golden in the shower, the villages with their smoke, the little houses hidden in the thorn hedges, the peace of the falling evening and the children playing on the doorstep. He has loved all that humanly, after the manner of men, but as no man has ever loved it before, would ever love it again. So purely, so intimately, with the heart he himself has made, just for that, with his own hands.[4]

The tender loving of Christ for our life at its humblest, His sensibility that was ever ready to sympathize and share our suffering, are a sign of something more than merely a finely attuned nature that had been prepared by centuries of suffering, faith, and compassion. They also point to the mystery of the redeeming God and the passionate concern of the Creator for man who is His child. The Greeks regarded it as beyond question that God is impassible and sovereignly indifferent to all that happens in the world. Against this view, Origen spoke of the true God's "passion," the passion of love:

> The Saviour came to earth out of pity for mankind. He experienced our passions before suffering the cross and even before He deigned to take our human nature to Himself. For, if He had not first experienced them, He would never have come to share our human life.
>
> What is this passion that He first underwent for our sake? It is the passion of love.
>
> But what of the Father Himself, the God of the universe, who is the long-suffering, merciful, and compassionate—does He too not suffer in some fashion? Do you

not realize that when He turns His attention to the affairs
of men, He suffers a human passion? "For the Lord, your
God, has taken your ways upon himself, as a man takes his
child on his back" (Dt 1:31). God therefore takes our
ways as the Son of God takes our sufferings. The Father
Himself is not impassible! If we pray to Him, He has pity
and is compassionate. He suffers a passion of love.[5]

The suffering in question is far from reducible to a simple
compassion for man's misfortunes. It is rather a passionate will
that man should succeed. Every failure of a man is a personal
setback, an unbearable wound for God. The source of Jesus'
human sensibility and of the movement that instinctively takes
Him out to meet suffering human beings and sends Him in
search of all that is lost (sinners and tax collectors, prodigal
children and prostitutes) is the Father's jealousy in regard to
His work, His anxiety at the dangers men run, His deep feeling at finding, after so much anxious searching, the son who is
hardly recognizable but still alive.

It is the human sensibility of Jesus that suggested to Him the
parable of the prodigal son, but He discovered it only while
His gaze was fixed upon the Father, since "the Son cannot do
anything by himself—he can do only what he sees the Father
doing. For whatever the Father does, the Son does likewise.
For the Father loves the Son and everything the Father does
he shows him" (Jn 5:19-20). What the Father does, what He
never ceases to bring forth from all eternity, is His only Son.
What He does on earth throughout all history and into eternity
is again and always His only Son. But all the joyous pride the
Father had derived from the love shown Him by His only
Son, He now derives, no less pure and total, from the Son as
man, living the life and dying the death of a man.

In Jesus Christ and in all who live by His Spirit, the human
race is for the Father a source of divine joy; the race meets all
His expectations, and creation is a success. There is a simultaneous success on both sides: God's success is the success of
man. God's success does not consist in God's first obtaining

His own satisfaction and then allowing man to enjoy it in turn. The joy of Jesus Christ, the joy of this man who is welcomed by His Father as He breathes His last, and the joy of all who die in the Lord—*that* is God's own joy which has become the joy of mankind, the joy for which we were made, the joy that is ours in spirit and in flesh.

God's Victory, Man's Victory

We must realize, however, that if God's success and man's are inseparable, Jesus does not speak of both in the same way. This difference in His words and evaluations raises a question. If Christ is so sensitive to our failures, if He has such a tireless, spontaneous sympathy for us as men, if He wants man's success with all His heart and is even willing to die for it, why does He have so little to say of it? After all, there is a vast difference between the place the Father has in his life and the place man has. In comparison with the Father's importance for Jesus, in comparison with the way Jesus thinks of Him and loves Him, can we say that man counts at all?

There is no doubt, of course, that Jesus is sincerely interested in men. But that interest, however deep and full of feeling it may seem to be, is also, we might say, marginal and secondary. When all is said and done, does the Gospel not confirm the accuracy of the diagnosis so many unbelievers make of Christianity: that it is alienating? Oh, indeed the Christian intends to serve man, and his intention is sincere, but it is necessarily ineffective because it is not wholehearted and unconditional and cannot wager everything on man. Why? Because the Christian persists in putting God first and can also be consoled despite man's failures, provided God succeeds. Yes, the Christian who is faithful to the Gospel is sensitive to human misfortune, and the Church is always ready to open hospitals, and its interest in programs of scientific and social development will always be polite and deliberate, but also remote.

The facts themselves are beyond doubt. Deeply attentive though He is to man, Jesus never speaks of them as He does of

His Father. This is not simply because He cannot put the Creator and his creation on the same level; that, after all, is perfectly understandable. It is also because He cannot drag His
eyes away from His Father and has no food other than the
Father's will, no possible objective in life save His plan, no joy
save His; consequently, nothing to be found in this world can
be the real goal of His life. Never once does Jesus offer us
mankind as a goal; never once does He see mankind happy
and united save in His Father's house, at the family table.

But this image of a meal which is so important for Jesus as
well as deeply human, earthly, and familiar to us, should point
the direction in which the solution of our problem is to be found.
It is strictly the fact that Jesus can focus His will on the Father
alone and that any divided allegiance is unthinkable for Him.
But the Father who is everything to Jesus is also the God who
loves men, and loves them to the point of giving His Son over
to death for them! In becoming man, being born of our race,
and accepting our instinctive sensibilities and reactions as His
own, the Lord does not turn away from the Father and look to
our human race for a new center of His existence. The only
center for Him is the Father, but, precisely because He cannot
turn away from that center, He is connected with us by a unique
and eternal bond.

He is linked to us by the whole of His human nature, that
is itself complete, integral, without limitation, sensitive to everything that affects us, and open to everything that appeals to us.
But this unbreakable and all-embracing bond that is the very
substance of His being as a man is the fruit of His filial love for
the Father; it is the fruit produced by the Holy Spirit. The fruit
cannot perish; the bond is unbreakable. If the bond consisted
solely of His human nature, we might well wonder how strong it
was; after all, what man has never betrayed his brother and
harmed mankind? Yet in Jesus, and in Him alone, human nature
has never yielded to evil. In the blackest hours of His Passion,
when He was victim of a monstrous injustice, surrounded by sin,
handed over defenseless to all the evil that cruelty, meanness,
fear, or hatred can evoke from our defiled hearts, and witness

to the worst human degradation, Jesus says not a single word of rejection; not by a single gesture does He fend us off. Instead, having experienced our sinfulness to the utmost, He dies with words of pardon on His lips, still finding reason to love us. The secret which alone explains such love and fidelity as this is the Father: "I have loved them as you have loved me" (Jn 17:23). That we might really be the sons of God and mankind His daughter, the Son had to be bound to men by the same bond that unites Him to the Father; His human nature had to be the work of the Holy Spirit.

We can now understand why mankind could not be the end and goal for Jesus. He can see mankind only as embraced by the Father's love and as sharing the joy of the Three Persons. But it would be a blasphemy against the Gospel to suggest that the silence of Jesus is due to an unwitting forgetfulness or to indifference. Christ has the same love for mankind that He has for His Father; His desire for mankind's greatness is one with His desire for the Father's honor, and He cannot serve the Father without becoming the servant of all men. It is but a single step, direct and immediate, from love for the Father to love for men; and it is in the Father's name that He takes the step.

His answer to the question about the greatest commandment is characteristic of Him: "You shall love the Lord your God with your whole heart, with your whole soul, and with all your mind. This is the greatest and first commandment," and the commandment that comes spontaneously to His lips, justifying His whole existence and attracting all of His attention. But He goes on directly to say that there is a second commandment. This other commandment cannot come before the first, because what would God be if He were not first? And what kind of love for man would it be that did not reverence God in him? The second is, rather, "like the first," not marginal or secondary but just as comprehensive and just as urgent: "You shall love your neighbor as yourself" (Mt 22:36-38).

This then is why the victory of the risen Christ is mankind's victory. Not only has Jesus Christ triumphed over the iron boundary-walls that kept mankind prisoner—the walls of division, hatred, separation, and death. Not only can He now be for every man, on all the roads men walk and at every moment of history, the companion at work and on the journey, and the friend who is always near. More than all that, He has now become the "life-giving spirit" of a new human race (1 Cor 15: 45). He was born of our race as a son of the first Adam and heir to our sorrows and our sins; now He is the second Adam and head of a new human race, a race which is still ours, made of the same flesh and subject to the same death, yet already triumphant over the flesh and over death.

Now that He is risen, Jesus Christ embraces and is united with the whole of mankind, not only as His inheritance and a sphere of influence but as His own Body that is animated by His own Spirit. Through the patient suffering of the poor, the efforts of the peacemakers, the tears of those who mourn, the charity of the saints, through the slow advances and the tragic setbacks, the conquests and the crises, Jesus Christ is gathering the generations and forming mankind. He is making man, for He is man.

Chapter 2
The Growth of Jesus

The growth of the young Jesus, and the growth and building up of Christ's Body "till we become one . . . and form that perfect man who is Christ come to full stature" (Eph 4:13), are developmental themes we find congenial today. The reason for this is not simply that they suggest positive perspectives and supply grounds for hope. It is also that they attribute a real value to the created order, an inner coherence to the work of time, and thus a meaning to the world: the world does not simply perdure without purpose but is making laborious preparation for a new dawn brighter than anything we could dream of.

We are, then, keenly sensitive to themes of growth, and it is therefore all the more important to handle them with great clarity and delicacy. A few phrases from the Gospels and St. Paul reveal the whole mystery of the Word made flesh, with its human reality and its divine paradoxes.

A God Who Is a Child

What depths there are in the eyes of a child! They do not come from the child's experience or personal discoveries, but are with him from birth. There is a living light in his eyes even before he has learned to look into his mother's eyes and return her smile. There is a unique something there, a depth out of which the mother elicits his first smile. That something is the presence of a human soul. In the case of Christ, the depths are the depths of God, infinitely greater than any to be found in a merely human child, and yet they are revealed to us through an authentically human childhood.

The Gospel of Christ's infancy and childhood terminates, in St. Luke, in an incident in which Jesus tells His parents, in an unambiguous fashion, that His childhood is over. On His own initiative He stays in Jerusalem and let's His parents set out for Nazareth without Him. In answer to His mother's anxious and reproachful question, "Why have you done this to us?," He enunciates the "must" that will later lead Him to His Passion, because that "must" comes to Him from His Father: "Did you not know that I must be busy with my Father's affairs?" (Lk 2:49 JB).

This scene, with its clear manifestation of Jesus' consciousness of belonging directly and personally to the Father, is framed by two sentences, or, more accurately, by the same sentence repeated in almost identical words: "The child grew in size and strength, filled with wisdom, and the grace of God was upon him" (Lk 2:40); "Jesus, for his part, progressed steadily in wisdom and age and grace before God and men" (2:52).

The evangelist's aim is clear. He intends to highlight, by contrasting them, two simultaneous facts, each of the utmost importance: this child, who grows up like all other children and is distinguished from them only by growing in a more perfect way, is also a person who, without having learned it from anyone else, knows Himself to be the Son of God and also is aware of the life God has determined for Him. If, then, we are to be faithful to the Gospel, we must keep a firm hold on these two essential facts which manifest His authentic humanity and His authentic divinity. But we may also perhaps push a little further and, by observing the life of this child as he grows, hope to discover something of the mystery of God's Son made man.

Jesus Grew

The Gospels tell us nothing of the hidden years of Jesus ex-

cept that He obeyed His parents and that He grew. At first
sight, the statement is a commonplace, and "size, grace, and
wisdom" are specifications that do not tell us very much. But
the very triteness of the statement is valuable, because it shows
that Jesus's life at Nazareth was not simply an "example" for
men. The thirty years there do, of course, give us the example
of a poor and hidden life, and the example has in our day taken
on a new power and urgency that deeply affected a Charles de
Foucauld and made his experience significant for the world at
large. In a world in which the distance between the rich countries and the poor countries is widening every day, Nazareth
reminds Christians that Christ lived the kind of life which the
inhabitants of the poor countries are living today. It is surely
not by chance that we are being taught this lesson.

But the power of the example comes from the fact that God's
primary intention was not simply to teach us a lesson but to
impose a necessity on His Son. The life Jesus lived was the life
lived by the vast majority of His fellow countrymen, and this
fact does not seem to have struck the first Christians as anything extraordinary. Even before His disciples came on the
scene, Jesus Himself needed those thirty years for the sake of
the work He had to do and the man He had to become.

To all appearances, they were empty years, taken up with
tasks any worker could have done in Jesus' stead. But what
dubious conclusions people have drawn from this fact, as
though it proved the worthlessness of all human undertakings!
These people forget, first of all, that Jesus' work, like any other,
served those who profited by it, and that this service was already
a justification of the toil. Otherwise, what justification can we
find for the labor of millions of men who live in similar conditions? But those who draw pessimistic conclusions from the
hidden life forget, above all, that, for Jesus as for any other
man, the life at Nazareth—which was like the lives of millions
of others, with its work like that of other workers of His social
condition and time, with its Israelite traditions and culture in
the setting of a small Galilean village, and with its daily contacts with others of His social class—had a deep meaning for

Jesus, just as it did for others who experienced it.

Jesus contributed both His work and His personal presence to the human community of which He was a member. The life He lived there, hardly distinguishable from the lives of others, provided Him with factors indispensable to His growth. It was there that He acquired His physiognomy, His personality, His culture. We tend to isolate the hidden life of Jesus (in which we think of Him as living a double life, hiding His real self behind the outward mask) from the public life, in which at last he could show Himself as He really was. But the prophet of Capernaum was formed at Nazareth; it was at Nazareth that He learned to speak, to think, to deal with men, and to communicate. He needed those thirty years in order to become what He was: a man of His people and time, a man sharing our humanity.

If Jesus had begun his public ministry a few years earlier or a few years later, He would not have been the same man. His manner would have been different: livelier or weightier. His words would have had another cast. All these things would have been different, and so would our history and the human race. In short, it was because of the way He grew that Jesus became the man He did; to that growth we owe the man we now know, the man in whom God reveals Himself to us. He is not a young man nor an old man, nor even a man already mature. He is a man whose energies are just being tapped, a man who has just finished learning to be a man.

He Learned by Experience

To grow is to acquire; it is to take from outside and assimilate. To grow means to be poor and depend on the outside world, on events as they happen, and on the people we meet. It means to conquer and make our own, but also to undergo, to be passive and receptive. Jesus grew in size and wisdom; He developed and opened out in every area, physical, moral, and spiritual. This is the first thing we think of when we speak of growth, and it is the first thing to which the evange-

list wants to call our attention. Jesus was a man in full possession of His gifts and the means at His disposal; He profited
fully by all His experiences.

But He had to acquire these experiences, and this He could
not do without undergoing and suffering. Like every human
being, He lived in time; events, happy or unhappy, came upon
Him, fell upon Him as it were, and surprised Him in the literal
sense of that word. He knew the future, but He did not know
it by a kind of second sight (something of the natural order),
as though He saw a magic ribbon unfolding with future events
recorded on it before they happened. No, He knew the future
in the way God made the future known to His prophets. This
is to say that God made it known at each moment as something
ever new, made up of His creatures with their former, now
irreversible actions, with the inevitable consequences, fortunate
or tragic, of these actions, with their actions at this moment, but
made up also of God's own resources, His inexhaustible mercy
and creative love that is always effective and always able to
create a new future.[1]

When the future was known in this way—as God creates it
and as it is already effectively present in the reality of each moment—it was for Jesus, as for the prophets, a real future. It
was not a past magically projected ahead of Him; it was
rather what the future is for us: something not yet experienced.
The experiences Jesus had are the experiences we have; they
differed only in being immeasurably deeper and more "trying"
for Him than they are for us. The amazement, despondency,
indignation, and weariness that He felt in the face of unbelief,
hostility, or bad faith (Mk 3:5; 6:6; 9:19; 10:14) were not a
pretence, but arose from a heart that never became accustomed
to evil, however sharp-eyed it might be in detecting it.

Day after day Jesus saw passing before Him the sad proces-
sion of human distress, in the form of illness, weakness, and
death, and each day the powers He exerted were activated by
a new sense of compassion. The faith of the centurion really
amazed Him, and the sight of Jerusalem that was soon to be
destroyed really moved Him to tears. The Passion had been

for months on the horizon of His mind and in the background of
all He did; He was preparing His disciples for it; it was inescapable because the Father willed it. Yet when it came, it
took Him by surprise as though He had done nothing to prepare
Himself for it.

Jesus was genuinely a man, and it is an inalienable part
of man's nobility that he can and must freely plan his
existence for a future which he does not yet know. If this
man is a believer, the future into which he casts himself
and projects the plan for his life is God in all his freedom
and immensity. To deprive Jesus of the same opportunity
and to have Him move toward a goal known in advance
and distant only in time, would be to deprive Him of His
dignity as a man. The saying Mark records must indeed
be authentic: "As to the exact day or hour, no one
knows it, neither the angels in heaven nor even the Son"
(13:32).[2]

The Growth of the Son

Is it possible, however, to reconcile this picture of Jesus as
a man who passed an apprenticeship in the school of human
existence and learned by experience that obedience ((Heb 5:8)
which is the innermost secret of His life and person, with the
picture drawn for us in the Gospel of John? In the fourth Gospel, there are no surprises, nothing happens that was not anticipated. From His very first public manifestation, from His first
recorded words, Jesus knows exactly where He stands and
where men stand, whether the latter be disciples or strangers:
"My hour has not yet come" (Jn 2:4); "I saw you under the
fig tree" (1:48); "He needed no one to give him testimony
about human nature. He was well aware of what was in man's
heart" (2:25).

As the passion draws nearer and those opposed to Jesus
seem to be dominating the scene, the evangelist and Jesus Himself take ever greater care to show that He has the final say

about His own fate: "I lay down my life to take it up again. No one takes it from me" (10:17-18). In fact, the most solemn and categorical assertions come at the point when He seems to have been handed over to the powers of evil: "Jesus realized that the hour had come.... The devil had already induced Judas, son of Simon Iscariot, to hand him over; and so ... Jesus, fully aware that he had come from God and was going to God, the Father who had handed everything over to him...." (13:1-3). But could things possibly be different? Could anything be outside the Son's control ever since the moment when "the Father loves the Son and everything the Father does he shows him" (5:20)?

Is it possible that behind this hieratic mask with its unchanging gaze we can find the face we saw earlier: the face marked by our hopes and troubles, the face alive with feeling or concentration, alert or disappointed, stern or relaxed? But what can be wanting in someone who knows in advance everything that will happen to Him? And what can the meaning of the Passion be for one who knows that in a few hours He will be welcomed by His Father? How can these two faces be harmonized? Can we do anything but choose between them?

But we must refuse to choose; we must refuse to admit that there are two faces. Undoubtedly, the one face is seen in different lights, and John is more concerned to emphasize the divine side of the Lord, the glory He has from His Father that marks His every movement. But this same John deliberately draws our attention to the weariness of Jesus at the well of Jacob, His thirst on the cross, and His emotion and tears at the tomb of Lazarus. This Jesus is the same as the Jesus of Mark and Luke. He is not to be explained by our choosing one Gospel against the others or one tendency as opposed to others. We can explain him only by taking all His traits into account, especially those most difficult to reconcile with one another. As long as we have not grasped the deeper harmony among them all, we will not grasp the mystery of Christ.

As a help to understanding how the experience and growth of Jesus can be those of the Son of God and yet not lose their

genuinely human character, it will be worth our while to go
back to the incident involving the twelve-year-old Jesus and
His answer to His parents: "Did you not know that I must be
busy with my Father's affairs?" (Lk 2:49 JB). We must also
observe how Luke frames this scene within the repeated reference to the growth of Jesus (2:40.52). He evidently saw a
connection between the incident and frame in which he puts
it, and we must try to understand this connection.

The connection seems to include both contrast and explanation. The child who suddenly asserts His own initiative at Jerusalem is a child like all other children: He grows gradually
and draws from His milieu the physical, moral, cultural, and
religious food He needs to turn Him into a man. Like all other
children, as He feeds upon His milieu, He develops a personality that has been present all along but in a latent form.
The growth of a child is not simply a matter of extending his
being as it were, that is, of enlarging his capabilities and the
range of his action. Through the enrichment that comes from
experience, he also becomes aware with deepening clarity of his
own identity; there is a progressive emergence of his personality.

A child is able at a very early stage to distinguish himself
from others and to say "I"; he can express what he wants and
what he rejects. But the "I" which asserts itself seems initially
to be hardly anything more than a bundle of desires and impres-
sions. He has hardly any grasp of the personality in him that is
stating its demands in a loud voice. It will take years before he
can look objectively at himself, separate himself from the milieu
on which he depends, and take responsibility for his own life.
But the moment when he emerges from childhood and takes responsibility for himself is also the moment when he confronts
others with the assertion of what he himself is at bottom: the
thing he has always been ever since he came into existence, but
has now become capable of grasping.

We have absolutely no intention of elaborating a psychology
of Jesus which can find no support in the Gospel texts. We believe, however, that this incident and the words of Jesus which
Luke records can help us, not indeed, to trace the development

of consciousness in the child Jesus, but simply to understand how the consciousness of this child could have been, from its very first glimmer, the consciousness of God's Son, and how, in the manner proper to His years, the child could already grasp this fact and be sure of it.[3] We need not conjure up a miracle, some privileged, miraculously illumined place within a consciousness that otherwise was still that of a child. It is clear that the statement Jesus makes to His parents at the point when He is leaving childhood behind and taking a stand in relation to His parents, could have come only from the Father. After all, what creature—even Mary!—could teach Jesus what He was or what the Son of God is? Mary herself could only stand outside an experience which was beyond her grasp; she could only point to it, in fact she could only remain silent about it.

Fully Aware That He Had Come from God

This experience, which Jesus has directly from God, cannot have been a sudden discovery, a revelation just received. You can inform a child, who is ignorant of the fact, that he was born a king's son, because to be a king's son is not part of this child's very being. He can live for years without knowing the fact, because before being the king's son he is first of all himself. But Jesus was Himself only in being the Son of God. If He had to learn the fact at some later point in life, this means that He was not God's Son up to that point, and if He wasn't, neither could He become it! This absolutely fundamental fact about His being must therefore have been present in His consciousness from the very first instant that He became aware of Himself.

This does not mean, however, that this basic datum took the form, from the beginning, of an intellectual certainty, a distinct idea; in fact, this is highly unlikely. Before a child can speak, even before he opens his eyes, he has a human consciousness; a personal will is emerging, and a thrust outward to others. We need not expect that when Jesus came into our world, His consciousness was more developed than that of

other newborn children. The only requirement is that the thrust
outward and the shaping will within were from the first moment
infallibly directed toward God, and that they were assured by
God of a unique attention and love on His part. Then, as the
growing Jesus learned to see in the faces around Him the faces
of His neighbors, His relatives, His mother, and Joseph, He
learned at the same time to recognize the inner voice that told
Him in accents of certainty and love He heard nowhere else,
not even on His mother's lips: "You are my beloved Son. On
you my favor rests" (Mk 1:11). And in order to give answer
to this voice and to express in return the tender love and joy
it roused in Him, the child Jesus learned to repeat the word
which all children of His age used when they met their father:
"Abba, daddy."

There came a day when the apprenticeship was over. Jesus
left His childhood behind, for He was now able to say what
He was and what He had to do. Mary and Joseph were surprised and disturbed, but they were also capable of understanding the source of the mystery whose requirements Jesus was
telling them: "Did you not know that I must be busy with my
Father's affairs?" Jesus could have derived this idea only
from His Father and from His certainty of being the Father's
only Son, but He could not have expressed it except in the
language He had learned from His parents and on the basis of
the experience with which His milieu supplied Him. The growth
of Jesus Christ was, therefore, a thoroughly genuine human
growth, and the indispensable, irreplaceable means by which He
became conscious of His divine personality and His status as
Son of God.

Chapter 3
The Chastity of Jesus

There are so many misunderstandings connected with the word chastity that it might seem impossible, or at least improper, to apply it to Jesus. It is quite certain that He was not married, and His life is a proof that He never had sexual relations with a woman. But to define chastity by the absence of carnal union is to empty it of all meaning. Such an identification reduces chastity to a mere law; it is a giving in to that instinctive fear of one's own body and of the other person which conceals all kinds of alienation and walls the person off into a narcissistic concentration on himself; it ends up in a condemnation of marriage and human love, and shows a complete ignorance of the power and freedom which the Gospel bestows. In addition, by an infantile reaction, it gives rise to the type of aggressive attack we see today on all forms of sexual control.

It is true, moreover, that Christ hardly ever speaks of chastity. The word itself does not occur in the Gospels and is not part of Jesus' vocabulary. He urges His disciples to meekness, poverty, forgiveness, and faith, but does not seem to have directly called them to chastity or to have pointed to His own chastity as an example. About all we can say is that on one occasion He makes a mysterious allusion to "some who have freely renounced sex for the sake of God's reign" (Mt 19:12). And He adds: "Let him accept this teaching who can." This enigmatic exhortation prevents us from taking lightly a secret

that must have been important, but does it justify claiming that
we have here a basic theme of the Gospel?

Perhaps it is precisely this reticence that should alert us and
make us attentive. If Jesus says so little of chastity and does
not think of offering His own chastity as an example, may this
not be because chastity was not only something natural and
spontaneous for Him, but something basic and essential to His
person? He was free from all fear and desire; He lived every
human situation to the full and was at home especially in all
those situations in which human beings encounter and love one
another; He rescued men from eroticism so as to make them
free to love. Consequently, He did not have to preach chastity. Part of His true self was a radical chastity: a chastity
that is the root of His unique power of giving Himself and of
understanding others and accepting them. If ever a man chose
to renounce sex for the sake of the kingdom, it was He. And
if that choice was ever spontaneous, genuinely personal, and
free of any tension or alienation, then it was such in the case
of Jesus. He did not choose to be chaste in obedience to a
principle or in the name of an ideal or in order to accomplish
something; He simply chose to be Himself.

In this matter more than any other, we must sternly resist
the temptation to draw a character portrait or delve into psychology. Our aim must be a modest one: to examine some in-
cidents in the Gospel and to open ourselves to the reality of
Christ.

*"Did you not know that I must be busy with
my Father's affairs?"*

These are the first and only words we have of Jesus during
His first thirty years (Lk 2:49 JB). They are the words of
one who is still a child; they are a child's answer to His mother
—but in them we already have Jesus whole and entire. His
Father's affairs are something so demanding and absorbing that
nothing else is important in comparison with them. Has Jesus
just made the sudden discovery of this fact? Everything sug-

gests the contrary: He seems to be stating something perfectly clear to Him, something so natural and simple that the only surprising thing is that His parents should be surprised.

Yet their surprise was probably quite natural. Jesus was a child still growing up, a point that Luke emphasizes. The child was not like other children in that He was the Son of God, but this Son of God had become a man, and His consciousness was that of a child. He knew, of course, that He was the Son of God; He had known it since birth. For, if He had not known it since the time when He came into our world, He would have had to learn it from someone else. But how could any creature have taught the Son of God what He was? He must have derived the knowledge from within Himself. But this point we have already discussed.

He knew, then, who He was, and this is why His reactions in regard to God were immediate: He could not but belong completely to the Father. He knew this and had always known it. But, as long as He was still a child, as long as His consciousness of Himself was wholly spontaneous and incapable of reflection, as long as His life, like that of other children, unfolded in the shadow of His parents, He could belong completely to His Father without having to draw away from them at all. A day came, however, when this child, like other children of His age, was ready to assert His own personality. It is this moment that is recorded for us in the episode of Jesus' stay in the temple at Jerusalem. He stated that He was the Son of God and wholly absorbed in His Father's affairs, and this was as real and natural for Him as it was to acknowledge Mary as His mother and to answer her question.

These first words of Jesus show us what was to be from this point on a basic trait of His personality and a major aspect of His chastity. From this point on, Jesus showed himself really free, free enough to confront His parents with a decision that seemed strange to them, but free enough also to go back to Nazareth with them and continue in the obedience and maturation proper to an adolescent. Though He stood off from His parents as an independent being, He did not move away from them: they were still His parents, and He still treated them as such. They had a right to know what was going on within him, a right to know the secret of His being. They were the first ones to whom He revealed that secret. It was to take them time to understand it, and even Mary would have to meditate for a long time on these disconcerting words. But her meditation would feed on the assurance that her Son had told her a secret which was uniquely His, yet which was also meant for her.

This secret—His filial intimacy with His Father—is only one element in His chastity, but it is the primary one. Later on, at the age when a man takes His place among men, Jesus will have His own way of entering into their midst and establishing contact with them. His freedom in relation to them, like His inexhaustible concern with them, will have its roots in the certainty that He belongs to His Father, that He gives the Father the proud joy He expects from His Son, and that He must tell all men that the same joy is meant for them, embracing all men in the love He has Himself received.

Jesus' chastity, then, bears no marks of a fear of others or a rejection of life. As with every authentic human being, be he religious or layman, celibate or married, so also with Jesus is chastity a capacity for self-giving and attention to others, for self-assurance and freedom.

"It is the groom who has the bride. The groom's best man waits there listening for him and is overjoyed to hear his voice"

These words of John the Baptist to his disciples, who were worried that Jesus' success might overshadow their master (Jn 3:29), do not, like the words of the twelve-year-old Jesus, give us access to the immediate lived experience of the latter. It is even difficult to decide to what extent the words represent the memories of John's former disciple who has since become a disciple of Jesus, or are an echo of the words and soul of the Baptist, or spring from Christian meditation on the person of Christ. But in the last analysis it does not matter very much whether the words came from John the Baptist, the evangelist, or an anonymous Christian tradition. The important point is that the words could not have come into existence except through contact with Jesus on the part of men who had direct experience of Him.

Jesus is the bridegroom, and John the Baptist is His best man. John was a prophet, the greatest of them in fact. The prophets had never forgotten the astounding revelation the Lord had given to Hosea: that He loved His people Israel with a passionate love; that He had chosen to make His people His bride; that, in order to speak to His people, He had sent the prophets, to whom He had entrusted His secrets, opened His heart, and given His friendship.

If Jesus is the bridegroom and sends His best man to prepare the bride, then there can be no doubt that the bridegroom is chaste and a virgin. The image of Christ as bridegroom, true, restrained, and powerful though it is in the New Testament, could have compelled acceptance only if it was based on a genuine experience of Jesus that prolonged a basic experience of the Old Testament people. To Israel, the bridegroom meant the bridegroom of whom the prophets had sung: the God who was passionately desirous of union with men, even though no one could have thought of Him as having for companion a sister- or mother-goddess. All the gods of the East had consorts, and the loves attributed to them were marked by the blind violence and instinctiveness proper to forces of nature. The God of Israel has no spouse save on earth, and He can be united to her only in tender love, fidelity, and chastity. Now, however, the bridegroom is Christ, who speaks to man's heart words he has never heard before; who does not speak in the name of an Other but reveals the secrets of His own heart; and who comes not to remind a distracted or faltering spouse of her commitment but to awaken in her a love that is wholly new.

"How can wedding guests go in mourning so long as the groom is with them? When the day comes that the groom is taken away, then they will fast"

Christians could not have thought, by themselves, of calling

Christ a bridegroom. Would they have dared do so, if the master had not bidden them? The saying just quoted, which sounds so authentic, must have come from Jesus Himself. It bears all His marks: His mysterious way of referring to Himself in the third person, as when He speaks of the Son of Man or simply of the Son; His way of voicing His own fate through a figure we would have thought of as distinct from Him, but which expresses His own innermost being; the inner call which is part of Him and always guides Him; His certainty of being both doomed to die and destined for some indescribable joy and encounter, the time and manner of which are for the Father to decide, but which will make evident to all mankind what He really is.

The communication we have quoted is a mysterious one; indeed it seems almost involuntary, since it so far transcends the occasion, which is the limited question of the scribes as they criticize the way Jesus' disciples live. For that very reason, it is all the more precious to us, since for a moment Jesus reveals what is going on in the depths of His mind and heart (Mt 9:15).

His heart is a human heart; it has been made for the deep joy of loving and being loved in return. If He attends a wedding banquet and even gives a miraculous present, as in the wine of Cana; if He speaks so often and so naturally of weddings in His parables and discourses, this is neither accident nor simply a pedagogical device adopted by a clever teacher. The point is rather that He feels at home with weddings; He is personally interested in them, and His presence lights up every wedding that takes place in our world.

How can He be present at every wedding without being out of place? Without breaking in upon the intimacy of the newly united spouses? How can He be everywhere the bridegroom, while yet leaving all spouses free in their encounters and union? To accomplish this, this bridegroom must possess unheard of, superhuman understanding and tact. In Christ, the understanding and tact are those of God, and this is why we take them for granted and are not surprised any more. And yet, in order to gain a better knowledge of the Lord, it may be worth our while to observe His behavior a little more closely.

He is perfectly at ease when He speaks of marriage and all that goes into it. With complete assurance and, we might say, the utmost competence, He points out God's original plan that had been distorted by human weakness: God's plan was that two beings should become one. With sovereign authority He reveals the dimension of the holy in their union: "Let no man separate what God has joined" (Mk 10:9). The flesh, the heart, temptation, and the unbreakable bond fashioned by God—all are summed up in these few words. Christ knows what He is talking about.

But He speaks of it with remarkable discretion. He has no need of breaking in upon and examining the intimate relations of the spouses; but neither does He give the slightest suggestion that He is either envious or afraid of it. Without ambiguity and without embarrassment He can speak of marriage and be present at all marriages, and this not only because He is God but also because He is a man fully and perfectly chaste.

"You see this Woman"

The whole city knows this woman: she is a sinner (Lk 7:39-44). When she passed by, eyes lit up with lust or were lowered because scandalized. But here Jesus sees this woman, whom others look at only in desire or condemnation, laying at His feet all her weapons of seduction: tears, hair, perfume. Christ is deeply sensitive to this deeply feminine gesture and hides neither His emotion nor His admiration; but He also lays bare the almost miraculous secret of purity. There is no question here of a woman formed for seduction nor of a victorious male, proud that all can see his triumph. There is only, on the one side, a bewildered heart that has suddenly learned how to love supremely, and, on the other, a heart chaste enough to be able to recognize, reach out, and liberate.

The most extraordinary thing about Jesus' dealings with women is certainly the complete naturalness of them. On more than one occasion, others are amazed at how uninhibited He is.

At the well of Shechem He engages the Samaritan woman in
conversation, without worrying what others will think of Him
(Jn 4:27). He lets sinful women approach and touch Him; He
offers prostitutes as an example, thus shocking those around
Him. Yet no one will ever dare accuse Him or even suspect
Him of inciting such women or of finding an ambivalent pleasure
in their company. His favoritism toward sinful women was so
well known that the scribes and Pharisees could make an obvious allusion to it when they brought to Him the woman caught
in adultery: "In the Law, Moses ordered such women to be
stoned. What do you have to say about the case?" (Jn 8:5).
But those who are strongest in condemnations of His preferences and reactions find themselves forced to admit, in His
presence and that of the woman, that the real sin is in their
hearts, not hers. One after another they drift away, leaving Him
alone with the guilty woman.

Jesus, though He chose to live in the company of twelve men
whom He called to join Him, welcomed every woman who
crossed His path or came to Him, and we find no trace of reticence or embarrassment, of attraction to them or preference of
one over the others. The women who drew His attention were
typically feminine in their actions and their concerns. The
widow who wept for her only son, the housekeeper who turned
her house upside down looking for a lost coin, the poor lady
who had just put all she had into the collection-box in the temple, the sick woman who had been half paralyzed for years,
the incurably ill woman, the Samaritan woman who was an im-
pertinent chatterbox, and the attentive friends at Bethany, the
sinners and the pious, those easily moved to tears on the road
to Calvary and those who remained, supremely faithful, at the
foot of the cross—Jesus met, looked at, and listened to all of
them, scorning none and flattering none. He was free of the
misogynist tendencies to which St. Paul, for all his genius and
liberty of spirit, was to some extent still captive. The freedom
of Christ is of a different order. It does not derive from princi-
ples or formulas: "There does not exist among you . . . male or
female" (Gal 3:28); "Woman is not independent of man nor

man independent of woman" (1 Cor 11:11). It is the freedom of a person for whom sexual union is something provisional that will have no place after the resurrection (Mt 22:30) and that one can choose not to experience without thereby ceasing to be a genuine man or woman (Mt 19:12). Yet, even when He himself has risen from the dead, He continues to call a woman by her name and to appeal to her heart: "Mary!" (Jn 20: 16). He is completely chaste and completely a man.

"Whoever does the will of my heavenly Father is brother and sister and mother to me"

This saying is one that should shed some light for us on the chastity of Christ (Mt 12:50). We would be falsifying this chastity and reducing it to what it only too often means to us if we limit it to the realm of sex and marriage. The balance, assurance, and freedom from ulterior motives that He shows on these matters are inseparable from a more general attitude that reaches far beyond His dealings with women.

It would be possible, of course, to see in these words only an expressive contrast. Jesus is speaking, with His disciples around Him. Suddenly, someone comes and tells Him: "Your mother and your brothers are standing out there and they wish to speak to you."[1] In order to show His independence of His natural parents, Jesus could quite well repeat the words just addressed to Him and say: "Who is my mother? Who are my brothers?" and, pointing to His disciples: "There are my mother and my brothers." He is a master in the art of the shrewd reply and the telling contrast; perhaps all we have here is a fine example of His presence of mind.

In all probability, however, we must go further than that. For an Oriental or a Jew of Christ's day, family ties were solid, indestructible, and indispensable. The isolated individual could not survive; if excluded by one group, he could continue only if he could attach himself to another. Jesus' words therefore are more than a clever formula; they are a creative act that calls a new reality into being. If Christ breaks His links with His family group, He does so in order to create a new unit with Himself at the center, a new and different kind of family.

The members of this family have a unique relation to Jesus. They are brothers, sisters, and mother to Him. Between them and Him there is a deep bond that is strong enough to cause a breaking of natural familial ties, and intimate enough to ground a genuine kinship. If a person can count on his family, on the support of his brothers and sisters and the understanding of a mother, he is able to stand up to life; he is accepted for the same reason as the other members, that is, not because of his own gifts and abilities, which are necessarily unequal to those of many other people, but simple because he belongs to the same family.

In this new family Christ is the center, and the scene as the evangelist portrays it makes the reality very concrete. Jesus speaks with His disciples around Him; the group which they form is real and visible, and sizable enough to keep Jesus' natural family from reaching Him. In fact, this group includes infinitely more than the little crowd which has the Twelve for its nucleus. Wherever there are men and women who do His Father's will, Jesus recognizes brothers and sisters.

All are in direct communication with this center, and the link is a personal one: *my* mother, *my* brothers. Yet Jesus is not the source of the bond, for that comes from the Father. He it is who begets these children, gathers them, and gives them life. Christ's words to this effect are explicit, even if surprisingly brief. The thought is more fully developed in the fourth Gospel, but it is the same thought: "All that the Father gives me shall come to me; no one who comes will I ever reject" (Jn 6:37); "I have made your name known to those you gave me out of the world. These men you gave me were yours. . . . They are really yours. (Just as all that belongs to me is yours, so all that belongs to you is mine.)" (Jn 17:6.9.10).

In order thus to be at the center of this family in which the Father gathers His children, to be a brother to each of them and to treat each as His brother or sister, Jesus must have an inexhaustible capacity for attachment to others coupled with a total respect for each. A total belonging to all His brothers and sisters, so that all in turn can belong totally to Him: that is the secret of Christ's love, and it is also the secret of His chastity. If a father and mother are to be able to give each child the love each needs, a different kind of tender affection for each, and to make no distinctions but to treat all equally as brothers and sisters, the parents must purify their own love of all preference and self-satisfaction. Their paternal and maternal love must be truly chaste, free of sentimentality and possessiveness, while the love between the spouses must likewise be chaste.

If parental love and conjugal love require chastity for their perfection, the Lord's love for His own, a fraternal love lived under the Father's eye, is chaste in its very root. It is a freely offered share in a love that comes from the Father and returns to Him. It never turns into domination, never makes self-centered demands, but always takes the form of acceptance and communication of self. The chastity of Jesus and the secret of His freedom toward and power over women is at bottom His manner of approaching every human being, giving Himself wholly to that person, sharing with Him all His own experience and wealth and attention, and calling Him to a total response in return. He is incapable of asking for anything less than the other's whole heart, and incapable, too, of pressuring the other in any way; He thus makes it possible for each person to be simply himself or herself.

His love for His disciples is friendship of a deep, virile, tender kind. He counts on their friendship, feels their weaknesses keenly, and values their fidelity; He suffers greatly at being separated from them, asks them to leave all and follow Him, and lives His life in their presence and company. He even has His favorites and does not try to hide this special intimacy. Yet never does He show Himself as complacent, easily offended, or selfish. He belongs wholly to all. In a word, He is chaste.

"The wedding feast of the Lamb"

The Apocalypse brings together the vision of the Lamb slain

in sacrifice (5:6) and the vision of the spouse who is purified
by the Lamb's blood: the new Jerusalem, the holy Church
(19:9; 21:9). The hour when the wedding feast of the Lamb
is celebrated is the hour of the cross. This is not a visionary's
fantasy. For, in the Letter to the Ephesians, Paul too reminds
us that Christ loves the Church as a man loves his wife and
that, in order to prepare her for this union, "he gave himself up
for her" (Eph 5:25). Christian tradition has always meditated
on these images and endeavored to plumb their depths, with
a view to understanding better the mystery of the union of husband and wife in Christ and the mystery of virginity consecrated
to the Lord.

These images are heavy with meaning and tell us a profound
truth concerning Calvary, a truth that is an essential part of our
faith: God's love is revealed in the passionate love that brought
the Son to the cross, and the secret of this passionate love is
also the secret of His chastity. In order to penetrate the secret,
we must, with great reserve and deep respect, look both to the
discourses at the Supper and to the sequence of events in the
Passion. The accents differ in the two places, but it is the same
man who gives of Himself, and the same love that is manifested.

In the supper room, Jesus is more serious than ever before,
but He is also relaxed and opens Himself to His disciples in
ways they had not thought possible. Admitting them completely into His confidence, He reveals the secrets of His heart:
"There is no greater love than this: to lay down one's life for
one's friends. You are my friends" (Jn 15:13-14); "I have
greatly desired to eat this Passover with you. . . . This is my
body to be given for you" (Lk 22:14.19). But His attitude is
marked by the same perfect purity as always, for, while He cannot hide His feelings and shares them with His disciples as
though such feelings belonged to them, He never for a moment
plays upon these feelings; He does not dwell on them or exploit them so as to control the disciples. Everything belongs to
them: all His love, His life, His death, His future in God—,
but they will never enter into this mystery until He brings them
there through the door of faith. They will never understand

the gift He gives them if they confuse it with the tender feelings of the moment.

Jesus therefore gives Himself in the humble and most chaste form possible: bread, wine, everyday and very substantial foods. That is the way He has given of Himself all His life long, and it is the way in which He will now give His very life itself. He who eats His flesh and drinks His blood will enter into the mystery of detachment and self-giving; the Lord will lay hold of Him and unite Himself to Him more fully and deeply than any husband and wife. He will unite Himself to His follower as He is Himself united to His Father.

Throughout His human life Jesus has, day after day, given His disciples His selfless attention, silent dedication, unobtrusive strength, light, and chaste love. It is all part of His being, of His very flesh and blood, and tonight He gives it all in a single gift. At the same time, He gives all who receive Him the power to receive His gift in pure faith. He gives them the power to draw nourishment from Himself and His word and His life, but without being able to taste the gift and without expecting it to be accompanied by any sensible sign.

The cross is the source of this purity and the heart of the Eucharist. On the cross, Jesus dies for men. A man must have a great deal of love in order to be able to give his life. His love must be truly chaste if he is to be united to someone at the very moment when he must surrender all hope of meeting that loved one in the flesh. A man's love must be totally pure if he is to be able to give his life for his enemies. Such was the Lord's love for us. On the cross Jesus received from our human race only the vilest and most hateful things we had to give: hatred itself, arrogant pride, cruelty, cowardice, lies. All the faces that passed before Him bore the hideous marks of sin. Yet for these wretches and for all of us, who are no better, He gives His life. He does it because He loves us; because He is able to enter deeper within us than our sins and rejections of Him and find a buried spring which is still capable of flowing and from which He can elicit a pure stream of water; in short, because He is chaste.

"Do not cling to me"

Of all the words the Lord spoke, these which He spoke to
Mary Magdalene on Easter morning (Jn 20:17) are doubtless
the ones in which we can most easily see what we usually think
of as chastity. Mary has just recognized the Christ whose body
she was looking for; she falls at His feet to embrace them, but
Christ checks her action and refuses the contact. That is how
chastity reacts, isn't it?

The really surprising thing is that Jesus, who during His
mortal life never seems to have been embarrassed by this tender,
intimate action but gladly accepted it and defended it against
criticism, should regard it as out of place now that He is risen.
We cannot think that He must now take precautions He never
had to take before! We cannot believe that He wants to emphasize the distance between Himself and Mary, since He was
never closer to His own than after the resurrection. When He
wishes to appear to them, He seems almost to take advantage
of the fact that they are at table: He eats what they have left
over; He receives them at the lakeside by a fire on which some
fish are cooking, and invites them to eat; in order to make
Mary Magdalene recognize Him, He uses accents of familiar
intimacy by which she immediately sees who He is. All the
actions of the risen Lord show that despite the new conditions
in which He lives, He has in no way changed: He is just as
human, just as simple, and is even closer than He ever was before.

If, then, He eludes Mary Magdalene's embrace once she has
recognized Him, and will not let her hold Him, the reason cannot be that He wishes to withdraw from her or weaken the bond
between them. His purpose is rather to give the bond a new
value and a new dimension. From now on, neither life nor
death, neither the present nor the future, nor anything else
will be able to separate Mary from the love of her Lord (cf.
Rom 8:38-39). He has passed through death in order to come
to her, and will be with her always until the end of the world:
with her and, simultaneously, with all His brothers and sisters.

The risen Jesus here reveals the secret of His chastity: a heart open to every creature, an intimacy compounded of both tender love and freedom, a capacity for welcoming all persons by name and uniting them all in the Father's house in the joy of the wedding feast. From this point on, Mary Magdalene, Augustine, Francis of Assisi, Thérèse of Jesus, saints and sinners, spouses united in Christ and celibates consecrated to the Lord—all will be living proofs in the world of the chastity of Jesus Christ.

Chapter 4

Jesus, Sickness and Death

Sickness and death bulk large in the Gospel and the Scriptures as a whole, as they do in man's life. Healing too has a place, but it is difficult to grasp and follow the process of healing. The treatment of illness and even the fact of regeneration are usually noted only when they are completed and the healing has been accomplished. In the Gospels most of the cures mentioned are narrated as miracles, that is, the natural processes which a specialist would be interested in observing have been bypassed. And yet, if we look more closely, we will find, even in the miracles, a number of points that will be of interest not only to Christians but especially to those who work for man's health.

The order we shall follow may seem somewhat naive, yet it reflects an important truth. We shall ask what sickness, death, and healing are, first in the Old Testament, then in the New. There is nothing original about this scheme, of course, but it does enable us to see, first, the spontaneous reactions of a believing people, and, second, the new element introduced by the coming of Jesus Christ.

1. Old Testament: Natural Death and Tragic Death

In the Old Testament, sickness and death are viewed both

as inevitable natural occurrences, and as tragic, even scandalous events. It is natural for man to die; the elements that make him up will inevitably be destroyed; yet it is abhorrent that a being who is the object of affection and an integral part of the life of those near and dear to him should be brutally snatched away by a set of blind circumstances. Old Testament man accepts both of these aspects and does not seek to pass over one of them and concentrate solely on the other. The difficulty is to combine the two in a way that does not do violence to reality.

What might be called a natural kind of death, that is, a death which raises no problems, is the death that comes without violence at the end of a long and happy life and at the point when life has become chiefly a burden. Such was the death of the patriarchs, those great models of life in Israel. In the evening of a fruitful life, surrounded by children, grandchildren, and great-grandchildren, these men fall asleep in death and go to join their ancestors, in the same tomb where they had laid their parents before them. The emphasis here is on the gathering: the living gather around the dying man, while he goes to be united with the ancestors who went before him.

There is no question, at this period, of hoping for an eternal life. The existence that follows upon our present life is a shadowy existence that has nothing in common with what the Christian hopes for. The important thing about these exemplary deaths is that they bear witness to the importance of life. A man must indeed go when his time is up, but if he has begotten a numerous progeny and has given them security and a sense of oneness as long as he had the power to do so, then he has done his work and can go to join the generations before him who in their own day accomplished that amazing and delicate miracle, the transmission of life. The people gathered around the dying person are not simply united to him in affection; they also bear witness to the power of life.

But there are other kinds of death, and they are tragic. There are the young and vigorous who are cut down before they can in their turn give life to others: the daughter of Jephthah who must die while still a virgin because her father foolishly made a stupid oath; Jonathan, son of Saul and friend of David, who is killed beside his father in a hopeless war. When fate thus strikes down the sinner, the man who has spent his life destroying within and around him the forces of God in our world, that is simple justice: the sinner, who uses his talents to destroy life is doomed to die. But how many innocent people, people fully alive, die young and depart alone! What can we do then but weep?

How did the heroes fall in the thick of the battle?
O Jonathan, in your death I am stricken,
I am desolate for you, Jonathan, my brother
(2 Sam 1:25 JB).

There is a loss here that cannot be repaired. The Israelite does not rebel—at least not yet; that will come later—but he cannot fail to weep.

Why? Because death is irreversible. There is continuity among the living, but death means a defensive break in this continuity. In many archaic religions, indeed, there is an ongoing communication between the living and the dead. Ethnologists tell us of African villages where only a part of the community is in open view, while the far greater part consists of the countless ancestors who, while living in their own mysterious country, always accompany the living. Africans who have become Christians claim that the meaning of these beliefs is more specific than that, and maintain that there is in them at least a distant glimmer of Christian hope. Communication between the living and the dead—they say—does not involve anybody and everybody indiscriminately; rather, the dead who continue to have a place among the living are those who played an effective role among the living when they are themselves alive. This conception is probably fairly close to the biblical view of the dead patriarchs.

The Old Testament nonetheless prescribes severe penalties for any attempt to establish communication between the living and the dead. The intent was probably to safeguard against attributing divine powers to the dead. In any event, Israel's strictness on this point preserved a healthy realism about death as a decisive and definitive occurrence. There is no returning from the land of the dead, and no one lives his life twice. Man is put on earth to play the part life assigns him. Jesus will say that he is put here to win his life or lose it.

Loneliness of the Sick Man

Sickness, like death, is both natural and scandalous. The worst thing about sickness is really not suffering as such. The Israelites, like all peoples whose life is hard, were inured to suffering and did not dream of rebelling when it touched them. Suffering, sooner or later in life, was the common lot of mankind, and only a fool would think he could avoid it.

But there was an aspect of illness which the Israelite felt keenly, to the point of being crushed by it: the loneliness it brought. The sick man found himself shunted aside and, in extreme cases, even excluded from the society of men. They did not speak to him; they avoided him. They took advantage of his absence to make decisions he would have prevented. In this sense, to experience sickness is already to experience something of the solitude death will bring. The sick man sees himself as already dying, not only because he feels his strength draining away and his flesh beginning to corrupt, but also because he is cut off from the disputes and the joys of men. And, as is natural in so closely knit a society as that of the Israelites, the empty place left by a sick person is immediately filled by competitors and rivals. This is why we so often find in the psalms complaints against enemies and the envious put on the lips of sick people. The most characteristic psalms, in this respect, are Psalms 22, 30, 41, and 88.

But I am a worm, not a man;
the scorn of men, despised by the people.
All who see me scoff at me;
they mock me with parted lips, they wag their heads

(Ps 22:7-8).

This is the psalm Jesus prayed on the cross. His terrible suffering is not to be separated from the distress of so many sick people.

Sickness, then, is the beginning of death, and it excludes from the society of men. These two traits are especially evident in contagious diseases and, in particular, in leprosy, the sickness which in Scripture symbolizes all the others. Its destructiveness is evident; it inspires terror; Israelite law provides penalties for it. Even while still living, the leper is as unclean and untouchable as a corpse, which cannot be touched without defilement, and the resultant need is careful purification.

These psalms say, further, that the sick man and those around him often see his condition as a sign that God has abandoned him, and, therefore, as a sign that he has sinned. How could God abandon a man to suffering and solitude if the man had not sinned? This attitude seems to reflect a spontaneous human reaction. The sick man is alone, and if he is alone and his friends have left him, that is attributable to him, not to them. There is something about him, then, that causes friends to leave him and has already caused God to abandon him. For the same reason, his enemies, who have been waiting for their opportunity, see themselves justified now in attacking him. The sick man becomes a condemned person, rejected by society and abandoned by God. More than one psalm is a cry of innocent people who find themselves in this painful situation.

God's Presence in Illness

But if the Old Testament gives expression to this kind of instinctive reaction, it also voices strong protest against such fatalism. It confronts these traditional notions and passionately asserts that they are false and that in the depths of sickness and loneliness God is present and concerned, invisibly indeed, but with the whole force of His creative will. The sick man, despite appearances, is not abandoned by God and separated from Him. On the contrary, he may be the very one in whom God is mysteriously carrying out His most precious work.

The figures stand out here as highly important in the Bible: Job and the nameless personage described in the Book of Isaiah, who has his true name from God: "My servant" (Is 52:13-53:11). Job is the prototypical sick man we described above: a man disfigured and ruined by illness, a man misunderstood by his best friends and finally condemned by them. How, they ask, can there not be sin where illness and suffering such as these befall a man? Look for your sin and you will find it. Job's answer is unvarying: I am innocent, I have not forgotten God. No matter how He treats me, the one thing I cannot surrender is my consciousness of being on His side. God has seemingly abandoned him totally. He allows Job to suffer so terribly that he curses his life and the day of his birth. Yet Job wants God to be with him, and he finishes by coming out on top. At the end God finds Job right and his opponents wrong: God was indeed with His servant all along. He does not explain why or to what purpose He treated His servant as He did; He does not take away the mystery from suffering, but says only that He was there with the sufferer.

The "suffering Servant" of the Book of Isaiah is also described as a sick man who is disfigured, cast out by men, a revolting sight that evokes not pity but pure horror. Then, in a divinely effected reversal of roles, this man who was thus rejected by everyone proves to be the one who bears the sins and diseases of everyone else. Though imprisoned in his infirmities, he is really at the center of the sick human race, and he saves it. Though he dies as an outcast, he proves to be the focal point upon which all other lives converge. In this personage, God is not simply present and completely silent, as he was in the case of Job. Here, instead, He makes the suffering of His servant the point of departure for the healing of mankind.

Healing

It is much more difficult to follow in detail the process of healing. In almost every case, the cure is noted when it is complete. The most striking thing about a sick person who is waiting to be healed, is the role played by his restoration to the society of his fellows. To recover means to be able to take one's place among one's fellows, to meet their eyes, to regain face with them. A cure means the triumph of those who had continued to support the sick man, and the defeat and confusion of his enemies.

To recover also means to enter again into communication with God and to get back one's place in "the land of the living." For an Israelite, the land of the living does not mean the other world; it means our world, the place where we live and experience the gifts of God, where we can praise Him and pray to Him. To be cured is to escape death and feel the blood coursing energetically in one's veins again; it is to enjoy the beauty and power of the world; it is to see in this new returning spring the glorious generosity of God.

2. The Gospel: Positive Meaning of Illness

Sickness has a large place in the Gospels; we might even be tempted to say its place is disproportionately large. On almost every page we read of the sick and the infirm. True enough, all these sick people come looking for, and find, the miracle that cures them. But one of our difficulties with miracles is that they seem alien to life. The fact that miracles seem to contradict the determinisms of nature may be a decisive objection for the inflexibly scientific mind, but that type of mind is not very common. The most serious difficulty for most people is that miracles mean the laws governing human existence are not being taken very seriously. To expect or perform a miracle seems to be a way of scorning the basic rules governing the progress of mankind: application to work, patient study and research, careful application of means.

But if we read the Gospels carefully and listen to Jesus explaining the meaning of the miracles He works, we find that, though He does actions He alone can do, they are not an alternative to what men do when faced with illness. On the contrary, they are His unique way of performing the simple actions of men, the elementary actions of the doctor and the nurse. "Which of you would not do as much even for an animal?" That is the first argument Jesus uses against those who blame Him for curing on the sabbath. If I have the means of "preserving life" (Mk 3:4), it would be criminal to stand by and do nothing. The miracles of Jesus are not offered as a substitute for the doctor's art, but, on the contrary, set a seal of approval on it. If a man can do something to cure the sick, he has no right not to do it.

By this very fact, illness can take on a positive meaning. In the Old Testament cases of illness having a positive meaning were indeed striking—Job and the suffering Servant—but they were also exceptional. In the Gospel, they are frequent. In at least two cases—before healing the man born blind (Jn 9:3) and before raising Lazarus (Jn 11:4)—Jesus makes the point explicitly: "This sickness . . . is for God's glory." These are words of major importance, for they are a categorical rejection of the explanations that are always fairly close to the surface in men's thinking: if he is ill, if he is struck down and humbled, he must have sinned, or, if not he, then his parents must have sinned (Jn 9:2). No, says Jesus: neither he nor his parents.

But, then, why? So that God may manifest His glory, that is, His own way of acting. Jesus is here effecting an important reversal of perspective. The spontaneous reaction of people, evident in the Gospels even in the circle of those closest to Jesus, is to look to the past and to explain illness in terms of hidden guilt. Jesus' reaction, on the contrary, is to look to the future and to ask why the illness exists and what profit is to be drawn from it. His answer is: It is for God's glory. It is easy enough, of course, for Him to think that way, since the illness provides Him with an occasion for working a miracle. But He connects the miracle with the lesson: Here is an illness, and we must do something about it, namely, cure it so that God may be glorified. From our side, things are admittedly more complicated. If we are to care for a sick person, we must make a precise diagnosis of the trouble and its causes. We cannot neg-

lect the past, but we attend to the past in order to make use of
it and to work toward the future.

Illness, then, is meant from Jesus' viewpoint as a way of
manifesting the greatness and goodness of God. It would be
a mistake, however, to conclude from this that God's work requires illness and that the God of the Gospel wills sickness and
needs it in order to accomplish His own work. Everything Jesus
says and does makes it clear that God's glory is manifested in
the cure, not in the illness. Admittedly, we cannot help thinking it would have been better not to let sickness happen in the
first place. There are questions we instinctively ask, and in answer we can only point to one clear fact. It is evident that
Jesus does everything He can in order to cure people; it is
also clear that in so doing He knows Himself to be manifesting
the attitude of God Himself.

Jesus the Physician

Not only does Jesus manifest the attitude of God. At the
same time and by that very fact, He also embodies the instincts
and gestures of the human being who seeks to heal, be it a doctor or a nurse. Jesus presents Himself as a physician, and, in a
way, thinks of Himself as one. This way of looking at Jesus
may help us as much as an understanding of His explicit teaching. Rarely does Jesus define what He is and what He comes
to accomplish. His normal procedure is to act in the presence
of witnesses and patiently lead them to the discovery of who He
is. Here we have the sense in which His life can be said to be a
revelation: through the words He speaks, yes, but above all
through the way He lives. He usually leaves it to His disciples
to uncover the meaning, but on several occasions He says that
He is a prophet or allows others to give Him that title, and at
least twice He presents Himself as a physician. In the synagogue of Nazareth, when His fellow townsmen find it hard to
believe in Him, He quotes the proverb: "Physician, heal yourself" (Lk 4:23). And when the Pharisees reproach Him for
accepting invitations from sinners, He answers: "The healthy

do not need a doctor; sick people do" (Lk 5:31).

   These answers are obviously to some extent expedients, reflecting the presence of mind of a man who cannot be caught
because He always knows the right answer. At the same
time, however, the answers are spontaneous and come from a
man who thinks about what He is doing the way a physician
thinks about his job. Jesus is not simply comparing Himself
to a physician, however. It is true that the sickness He comes
to treat is neither physiological nor psychological; it is an affliction of the soul, the sin that destroys man. But the fight against
sickness is not foreign to His mission. Many scenes in the Gospel show us Christ confronting illness and struggling against it
as a physician does. More obvious still is the resemblance of
Jesus to the doctor who cares for people sick in body or mind.
Jesus' life is to a large extent filled with contacts with sick
people. From morning to evening, no matter where He goes,
He is approached by the sick and the infirm. He lives in their
world.

   Jesus is very different from the wonder-worker. There have
always been wonder-workers, healers flaunting extraordinary
powers. But in the description of such people and their activities, one striking fact is to be observed: They do not themselves fall sick nor go about with sick people, but live in another world. From above, effortlessly and without any genuine
compassion, they exercise their powers.

   Jesus too has power over sickness, but His power causes
Him first of all to enter into the world of illness. Like a physician, He lives among the sick. A reading of the Gospels shows
us that Jesus' life is taken up with two basic activities: one is
speaking and conversing with men in a great variety of ways,
and the other is living among the sick. For He is indeed in
their midst: they beset Him, crowd around Him, deafen Him
with their cries. If, in order to eliminate the miracles that em-
barrass us, we were to suppress the accounts of Jesus' dealings
with the sick, we would reduce Him to a simple preacher, a
talker. But, in fact, He did not stand above and outside our
life, but made it His own. He mingles with the sick, but not

in order to display His generosity. He does so because, if He is to heal, He must first be moved to compassion and take upon Himself the evil He wants to get rid of.

Thus Matthew, the evangelist, after telling how Jesus cured all the sick who were brought to Him, ends with a surprising juxtaposition: "He . . . cured all who were afflicted, thereby fulfilling what had been said through Isaiah the prophet: 'It was our infirmities he bore, our sufferings he endured'" (Mt 8:17). But in the Bible, the man who bears our infirmities is the suffering Servant in the Book of Isaiah ((Is 53:4). Thus the power of Jesus to heal the sick cannot be isolated from His compassion: He takes upon Himself the evil from which He frees us, and spends His life in the most painful areas of our human existence.

Healing

For Jesus, to heal is by that very fact to restore to a former position. Sickness cuts men off from society; the person healed regains his place in society. We have an expressive sign of this restoration in the healing of the leper (Mk 1:40-45). The evangelist calls attention to the compassion of Jesus; he also records the amazing and, in fact, forbidden action of Jesus in touching the sick man. Jesus' touch is a sign that in this sick man life is stronger than death. It is also a sign of the contact with men that is being restored and that the priest will approve when he verifies that a healing has occurred and the man, now cured, may take his place once again in the community.

For Jesus, healing also means the involvement of His own being and person. We cannot determine, of course, what exactly constituted His miraculous power. For one thing, such a power will not fit into any of our categories; for another, the exercise of it is perceived and described by men living in a cultural context quite different from ours. Some points, however, are meaningful for us. For example, there is the reaction of Jesus when a woman, who does not dare stop Him as He passes, manages to touch His garment and finds herself healed (Mk 5:25-34). Jesus immediately halts, for He "was conscious at once that healing power had gone forth from him." The language the evangelist uses is rather primitive, for it suggests a kind of magic fluid, but his intention is clear. What Jesus became aware of was a presence and a faith, and that is what He wanted to find. He cannot let this woman go away thinking that to touch Him was the only thing that mattered. She must be made to understand that the miracle was due to her faith.

But what is faith? Is it simply a blind confidence in the healer? Confidence does play a role, but only as part of a larger whole. The sick person seeks in Jesus something more than a healer. For, Jesus' whole action makes it clear that He is the representative of God's will and the instrument of God's action. The sick person who approaches Him can only take Jesus as the latter presents Himself. The sick man asks for a cure, but the only cure he will get is the kind of cure Jesus gives, a cure which is a sign from God and a call to change his way of life. Where this wider acceptance—faith—is lacking, even Jesus cannot work a miracle. That is what happened at Nazareth, His own town (Mk 6:5).

Another incident shows how careful Jesus is to present Himself as He really is; it is the cure of the paralytic whose stretcher-bearers lower him through the roof (Mk 2:1-12). When Jesus sees the faith of the attendants, the first thing He says to the sick man is, "My son, your sins are forgiven." He is not refusing to cure, but simply putting the most important thing first. The rest follows of necessity: You will be cured. The proof of this is that Jesus says not a word to justify Himself in face of the scandal His words have caused. He simply adds: "That you may know that the Son of Man has authority on earth to forgive sins, I command you: Stand up! Pick up your mat and go home." Thus He not only gives an irrefutable sign, but also shows that there is a connection between the two actions.

The cure of illness is not only an expressive image for the forgiveness of sins; it is also, to some extent, a consequence

of and a seal upon forgiveness. The person who receives forgiveness of his sins from Jesus and thus experiences Jesus'
regenerative, revitalizing power, sees himself profoundly transformed within, in ways that affect his whole person. There is
certainly a substantial connection between the action of Jesus
within men that enables Him to touch sinners, and His power
over sick bodies. To cure is to practice a careful technique and
to work on specific factors; but it is also to be involved with
a sick person, to encounter a human being and save him.

Chapter 5

Jesus as Penitent

Jesus Christ calls us to repentance. We would have to block our ears not to hear His summons in the Gospel. The first words He is recorded as speaking in His public ministry sum up that ministry as a preaching of repentance: "This is the time of fulfillment. The reign of God is at hand! Reform your lives and believe in the Gospel!" (Mk 1:15). And among His final words before death is a warning to the women of Jerusalem, who are weeping for Him, that they should weep rather for themselves and their children (Lk 23:28), and a welcome to the repentant criminal: "I assure you: this day you will be with me in paradise" (Lk 23:43).

But there is another aspect of this call that is less visible in the Gospel or, in any event, is less striking to us because it seems quite natural and we are only too accustomed to the way the Lord acted. I am referring to the fact that the call to repentance comes from one who is Himself a "penitent," one who before giving us a share in His paradise first comes to share our repentance. If we become more conscious of the Lord's own penitence and the place penitence has in His life, we will be better able to understand what He is saying and to become penitents ourselves.

Jesus Among the Penitents

John the Baptist, last of the prophets and more than a

prophet, preached repentance, as had all the prophets before him: "Reform your lives! The reign of God is at hand" (Mt 3:2). From all over the country people came to him to be "baptized by him in the Jordan River as they confessed their sins" (Mt 3:5). "Later Jesus, coming from Galilee, appeared before John at the Jordan to be baptized by him" (Mt 3:13). In the crowd of sinners who had come to confess their sins and perform the action that would commit them to a new life of obedience to God, Jesus took His place. He too presents Himself to receive the baptism of repentance. John is surprised; the reason for his surprise really doesn't matter, whether it was because he was already acquainted with Jesus or because he received a sudden supernatural enlightenment concerning Jesus. Jesus answers by invoking a principle that is provisional and yet has profound justification: "Give in for now. We must do this if we would fulfill all of God's demands" (Mt 3:15).

This answer sheds light on Jesus' behavior, even if it leaves it still mysterious and paradoxical. It is indeed unexpected that Jesus should come to John and ask for baptism, when He Himself should really be the one baptizing. Jesus does not deny the truth of this. He is following, however, another law than that of pure reason; He is for the time being subject to a law which He cannot evade and which has its own logic and consistency: "Give in for now." But "for now" does not imply that the action is superfluous and that Jesus is doing it out of condescension or to observe formalities and spare sensibilities.

The "fittingness" to which Jesus adapts His action is not that of human ways or human views, but is established by God and is no less demanding than the series of "musts" that will later determine His journey to Jerusalem and His Passion (Mt 16:21; 17:22; 26:24.54). The language here seems less categorical, but that is probably because the point at issue is not the well-defined goal of the "musts" but a style that is to characterize His life and personality, a principle that is to govern all His actions and give them their value and meaning. This principle is: to "fulfill all of God's demands." To speak of "God's demands" is evidently to speak not of what is merely desirable but of strict and fully specific obligations. The "justice" or "righteousness" of the Bible and the Gospel does not indeed, of itself, have the juridical aspect, the element of the calculable, which "justice" easily has for us in a civilization in which everything is anticipated and codified. Yet the justice of which the Bible speaks is even more strict, since it is always a demand related to the person. That is, it consists in treating each human being, not as a general law covering a multitude of similar cases would require, but as his unique personality and his special needs require. To be faithful to the ideal of justice is not simply to satisfy all the prescriptions of the law but to respond with our whole being to what others require of us.

When, therefore, Jesus comes to fulfill all of God's demands, He comes to respond to all that the Father expects of Him, to all that is involved in His being Son and redeemer, and to all that mankind needs if it is to be able to accept God's love and to love Him in return. If, moreover, in order to respond to all these demands, Jesus must mingle with sinners and at their side receive baptism from John, then His being a penitent must be something more than a gesture done as an example to others. It must be the expression of an essential law of His being and His life. He is the Just One, the only one to do justice to God, the only one capable of treating God as God, the only one in whom no sin can be found (Jn 8:46). But, in order to be just, He must place Himself among the sinners and become a penitent.

In our eyes, however, what Jesus does is more than scandalous, more than a bit of odd behavior that conceals a secret. It is simply a contradiction; it is radically unintelligible because it goes against all logic. We know what it means to be just or guilty, more or less just and more or less guilty; we know that all human justice is contaminated and shot through with guilt. Therefore we can understand a just man repenting. We can even understand that the greater his justice and his consciousness of what God and his brothers expect of him, the more conscious he should also become of his limitations and of the extent to which his interior sins corrupt the good he is able to do, and hinder the good that others might do. That the just man should have a greater need of repentance as his justice grows will, after all, seem quite right, once we reflect on it a bit.

But how can any of this apply to Jesus Christ? Nothing in Him is an obstacle to God's action. His every action and re-action are perfection itself; He is wholly transparent to the eyes of His Father and wholly dedicated to men. Nothing can distract Him from the love that is in Him; our rejections and our abhorrent ways cannot deter Him. What, then, can He repent of? What can "penitence" mean in His case? We do not imply, of course, that the whole thing is a comedy; we know He is not playing a game when he comes to receive John's baptism. But how else can we understand His action except as an example, a lesson in humility? How can it be what He apparently means it to be: an act of justice, an expression of what He owes His Father?

Well, what He certainly does not owe the Father is repentance in the sense of the need to ask pardon for His sins. The thought of this never crosses His mind. If He joins the ranks of the penitents, He does not do so because He is scrupulous, as though for greater security of conscience He wanted to be sure and wipe out any fault that might have escaped His attention and be now unknown to Him. No: Jesus knows that He always does the Father's will (Jn 8:29); He always hears the Father telling Him, "You are my beloved Son. On you my favor rests" (Mk 1:11). In His soul there is not the slightest trace of uneasiness before God, but only the certainty that He can never be separated from the Father, that He can never be alone (Jn 8:29) or distant from the Father. If, then, He repents, it cannot be for His own sins but only for ours. And if penitence is imposed upon Him in the name of a justice He must fulfill, then this penitence must express a profound need associated with His being and His mission. He can be what He ought to be, and can execute the task given Him, only if He becomes a penitent for our sins.

But how is that possible? How can a person repent, in any

proper sense of the word, for the sins of someone else? You can certainly suffer for the sins of others; in fact, that is a characteristic of human life. Think of all the children marked for life by the sins of their parents, who in turn had been the victims of preceding generations! To say nothing of the terribly cruel cases we can think of, every man sees himself daily oppressed by the sins and defects of those around him and by the accumulated weight of the evil in the world. But this kind of suffering is not repentance. It is imposed on us from without, whereas repentance can spring only from the heart.

What is impossible to men, God brings about in His incarnate Son. The whole weight of the world's sin lies upon Jesus Christ, to the point of causing His death. Because He is God and the Holy One, this crushing weight is not for Him merely what it would be for us: an amount of suffering to be borne; it is for Jesus what it is for God: a mass of sins, rejections, and offenses. But because the Son of God became man and one of us, the deadly weight of sin that should forever alienate Him from us has become, on the contrary, the bond of bonds uniting Him to us. Our sins are not foreign to Him, because, though He knew them in all their horror, He nonetheless came to us: not despite them, as though He managed to forget about them, but because, after experiencing them in an almost physical way, after seeing and touching them and contemplating them in the very depths of His soul, He brings us the proof that God can still love us. He proves that sin does not have the last word to say about mankind. How could it when He, a man of our own race, is capable of dying for mankind that is so wholly sinful?

This, then, is the mystery of the redeemer, the mystery of the lamb who bears the sins of the world and, bearing them, destroys them. The mystery is in large part a mystery of repentance. Just now we were asking how an innocent person could repent for the sins of others. The mystery of redemption supplies the answer by turning the question around. If repentance were simply regret for the evil that lurks in our sins, it would be our own personal affair, and we might think we

could repent on our own. But if repentance is to be able to
disavow and make reparation for the unsuspected depths of
the evil that is in us and that we spread throughout the world
(the evil that is like a vast submerged ice floe in our souls),
then repentance must arise in depths we cannot reach, in some
part of our humanity that sin has not been able to corrupt,
and therefore in a heart like ours, but perfectly pure, perfectly
transparent.

If, then, guilty men are to repent for their own sins, a sinless
man must repent with them; He must become the source of
repentance for His fellows. If the penitents who come to receive John's baptism are to obtain forgiveness of their sins,
Jesus must mingle with them. When Jesus comes to John as
a penitent, as the man who is already carrying "the sin of the
world" (Jn 1:29), He is beginning to turn John's baptism of
repentance into that baptism in the Holy Spirit which alone can
take away the world's sin. In order to do this He must first
undergo His own baptism (Mk 10:38); He must—if we dare
so put it in words we must immediately explain—perform His
own penance and make His life the logical consequence of this
first action of His public life.

With Sinners

Sinners came to John and asked him what they must do to
assure that their repentance was genuine. John welcomed them
and told them: "Let the man who has two coats give to him
who has none. The man who has food should do the same"
(Lk 3:11). Jesus went much further than John. Not only did
He welcome the sinners who came to Him, and tell them how
to live; He also shared their life and sat at their table. The
association proved scandalous: "Why does he eat with such as
these?" (Mk 2:16). Jesus' own answer shows precisely why
He acted as He did: "People who are healthy do not need a
doctor; sick people do. I have come to call sinners, not the
self-righteous" (2:17). Living with sinners was not simply
one aspect of His life, something fairly important and taking

up a certain amount of His time. It was His very mission, the thing He came among us to do; this was His true place in our world.

All this did not mean that He was in any way accommodating toward sin, or that He was in any way attracted by the "freedom" sin offers and the "rebellion" it represents. In the parable of the prodigal son He paints a very unromantic picture of the "freedom" which attracts the sinner: sin is born of selfishness and ingratitude and ends in degradation. Yet it is precisely the catastrophic situation of the sinner that explains His coming and His passionate desire to save us: "Suppose one of you has a sheep and it falls into a pit on the sabbath. Will he not take hold of it and pull it out?" (Mt 12:11); "Who among you, if he has a hundred sheep and loses one of them, does not leave the ninety-nine in the wasteland and follow the lost one until he finds it?" (Lk 15:4); "This son of mine was dead and has come back to life. He was lost and is found" (Lk 15:24).

The three situations are different, but the reaction is the same. It makes no difference whether the lost sheep was the only one the poor man had or was but one of a hundred. It makes no difference that the prodigal son had proved unworthy of his father. The reaction is the same: he was lost and has been found. To understand, one need hardly do more than be a human being, or at least someone who possessed something and then lost it: "Who among you . . . ?"

Jesus feels no attraction to sin; He makes not the slightest attempt to play down its seriousness. On the contrary, He sees the harm it does and the havoc it plays with man, for it means death and destruction for man Himself. And to make us understand how irreparable this destruction is, and, at the same time, to bring home to us what that loss means to God, Jesus invokes one of the most ordinary yet painful of human experiences. To lose something one values, even if it be of no great worth in itself (a few coins, for example) is always a cruel blow; it symbolizes the failure that threatens all we do and everything we love. Well, says Jesus, God Himself has had that experience! The joy He feels in pardoning and the thrill that is His when

He finds His children again are the emotions of someone who has seen the destruction of what He loved, and who still quakes when He thinks of what would have happened had He not recovered it.

Things did not go that far, and God has found His lost creature—but only because His Son went in search of that creature. He had to look for it where it was: crushed under its sins and ruined by its rebellion. "The Son of Man has come to search out and save what was lost" (Lk 19:10). This is why He ate with sinners and invited Himself into the house of Zacchaeus the tax collector. It was not the equality of their hearts and their love for Him that drew Him, since their hearts were still corrupt when He approached them. The sinful woman's many sins had to be forgiven her before she could show a great love (Lk 7:47). The Lord went to them *because* they were sinners and lost and because He wanted to lead them to repentance and conversion.

In order to make us repent, the Lord became Himself a penitent. He was not a sinner and could not be. Yet He lived with sinners and turned them into penitents, because He had Himself become a penitent. As a penitent He carried our sins, but not as though He considered them His own by an absurd fiction that would make Him guilty in our stead and take the responsibility away from us. He did so because the sins were indeed ours, yet, since He had become our brother and head of our race, whatever belonged to us belonged also to Him. This included our wretched state and the evil our sins do in the world, an evil that would touch Him more than anyone else. For Jesus, living with sinners meant suffering as only He could suffer; it meant suffering all the evil in the world, all that sin has brought about. Let us look again at some points made in the preceding chapter and reflect on them a bit further.

He suffered, first of all, from all that physical suffering has done to our world. The prophet had said of Him: "It was our infirmities that he bore, our sufferings that he endured" (Is 53:4). The prophecy does not apply simply to our moral illnesses, that is, our sins. It is also fulfilled in a literal though paradoxical way. St. Matthew's Gospel quotes this text when describing a scene that occurred frequently in Jesus' life: "As evening drew on, they brought him many who were possessed. He expelled the spirits by a simple command and cursed all who were afflicted, thereby fulfilling what had been said through the prophet Isaiah" (Mt 8:16-17).

It may seem strange to remind us of this text at the very moment when Jesus is manifesting His power over every kind of disorder and illness. Yet, while it is true that illness cannot stand up to contact with Him and that the sick need only come to Him and they will be cured, it is also true that He is the first to be affected, in the whole of His being, by the evil He sees before Him. For, the sick are brought right to Him, or come under their own power, so that He may touch them. If He wished, He could undoubtedly work miracles at a distance, as He did when He cured the centurion's servant and the Canaanite woman's daughter (Mt 8:13; 15:28). But He acts in this way only when faith, we might say, forces this unusual miracle from Him. Such cures are signs that nothing is beyond His power and that, if He wished, He could by a single act, and without any trouble, cure all the sick people in the places He passed through and even all the sick people of Palestine and the whole world.

But Jesus did not come to free mankind of its illnesses; He came rather to share those illnesses with men. It is true, of course, that He does cure illnesses and that sickness cannot stand up to His touch; He is, after all, the Saviour, the resurrection and the life, and is already giving us clear signs of this. But, while waiting to raise His followers from the dead and drying all their tears, He must learn what suffering, illness, and death are. He sees them everywhere. No matter where He goes, the same scene unfolds before Him: the line of litters, the wounds displayed, the inhuman cries, the faces distorted by suffering. He has not come in order to contemplate the marvels and masterpieces of our world, but to see its offscourings, its infirm, its poor. It is not that He has contempt for man's successes; there is not a single word in the Gospel to condemn them and justify others in devaluing them. His business, however, is to search out the failures and the lost, and to save them.

Rarely does He give us a glimpse of what all this costs Him. But all the evangelists do point out His sensitivity. Suffering of any kind touches Him and moves Him deeply. This is a recurring theme of the Gospels (Mt 9:36; 14:14; 15:32; 20:34; Mk 1:41; Lk 7:13; 10:33). At Naim, when He sees a weeping mother walking after the body of her son, His first reaction is not to bid the boy get up, but to tell the mother, "Do not cry," for her grief touched Him deeply (Lk 7:13). His reactions are just like ours: like us, He finds it easier to bear with suffering He does not see. Thus He can let His friend Lazarus die, provided He isn't there to see it (Jn 11:15), but when He sees Mary crying and the crowd in mourning, His feelings well up and He Himself weeps (Jn 11:33-36). He works miracles as He journeys, but He does not work them after the fashion of the wonder-worker who is anxious to use the power He has and eager to find people who can be affected by it. Jesus, on the contrary, is deeply moved by sickness and death before He cures or raises to life. Before He conquers them, He must know them and bear them. With us but with a taste infinitely more refined than ours, He savors the bitter fruits of our sin and experiences our repentance.

In the Power of Sin

But we have not yet come to the hardest part of His penitence. To a heart that is at peace with God, suffering, death, and the cruelest bereavements are indeed an agony, but the agony is fruitful and strengthening. It enables the person to accept God's ways in faith and to be assured even in the blackest night that the Father holds His children by the hand. Blessed are they who weep! And blessed will we be if we experience only these bitter but nourishing fruits of sin! The only real unhappiness, the only real sorrow, Léon Bloy used to say, is not to be a saint. We should not take this to mean: not to be, like the saints, sufficiently removed from the concerns of men that we are not vulnerable to their sufferings. Not being a saint means, rather, that we feel our heart to be always filled with the waters of sin, rising out of an inexhaustible fountain that cannot be cleansed; it means we continue to experience the spontaneous reactions that set us against God and imprison us in our selfishness.

Jesus had no experience of this sadness. Everything in Him came from God and was given back to God. His life was one of giving and communion; it was a bread received from God and wholly consumed. But Jesus was also a gift refused by men, a communion rejected, a bread profaned. The sadness of the sinner became His, because He came up against it and could not penetrate it; He could not batter down the barriers raised by our self-centeredness. "O Jerusalem, Jerusalem, murderess of the prophets and stoner of those who were sent to you! How often have I yearned to gather your children, as a mother bird gathers her young under her wings, but you refused me" (Mt 23:37).

Here we have the Lord's repentance in its deepest, bitterest, and most abiding form: He comes to turn sinners back to God, and He meets with rejection. When we read the Gospel, we hardly pay attention to the unremitting opposition Jesus encountered. We tend to think primarily of His miracles, His profound sayings, His splendid actions. We know, of course, that He roused violent hatred and an implacable resentment that led to His death, but we are too liable to think of it as a tragic but necessary episode, a conspiracy organized by a few people in authority.

It is undoubtedly true that a relatively small group planned His death and that we have no right to make the Jewish people as a whole legally responsible. It is also true, however, that as soon as Jesus came forward in public, He met with opposition and a lack of understanding. He was kept under surveillance and spied on; His every action was noted down; His words were given a distorted interpretation. The hostility was not universal, of course, but it was unrelenting; wherever He went, Jesus was sure of finding among His hearers some closed faces, watchful men weighing His words like judges planning the

sentence they shall pronounce. The Gospels make no claim to
present a precise chronology for Christ's ministry, but they are
certainly aware of the overall trajectory of His career and the
broad lines along which it evolved. When St. Mark tells us, at
the beginning of his third chapter, that after the sabbath cure
of the man with the shriveled hand, "when the Pharisees went
outside, they immediately began to plan with the Herodians how
they might destroy him" (3:6), he means to tell us that the
final prosecution of Jesus was beginning in the very first days
of His Galilean ministry.

If we want a full picture, we must go beyond these evidently
hostile men with their deliberate plans and look at the constantly vacillating crowds and His closest disciples, Peter and
the rest of the Twelve. The Jewish people as a whole and every
single inhabitant of Jerusalem bore a responsibility for Christ's
death, either because they wanted that death and asked for it
or because they let it happen. So we are responsible, each in
our place and degree, for the evil that is done around us. We
must take our place before the Lord with our sins and our
responsibility, we who spontaneously shout with the persecutor
or stay silent when an innocent man is unjustly slain or judge
Christian life inhuman when it leads to the cross. The greatest
suffering Jesus Christ endured was to see Himself encircled by
us sinners and to find among men only opposition or indifference
or fear. "To his own he came, yet his own did not accept him"
(Jn 1:11).

That suffering was repentance because it was caused by sin
and made reparation for sin. It would have remained mere
suffering if Jesus' life and Passion had been simply a new and
more striking occasion for sin to demonstrate its power and
prove that in our world innocence, justice, and love must in the
end go down to defeat. But Jesus, who died because of sin,
died as conqueror of sin. Our sins might band together to
cause His destruction: the vileness of Judas, the hatred of the
Sanhedrin, the cynicism of the politicians, the cruelty of the
mob, the fear of the devout, the cowardice of the disciples.
But they could not make Him utter a word of rejection or a cry

of abhorrence that would rescue Him from us and let us remain damned forever. After struggling all His life against our sins, and daily tasting the horror and irrationality of them, Jesus in His Passion endures all that can be done to Him, and remains whole under the attack. Not only does He save Himself and remain uninfected by the hatred and malice poured upon Him, but He saves us along with Him. He succeeds in doing so because He manages to go on loving us even at the moment when we give Him nothing but rejection and hostility. By dying because of our sins and for His enemies, He proves to us that God loves us and still finds something in us to love. Thus all the evil man can dream up as a way of rejecting God ends in showing that the love of God conquers all.

God's victory is not a victory won by being indulgent or by pardoning out of weakness. It is a victory of love, for it transforms men's hearts and turns sinners into penitents. The proof that Christ's death and resurrection were indeed a victory of His love is that guilty Jerusalem gave birth to the Church and that the disciples who had fled would find their joy in suffering for their Lord's name, and Peter would become a martyr. That is the proof that Jesus' death was not in vain, and that He was justified in clinging to us more strongly than we can cling to our sins. It is the sign that His repentance was effective, for it was able to make us repent in turn.

The repentant Christ, who is the source of our repentance, shows us what repentance really is. It is an understanding of sin as God sees it, with all its power to destroy and corrupt. It is the will to accept our share of the ruin and disaster which sin—ours and that of all our brothers—accumulates in the world. It is the certainty that Christ's work of redemption has succeeded and that, ever since the death of the Lord, God's love for the sinful world has been real, indestructible, and victorious. It is a felt need of responding to that love and sharing that victory by dedicating one's whole heart and strength to the restoration of the human race which had been lost but, thanks to the Saviour, is still capable of repentance.

Chapter 6

Love Your Enemies

Talk of love and the service of others can often seem empty and unconvincing, lacking in concreteness and interior power. The reason for this is frequently a lack of authentic experience and reflection on it. But frequently, too, the reason is a failure to take seriously the Gospel requirement: "Love your enemies, do good to those who hate you; bless those who curse you and pray for those who maltreat you" (Lk 6:27-28).

Jesus makes love of enemies the criterion for true charity and the sign by which the sons and daughters of God are to be recognized: "If you love those who love you, what credit is that to you? Even sinners love those who love them. . . . Love your enemy and do good; lend without expecting repayment. Then will your recompense be great, You will rightly be called sons of the Most High" (Lk 6:32-35).

The demands are very realistic and not made under the influence of illusions about the world. They are also ruthless and vast, and reveal to us the depths of God's love.

Your Enemies

We will always have enemies, and we would delude ourselves if we thought that a practice or policy imposed by the Gospel could do away with enmities. We must do all we can to lessen and suppress them, but the task is one that must be begun over and over again. The Gospel does not lead to a world free of oppositions and empty of enmities; instead, it requires that we love those who continue to be our enemies, and at the very time when their hostility is doing us most harm. The Gospel does not favor a theology of violence as though violence could be a revelation of the God of Jesus Christ, but it calls upon us to reveal God's love within a world where violence rules and where it may even be necessary at times to have recourse to violence.

The line of thought in the Sermon on the Mount is not political; the images Jesus uses are taken from daily life and relations between neighbors. He speaks of the importunate person who makes you lose time; He speaks of conflicts of interest, vain rivalries, and grudges long festering. We cannot conclude from this that the Gospel deals only with private life or that pardon and generosity should not be real objectives in national and international politics, objectives that deserve the commitment and hard work of Christians. But the examples Jesus uses do show us the unrivalled power of the Sermon on the Mount. The driving force there is not the hope of an idyllic world in which meekness disarms violence. It is something that is both more realistic and more mysterious: a call to treat an enemy as a brother even while he remains an enemy and continues to do violence to us, even while we are perhaps forced to resist him.

The true enemy, the one we find it most difficult to pardon and do good to, is in the last analysis the enemy who is closest to us. We can, therefore, see the point of Christ's examples, with all their familiarity and simplicity. Our enemy is not only the comrade who no longer talks to us, or the colleague who tricked us out of the job we dreamed of. He may live far from us, we may not even have ever met him, but he exists and we know him: he is the one who wants to destroy us, who cannot tolerate it that we should exist and live the way we do. He accompanies us everywhere. He may be a real individual with whom we have dealt, but he may also be a prototype whom we immediately spot behind the various masks where we encounter him:

the policeman, the communist, the integrist, the middle class citizen, the black, the Jew. The violence that characterizes ideological conflicts and the cruelty that is typical of civil wars are due to the fact that in them irreconcilable enemies confront one another and are less concerned to eliminate each other's physical presence than to annihilate the face that obsesses them, the will that is out to destroy them.

The conflict is not necessarily ideological or political. It may only involve one or more individuals in whom we find all the traits that are the source of our suffering, and all the reactions we abhor. Such enemies are frequently those close to us, the people who are familiar with our everyday life; their constant presence becomes an intolerable burden.

Forgive

Such is the enemy Christ requires us to forgive. The task is a difficult one that must be constantly begun anew, "not seven times; I say, seventy times seven times" (Mt 18:22). Why? It is not so much a matter of pardoning offenses received or bad treatment meted out to us, as it is of pardoning our enemy for being what he is, for being the person who here and now (whether our interpretation be right or wrong) embodies the most serious threat and the most ruthless opposition to our very being and to the way we live and think. To forgive means to become aware of all the evil we receive from a deliberate enemy, and all the distance that lies between us, and then to resolve to eliminate the distance and rise above the evil.

Nothing could be less like such forgiveness than the contemptuous indifference that proudly stands apart from people we regard as not worth our slightest attention. The distance we thus put between ourselves and those we are unwilling even to acknowledge is a refusal to pardon; it is an open declaration that the other can only be our enemy and the embodiment of a threat we cannot bear. Segregation is the opposite of forgiveness.

To forgive is to accept our enemy as he is and to will his

existence. It does not mean willing the evil he does, but it certainly means willing that this man who does evil to us should exist in order to do good. It means willing the good of which he is capable, and willing that he be the one to do it. It means willing this even when we receive from him—or think we receive from him—nothing but evil. In short, forgiveness is an act of faith, for, though we see in the other only the evil he does to us, we assert our certainty that he is capable of good, and we count on his doing that good.

We can see now why forgiveness is the real criterion of love, and why we cannot know whether we truly love our brothers as long as we have not encountered them in the form of enemies and forgiven them. It is not difficult to love the people who are on our side; as Jesus says, tax collectors and sinners do that (Mt 5:46-47). But what we love in such people are our own ideas, which they reflect back to us, and our pet preferences. It is much more difficult to dedicate one's life to the work of peace, as the "peacemakers" of the Beatitudes do (Mt 5:9), and to do all one can to overcome hostilities, remove barriers, and bring men together in a more than superficial way. Peace is something so precious, and men suffer so deeply from their divisions, that when they finally manage to meet as friends, their overwhelming joy is enough to forget the years of suffering and disappointment.

The hardest thing of all, however, is not to be able to obtain this joy, to meet with unalterable opposition, to fail to find in oneself the warmth or understanding or simple self-abandon that would cause the barriers to fall. For, after all, we not only suffer from our enemies; we also create them.

The only course left us in this situation is to forgive, and such forgiveness is the triumph of love. Our enemy is what he is, and we will not change him, any more than we can get out of our own skin. But when we are unable to change the situation and eliminate the enmity, when we are stymied by our own sins and those of others, forgiveness is a victory. Forgiveness does not seek to change the situation; it does not refuse such a change, of course, but it is not based on that slim hope. It is not a leap into an unforseeable future, but takes up its position in the midst of the real world as it now is. Though I am what I am, and he is what he is, this man, my enemy, is my brother! Even though I find in him nothing that does not repel me, I take the position that I was created in order to encounter him, and I now act in ways that make no sense except in view of this divinely determined relationship: I try to do good to him. I do not know and cannot know what effect my actions will have. I cannot count on their changing the situation. Yet, in doing them, I assert that the situation will indeed change and that it is for God to change it as and when He wills. Once again, love of enemies is possible only to one who believes in God.

Why so? Because it is not for my own sake that I forgive, or to live up to an image of myself that I have created. I must forgive for my brother's sake, and for the sake of the value he represents. Otherwise, I remain the prisoner of my solitude; I continue to be a sinner who has already received his reward and can do without God. The rule of God which Jesus proclaims means the end of hatred; it means a reconciliation that only God can bring about and that gives birth to a new world. But God already rules in the man who, after trying everything possible to make peace, has no way of overcoming hostility except by forgiveness and by the faith forgiveness is based on.

Jesus and His Enemies

What Christ proclaims, He also fulfills. The adversaries He promises His disciples run to meet Him and crowd together along the route He follows. Jesus experienced hostility. He saw it come into existence from the beginning, within His own family (Mk 3:21) and in His own town of Nazareth (Mk 6:2-6). He felt the inquisitorial gaze of people who were determined to catch Him (Mk 3:2). From the time of His first miracles and His successes in Galilee, and even while the stupefied crowds from all over Palestine pressed about Him, He knew that He was already condemned (Mk 3:6). To His very last day, He was to find in every group of hearers the hostile faces, the crafty questioners, the judges who were preparing their evidence. He did not live a sheltered life, protected by sympathetic people from conflicts and opposition. He saw hatred rising around Him, and the increasing determination to get rid of Him.

The Passion is the outcome of this torrent of hatred. His few friends run away, and the only faces He now sees are hostile or indifferent. The cold anger or outraged shouts of His judges, the cruelty of the guards, the contempt of Pilate, the insults of a weak and brutal crowd—that is the vision offered Him of our race, the image He has of Jerusalem. Doubtless it does not apply to all the inhabitants of the city; many must have stayed at home, ill at ease and troubled. But no one stepped forward, not a single important man intervened, even though Pilate would have been only too glad for someone to make a move that would have let him out of this business. Not everyone in Jerusalem was a criminal; but the city was full of men who were all linked to each other by their sins or their weaknesses. It was necessary that Christ should die, that He "be handed over to the clutches of evil men" (Mk 14:41), and that sin be able to exert its full power against Him, vent all its hate, and show its revolting face. It was necessary that the Son of Man live until we could hate Him, so that we might be sure He was capable of forgiving us everything.

Your Sins are Forgiven

What did the act of forgiving mean to Jesus? What went on within Him when He forgave? And what did forgiveness suppose in the forgiven at the moment they received it? How did Christ's forgiveness transform enemies into friends?

On these matters the Gospel are both suggestive and disconcertingly reserved, almost to the point of seeming indifferent, Two facts are clear, but they are difficult at first sight to harmonize. On the one hand, Jesus sees forgiveness as an essential part of His mission; on the other hand, we never see Him

dwell upon the action of forgiveness or enable us to see what
the sinner is like at the moment of being forgiven or in the
state of having been forgiven.

Jesus is bent on forgiving. When the paralyzed man is let
down through the roof opening of the house where Jesus is
speaking, Jesus sees his faith and that of his friends and immediately says: "Your sins are forgiven" (Mk 2:5), as if that
was the best possible response to such a faith. He acts thus
because His mission, His task as the Son of Man, is to forgive.
The miracles He works are only signs of that (Mk 2:10). This
is why we so often see Him in the company of sinners (Mk
2:15-17), why He likes to have them approach Him (Lk 7:37;
15:2), and why He describes the Son of Man as one who "has
come to search out and save what was lost" (Lk 19:10).

Jesus sees forgiveness as God's supreme activity, the activity
God has most at heart. Christ is extraordinarily reserved when
it comes to giving some idea of the divine life and what happens within God. He makes no attempt to describe the sight,
as it were, or even to suggest how we might attempt to imagine
it. He is completely untouched by the temptation to "mytholo-
gize" which people are at times too ready to see in the Gospels.
He raises no veils so that we may see God. He simply lives
His own life before men: if we know how to see Him aright
we will discover the characteristic features of the Father. There
is no need to see the Father, for we find Him present in every
movement of the Son.

When we note this reserve on Jesus' part and understand the
reason for it, we are all the more struck by the insistent way in
which, in the three "parables of mercy," He describes the joy
in "heaven" (an indirect way of saying "God") every time a
sinner returns to the Father. The joy of the shepherd who
brings back his sheep (Lk 15:7), the joy of the woman who
finds her lost coin (Lk 15:10), and the joy of the father who
sees his son returning (Lk 15:32) all joys in which the simplest
human reactions and man's deepest emotions are juxtaposed
and intermingled. Christ brings them together—adds them up,
as it were—to suggest the mysterious joy God feels when He

forgives. This is probably the only time in the whole Gospel when Jesus thus invites us to gaze at length upon the mystery of God and invites us, in a sense, to share the feelings of God's heart. These feelings are the joyous emotions that spring from the act of forgiving.

Jesus alone was capable of giving us some idea of that joy; He speaks of it with immense assurance and in just the right tone. Yet we never see Him experiencing it Himself. True, the Gospels never claim to be showing us the whole of Christ's experience, and we have no basis for supposing that Jesus never felt joy at bringing God's forgiveness to a sinner. But the way in which the Gospels often show us Jesus in His action of forgiving, yet say nothing about His reactions at such moments, must point to an important fact: Jesus pronounces God's forgiveness and must share at such moments in the joy of God who forgives. How, otherwise, could He speak in God's name and speak of the joy God experiences in forgiving? If there is anything Jesus can speak of only because He Himself immediately experiences it, it is this. For, to forgive sins is not only to exercise a power reserved to God, as Jesus' opponents know very well (Mk 2:7); to exercise the power as Jesus does supposes that He has access to the outlook and experience of God Himself. How is it, then, that we find no trace of this sharing in the divine joy? How is it that Christ's proclamation of forgiveness is reduced to a few words which admittedly say everything needed, but also lack the accents of divine joy that we would expect to find in them? There is nothing of this joy in: "Your sins are forgiven" (Mk 2:5; Lk 7:48) or "Sin no more" (Jn 5:14; 8:11).

One point should perhaps be made here: It is likely that these statements reflect formulas of absolution in use in the first Christian communities, and their unemotional character, like their wealth of meaning, is due to the nature of such formulas, which always aim at sobriety and a maximum elimination of emotional overtones. But even allowing for the possible derivation of these words put on Christ's lips from the forgiveness ritual of the early Church, we are still faced with a fact:

nowhere do we read of Jesus' joy in forgiving sins. The most we find is that after the departure of the Samaritan woman and the return of His disciples, Jesus makes a mysterious reference to the joy shared by both sower and harvester (Jn 4:36), with the implication that He feels this joy at the moment. Apart from this fleeting glimpse, the Gospels are silent, and their silence requires an explanation.

It is not hard to find the explanation. It is to be found in the situation of Jesus as being both man and God. He lives in an abiding communion with His Father; He has a direct experience of God and an infallible certainty concerning His outlook, actions, and reactions. But, insofar as we dare try to understand this mystery, we must say that this direct experience which dominates His whole being and existence is incarnated in the human experience of a human consciousness which has not yet reached the goal to which it is moving, namely, the coming kingdom. As long as He has not yet reached His hour—which is the hour of His death—Christ continues to be a traveller moving toward His destination. It already belongs to Him, and He is certain He will achieve it; He knows what its nature is; it remains only for Him to reach it and enjoy it. Consequently, His joy—which He constantly experiences—is the joy that comes from a goal still distant, even though present all about Him. This applies to the joy He experiences in forgiving: the forgiveness is now and is already given, but joy such as is experienced "in heaven" (Lk 15:7.10.32) is part of the kingdom which is still coming and will have come only with the death of the Son of Man.

Another reason why Jesus cannot have the full experience of the joy God derives from forgiving is that this joy is a shared joy, that unites the one forgiving and the one forgiven. The father's joy at finding his son is complete only when he has restored the son to his proper place in the midst of the celebrating household. God's joy in forgiving involves the joy of His forgiven creature. Christ cannot experience this joy as yet. At times He meets, as at the table of Simon the Pharisee, a sinner whose heart is transformed by forgiveness, and the account in the Gospel lets us glimpse the deep feelings Jesus experiences as He gazes on the woman at His feet. But pure and deep though His joy is on this occasion, it is still only a foretaste of the joy which God has and which He shares with the sinner whom He welcomes into His house.

Father, Forgive Them

The Passion of Christ is proof that the moment of forgiveness is not yet the moment of joy; that the fullest possible forgiveness does not immediately establish a communion with the pardoned sinner; and that forgiveness can be given to enemies even before they are reconciled with the forgiver. The Passion is the time when Jesus sees concentrated upon Him all the evil men are capable of, and when He is surrounded only by merciless adversaries. It is also the time when He forgives and when His forgiveness shows its full value. His enemies do not know what they do (Lk 23:34), but He knows it. He is completely aware of their sins. By the hatred on their distorted faces, He can see and estimate what sin can do to a human being. It is then that He forgives.

The forgiveness is expressed in a short final prayer to the Father (Lk 23:34), but it also finds expression in everything He does during the hours of the Passion. His attitude at this time shows most clearly what it means to love and pardon one's enemies.

Once He is in the hands of His foes, Jesus seems to make no attempt to soften their hearts, to reproach them, or even to assure them of His good will toward them. Evidently, at this time He makes no attempt at reconciliation; these men are about their business: "this is your hour—the triumph of darkness" (Lk 22:53). It is not always possible to bring about reconciliation with one's enemies. But the hour of His enemies is also Jesus' own hour; the hour of darkness is also the hour of forgiveness. Jesus forgives at the very moment when He allows sin to lay its hand upon Him and His enemies to commit their crime.

He forgives in everything He says and does. Although He does not in the slightest try to play down the seriousness of the act which victimizes Him, or to minimize the gulf between Himself and His enemies (on the contrary He points out their responsibility), neither does He do anything to alienate them further or increase the distance between Himself and them and their sins.

Yet Jesus was obviously capable of such action. He had often criticized the behavior of the Pharisees; He had been violent in His denunciations of their hypocrisy and duplicity; He had threatened them with God's judgment. Now, however, He says nothing more to this effect, and makes no gesture of revulsion, even when He is kissed by Judas, His friend (Mt 26:50). No longer does He try to keep His people from the sin they are going to commit; it is too late. Jerusalem has not accepted the message of peace (Lk 19:41). The sin is committed, and all Christ can do now is to carry it, take it on Himself, and see it envelop Him in its horror. This is why He remains silent during His Passion: He is too crushed by His burden and has no strength to speak. He will break His silence only to cry out to the Father in His distress and to assure us that we are forgiven.

Forgive, Because the Lord Has Forgiven You

It may happen that we, too, have no other way of loving our enemies and forgiving them than by being silent. But if our silence is truly to be filled with love and forgiveness, it must be a silence like that of Christ. A silence of indifference is alien to the Gospel, but so is a silence of mere powerlessness and discouraged rejection: "What can you do with people like that!" The Passion shows us that when it becomes impossible to act and be reconciled, it is time to suffer and endure. When the sin of the world had reached its climax and the world's resistance to God had become an unbreachable wall, Jesus took upon Himself the weight of that sin, and saved the world. True forgiveness, the forgiveness of enemies with whom we have not been able to effect a reconciliation, consists in patiently and peacefully taking upon ourselves the sin of our brothers.

But when we do this, it is not we who save him, but the Lord. For we are no more guiltless than our enemies. If we can carry their sins, we do so only by carrying our own as well, for we are all guilty. If we can forgive, it is not because we are good, but because we have ourselves been forgiven.

Chapter 7
Jesus and Politics

Was Jesus a Revolutionary?

It is only natural that the discussion of Jesus' relation to the political order should reflect current events and the divergent political positions men take. Not surprisingly, then, the subject "Jesus and politics" readily takes the form these days of "Jesus and revolution."[1] Several factors are at work here. The most evident is the importance attached to the idea of revolution in various Christian circles. To this must be added the reaction to the terrible results of anti-Semitism, and the questions Christians have been forced to ask themselves about the origins of anti-Semitism. Christians were accustomed in the past to a simplistic reading of the Gospels that tends to make the Jews completely responsible for the death of Jesus, while regarding Pilate's condemnation as simply an act of weakness he would rather have avoided. Nowadays, however, Christians feel the need of starting afresh and studying the trial of Jesus more closely.[2] Recent writings on the subject, though differing on many points, agree that greater importance must be ascribed to the Roman trial and the responsibility of Pilate.

As a result of this revision, Christians have also been led to examine the position Jesus took with regard to the various political currents agitating the Jewish world of His day.

The question may be asked: If Jesus could be charged with disrupting public order, must He not have given some grounds for the accusation? This has led to books that attempt to show the revolutionary character of His activity. As early as 1778, Hermann Samuel Reimarus, the founder of Gospel criticism, called Jesus a political agitator.[3] This view was repeated by the socialist, Kautsky,[4] and even by Wellhausen.[5] In 1929 Eisler took up the same thesis in an enormous work that provided considerable documentation but did not really prove the point.[6] In 1962, Carmichael wrote a sensation-mongering book on the subject, which was eagerly taken up by the press.[7] Then, in 1967, Brandon applied scientific methods in discovering as many similarities as possible between Jesus and the Zealots.[8] He did not turn Jesus into a Zealot, but he did think that, under additions and alterations intended to hide from the public eye a fact it would be dangerous to state openly, we can find in the Gospels traces of a persistent sympathy for the Zealot movement, and even traces, which have deliberately been removed, of a real uprising launched by Jesus for the purpose of seizing the temple.

In a recent article, Georges Crespy takes the facts used by Brandon and shows how they shed light on the death of Jesus. To explain His death, we must go beyond the usual moralistic interpretations which see the cause in the wickedness of the Jews, the cowardice of Pilate, and the cynicism of Herod. The death of Jesus (Crespy says) had a political meaning because Jesus Himself was pursuing a political goal. It was not exactly the same as that of the Zealots, but it was analogous.

> What Jesus has in common with the Zealots is the hope of a world in which the powers now reigning (Sadducees, Romans, the wealthy) will be defeated. . . . The hope is clearly a *political* hope, for it envisages an ordering of common life, of the "polis," and of economic relations as well as relations of power.[9]

Such an interpretation of the Gospels is indeed surprising.

Where do we find even a single word from Jesus to say that the kingdom of God cannot come to pass unless the political powers now reigning are destroyed? Where do we find any indication that He was for a certain ordering of human life in common? Nowhere. The striking thing is rather that He is so unconcerned with these problems and leaves His disciples free to do what they wish in these areas. Such a manner of imagining Jesus setting up institutions reminds us of what is weakest in certain strains of Catholic exegesis.

Attempts to make Jesus resemble the Zealots are based, moreover, on a dubious identification, too readily accepted, between the Sicarii ["stabbers," or assassins] and the Zealots or *qanna'îm*. But there seem to have been, in fact, two movements, not one, each of them admittedly inspired by fanatic religious nationalism. But Sicarii, formed in 6 A.D. by Judas the Galilean, were groups that conducted isolated strikes against the occupation forces until the war of 66 A.D. The Zealots, on the other hand, were the party that in the winter of 67-68, seized Jerusalem in the hope of forcing it to resist Vespasian who was preparing to march upon it. At this time, the priests in the resistance party attacked the Sicarii in the temple and killed their leader, Menahem. The surviving Sicarii fled and holed up in the fortress of Massada where they held out until 73; they played no part in the siege of Jerusalem. These two related but distinct movements should not be identified or confused: the Sicarii were outlaws, while the Zealots were the extremists of a national revolt. In the time of Jesus, the Zealot party did not exist, but the title of zealot was probably claimed with pride by those who imitated the "zeal" of Phinehas (Nm 25:11) and did not hesitate to kill the Lord's enemies.[10]

Jesus and Violence

But even when we have discovered the more or less tendentious character of the comparisons made between Jesus and the revolutionary movements of His day, a number of facts still remain to be explained.

The most important of these is the death sentence which the Roman governor pronounced on Jesus. It was imposed for the crime of rebellion to which the caption on the cross succinctly alludes[11] and was carried out by the Roman authorities. A further fact is that one of the twelve disciples was a man, Simon, who kept the nickname "the Zealot."[12] Even if, as is probable, the Zealot party had not yet been born, Simon's nickname seems to point in a certain direction.

It is also a fact that such actions as Jesus' triumphant entry into Jerusalem and especially His violent intervention in the temple show an open independence of the authorities. In His action in the temple Jesus seems to resemble the Zealots who rejected the worship and priesthood of the temple. Brandon thinks that Mark and, after him, the other evangelists, deliberately toned down Jesus' action so as to avoid awakening the suspicions of the Roman authorities. It seems much more likely, however, that Jesus' action was primarily symbolic, after the manner of the prophets, and that the evangelists, especially Matthew and John, tend to magnify the incident in order to bring out the significance of Jesus' self-manifestation in the temple.[13] In any event, by intervening so conspicuously in a place that was being jealously watched by both the Jews and the Roman forces of occupation, Jesus shows His freedom in regard to all the powers that be, and seems to be siding with those who challenge such powers.

The final words of the discourse at the Last Supper as recorded by Luke are these: "Now, however, the man who has a purse must carry it; the same with the traveling bag. And the man without a sword must sell his coat and buy one" (Lk 22:36). It sounds as if the time for violence has come and Jesus is giving His disciples the signal to act. But to see in His words a summons to join the Zealots would be to forget the whole of His preaching as well as His situation in His final hours.[14] Jesus is referring rather to the time after His death when the disciples will find themselves in difficult circumstances. Their equipment in the difficult days ahead will no longer be the light garb of the short Galilean missions during which they were traveling in a known area and among people who more or less welcomed them. Now they must dress as travelers setting out on a dangerous adventure into a hostile world.[15] It is to be noted, moreover, that the two references of Jesus to the sword, both at the time of His Passion, end in the same way—with a curt answer that puts an end to the discussion: "Enough!" (Lk 22:38.51). The abrupt termination makes the interpretation difficult, but it surely warns us not to see in Jesus' words a summons to continue along the path of the sword.

Jesus' answer to the question of the Pharisees and Herodians about the tribute to Caesar is quite clear on the essential point: "Give to God what is God's" (Mk 12:7). It is more difficult to determine the precise meaning of the first part: "Give to Caesar what is Caesar's." The words can be given varying emphases, ranging from a simple authorization: "If you wish," to an objective statement of fact: "Since you must," or a positive command: "Your duty is . . ."[16] If Jesus is not directly teaching obedience to the state, He is at least accepting a fact. Above all, however, He is asserting the priority of God over Caesar. He is keeping all that is valuable in the "zeal" of the "resisters," but applying it to a different end.

This is the conclusion which both Hengel and Cullmann reach. Jesus had not the slightest intention of supporting contemporary revolutionary movements, since they preached a violence He rejected, and unduly identified the kingdom of God with the kingdom of Israel. These conclusions seem beyond doubt, and they are important.

The Prophets and the Gospel

There is more to the subject, however. The conclusions reached by Hengel and Cullmann do not explain why Jesus had political importance and why His condemnation was a political act. They touch only a limited point—Jesus and the revolutionaries—and do not raise the more basic question of Jesus and the political order.

As a matter of fact, the question is not an easy one to answer. There is much to suggest that Jesus was no more interested in politics generally than He was in revolution. The free way in which He spoke about rulers who use their power to win the title of benefactor for themselves (Lk 22:25) or about Herod, "that fox" (Lk 13:32), hardly justify us in concluding to an opposition in principle or to a contempt for the whole business of politics.[17] His words seem rather to embody the spontaneous reaction of a man of the people, of one who is a political subject, toward those who govern him; individuals in the former position always tend to explain the behavior of their rulers in terms of concern for their personal interests.[18] In this reaction, Jesus would hardly differ from the mass of the people to which He belonged. The difference would chiefly be the standard that is applied. For most people, the politician is suspected above all of seeking personal profit at their expense; in Jesus' eyes, the politician is a man who is not looking for the kingdom of God. The viewpoint is different, but there is just as much alienation.

We can see the same distance between Jesus and the political world when we compare His person and teaching with those of the prophets. The prophets move in the world of politics. From Deborah to Daniel, they all pay close attention to the events which determine the lives of their people; all of them carry on a difficult but uninterrupted dialogue with the kings, princes, and priests who have political responsibility. All of them take off from the contemporary situation of their people and act as God's messengers in telling them what their duty is and what hopes they may entertain. The consciousness of events gives the prophetic message an urgency and relevance of which many people are sharply aware today.

By contrast, many people think the Gospel pale and sinewless. They look in vain for the avenger's voice of an Amos, the dauntless faith of an Isaiah amid universal collapse, or the radiant hopes of the prophets of the exilic period. The perspectives of the Sermon on the Mount seem cramped beside those of the prophets: estrangements and reconciliations among neighbors, minor problems, personal concerns: in other words, everyday

life with its realism and narrowness. And isn't this limitation of
outlook the source of the profound disinterest that characterizes
many Christians when it comes to action of a political kind?
See what a striking difference there is between Jesus and John
the Baptist! When John the Baptist learns of the sin of Herod,
he acts as Nathan once did when he faced up to David, or
Elijah when he confronted Ahab: he risked his life by intervening. Jesus, on the other hand, remains silent; in fact, "when
Jesus heard that John had been arrested, he withdrew to Galilee" (Mt 4:12), as though he were afraid of being compromised
by His dealings with the Baptist. How are we to explain this
difference of attitude?

First of all, we must take an essential fact into account. It
is true enough that Jesus does not come forward to make accusations, and is thereby different from most of the prophets.
Almost all the prophets had to denounce sin, especially the sin
that went unpunished, the sin people avoided mentioning: the
sin of the powerful. Whether they liked it or not, the prophets
were forced to get involved in politics. The sign that this was
their mission is the frequency with which in their preaching they
use the prophetic formula of condemnation: "The Lord says:
After murdering, do you also take possession? *For this, the
Lord says*: In the place where the dogs licked up the blood of
Naboth, the dogs shall lick up your blood, too" (1 Kgs 21:
19).[19]

Such, however, was not the mission of Jesus, for He came
not to condemn the world but to save it (Jn 12:47), and this
fact is reflected in His language. Apart from the reproach to
the towns along the lake (Mt 11:21-23) and His final warning
to the scribes and Pharisees —in which the words "All this, I
assure you, will be the fate of the present generation" (Mt
23:34-36) are in the style of prophetic condemnation—the
language Jesus uses is not that of the prophets but of the
"herald of glad tidings" (Is 40:9) typical of Deutero-Isaiah
(cf. Mk 1:14). He knows what sin is and He does not spare
the sinner, but His business is to go to him, "to search out and
save what was lost" (Lk 19:10). His silence about Herod is

not due to fear but to His sense of His own special mission. John the Baptist is a prophet (Mt 11:9); he must speak like the prophets and remind people of the Law. He is even more than a prophet, being the final messenger sent ahead (Mt 11: 10). Jesus, on the other hand, is the one who is to come; the one whose coming brings the kingdom of God (Mt 12:28); the one who saves and pardons. Without being at all indulgent toward the powerful, He does not confront them as a judge. For them, no less than for others, He is the one who comes to save.

Before we use words like weakness or surrender, we must be clear about what is implied in this new approach with its replacement of prophetic denunciation by the good news of the Gospel. The sign that Jesus' discourse is no less dangerous than the prophet's is that Jesus came to the same end as the prophets, and in even greater isolation and more complete failure. The kingdom of God came to pass through the supreme crime. The fate Jesus met was the doing of the politicians, both the Sanhedrin and the Romans. We can see, therefore, that although the Gospel is a message of salvation and supposes a refusal to condemn, it carries its preacher, no less than the prophetic message did the prophet, into areas where the politicians believe themselves to have complete control. This is evident in the life of Jesus and the reactions He provoked.

Jesus did not, like the prophets, come to denounce sin in the name of the Law or of the spontaneous reactions of man's conscience. Yet, when He proclaimed the limitless love of the Father and called for complete forgiveness, He pointed to the sin concealed in the heart and stripped the mask from all forms of hypocrisy. That is why all His hearers felt that the finger was pointed at them; that is why the people with political responsibility reacted. What would become of the Law if a woman were allowed to commit adultery with impunity? What would become of the sabbath if men were allowed to violate the laws passed to protect it?

Nor was the radicalism of Jesus any more favorable to the Law than the indulgence He preached. If an enemy is a neighbor, if the initial gestures of hostility amount to assassination,

if the cry of the wretched must be heard at any cost, how are
men to defend their national community and social organiza-
tion? The Sermon on the Mount, with its appeal to conscience
for action, forgiveness, reconciliation, and the finding of solutions, and its requirement that conscience never rest satisfied
with what it has already done, is in the last analysis far more
disturbing to a politician than any denunciation by the prophets.
For, the prophets raise an outcry when injustice becomes visible,
but they stop at the threshold of men's consciences.

This is the reason why Jesus' behavior provoked the hostility of the Pharisees and Herodians (Mk 3:6) while He was
still in Galilee and before He came into conflict with the authorities at Jerusalem. Neither the Pharisees nor the Herodians had
any political power, properly speaking. They represented tendencies that were often opposed and certainly quite different in
their inspiration. But in the Jewish world in which all law
comes from God, these tendencies were necessarily political.
Both groups felt threatened by Jesus and they reacted in the
same way: they joined forces in order to find a way of destroying Him.

The Messiah and the Politicians

Jesus thus came into conflict with the political powers and
with the political tendencies that supported them. He must
therefore have set foot in their preserve, and not have been
the stranger to these matters that we might think Him. We may,
however, still ask what the opposition signified. Perhaps it
meant only that with His sharp eye and untrammeled speech
Jesus upset the political applecart. If so, the defensive reactions
of the authorities are understandable. They do not prove that
Jesus had any interest in politics, but simply that politics is
necessarily a corrupt business that is incompatible with the
Gospel.

But Jesus' intervention was not simply that of a sharp-eyed
onlooker. He intervened as the Messiah; that is, as the one
who came to bring Israel the key to its own history and on-

going existence, and tell it what it must do and why it existed at all. His action, therefore, was necessarily political, since it was a matter of life and death for the Jewish people. Not surprisingly, then, the politicians reacted violently. Their reactions were not simply those of guilty men caught in the act, but betrayed a position taken on principle, a rejection that was strictly political in its nature. They also show that Jesus was asking for a political act on their part.

Jesus never presented Himself to His people as their Messiah. It took Him a long time to bring the twelve at Caesarea to acknowledge, in faith, who and what He was.[20] Even at the end of His life, as he stood before Caiphas, He accepted the title of Messiah only with reservations.[21] But the delays and qualifications are not caused by doubt, but, on the contrary, by the clear consciousness Jesus has of His mission. In His every act and word He intends to do the work of the Messiah, that is, to bring Israel the salvation God has promised, and show the way to it. That is why His starting point is the Law, which told His people what God wanted of them. He came not to do away with that ideal but to fulfill it ((Mt 5:17). The ideal was political; so too must its fulfillment be.

In more concrete terms, we are saying that the Gospel too contains its "politics." But they are not a politics like the others; they do not present a model like the others. They are not simply a more difficult, noble, and pure politics, which we may choose from among the others. The Gospel is a way of living the Law, taking it with complete seriousness and fulfilling its requirements without reservation. So too the Gospel is a way of living a political life that puts politics at the service of the Israelite people and their calling. Jesus does not do away with the sabbath or the laws protecting it; He does call on the politicians to see to it that the sabbath serves man (Mk 2:27). He does not come to destroy the temple or expel the priests in charge of it; He does warn them they must make the place "a house of prayer for all peoples" (Mk 11:17).

The proof that in coming forward as the Messiah Jesus was calling for a certain kind of politics is that He laid before His

people a choice whose outcome was political. The fate of
Jerusalem would depend on the choice it made: everything
will be safe if Jerusalem welcomes Him who comes to it; if it
rejects Him, it is doomed to destruction. This is the significance
of the last warning to the religious authorities—scribes, theo-
logians of the Law, and Pharisees—who deal with practice:
"All this, I assure you, will be the fate of the present generation.
O Jerusalem, Jersalem . . . how often have I yearned to gather
your children . . . but you refused me. . . . You will find your
temple deserted" (Mt 23:36-38).[22] It is also the meaning of
the prophecy about Jerusalem that is given to the disciples in
the "eschatological discourse" (Mk 13:2.14). The discourse
does not presuppose that Jesus has an exceptional gift of clair-
voyance, but is part of His prophetic and messianic mission.
Every time the prophets confronted Israel with a choice, they
also showed what was at issue in the choice, namely, the fulfillment of God's promises.

Now that Jesusalem must take sides for or against the Messiah, everything is inevitably at stake; the question is one of
life and death. How could any choice be more political? It
was to be expected that the Jewish authorities should come
together. The Jewish trial was evidently a religious trial, since
the question facing the court was whether or not to acknowledge
in Jesus the presence and summons of God. But the trial was
also, and inseparably, political, because the question was whether or not to accept His word and use it to interpret the Law
and the national vocation of Israel.

The Trial of Jesus

The choice is made first of all by the Jerusalem authorities,
but it is also the choice of the population as a whole. The population was not convoked according to democratic procedures, as
they used to be in a Greek city, but the event was public enough
for the whole people to be party to it, and in fact the event shows
clearly the political significance of both a choice and a failure to
choose. Undoubtedly, a large number of the citizens of Jeru-

salem did not agree with the decision of the Sanhedrin; at least two of them, Nicodemus and Joseph of Arimathea had the courage to come forward after the death of Jesus and claim His body from Pilate for burial (Mk 15:43; Jn 19:38-39). Without indulging in fanciful hypotheses or trying to figure out what would have happened if Jesus had received support from a couple of prominent men at the moment when Pilate was looking for a way to release Him (Jn 19:12), we can say quite simply that Jesus died because in Jerusalem that day no individual or group of men was to be found that was capable of coming forward and preventing the crime.

In reading the Gospels in this way, we are not throwing responsibility for the death of Jesus on the Jews alone. What we are showing, on the contrary, is that the event of that day, which has had a unique influence on the history of mankind, has been constantly repeated throughout history. It happens every time an innocent man falls victim to the conspiracy of sinful men.

Among the sins which led to the death of Jesus, one of the most evident was Pilate's. In the eyes of the four evangelists, even of Matthew and Mark who regard him as hardly more than the executor of a decision made elsewhere, the Roman governor bears the responsibility for the final verdict. The type of death Jesus died, the caption on the cross, and the presence of the two "insurgents" crucified with Him point quite clearly both to the authority who made the decision and to the nature of the decision itself as political. Pilate condemned Jesus because he found that this man, for all his inoffensive appearance, was a danger to his authority. We will even be surprised to find out how much the Gospels make Pilate emphasize the political nature of his decision. For, he says openly that Jesus is not a criminal and that the court finds no fault in Him. If Pilate nonetheless condemns Him to death, his reasons for doing so must be political.

Jesus went along fully with the game. He could have emphasized His complete innocence, shown that He was there because of a mistake, and demonstrated that the government had nothing to fear from Him because He never mixed in political matters. Jesus refused this line of defense. He must assert that his "kingdom does not belong to this world" (Jn 18:36), but, despite the distinction, He does claim to be a king and to have at His disposal both power and subjects who acknowledge His authority (Jn 18:37).

Such language may seem to proceed from a simple desire to be true to Himself, and the intention not to let those who come after Him think He had forgotten His own true dignity. In fact, however, the words have an immediate, concrete reference. He is addressing a man who has power and knows what power means; He is therefore telling Pilate that He Himself has genuine power. His power, unlike Pilate's, is not delegated and temporary but personal and inalienable; Pilate Himself is subject to it![23] Admittedly, Jesus' power is hardly evident at the moment: Pilate can put Him to death (Jn 19:10) and evade the invitations of Jesus with the words: "Truth! What does that mean?" (Jn 18:38). But Pilate cannot evade the power of the truth in question. The very presence of Jesus there before him is a judgment on his political action: his power as governor is given to him so that he may establish justice, but he uses it to commit injustice.

Jesus Saves the Political Order

There is a real parallelism between the invitation of Jesus to His people through an appeal to the Law (an invitation issued in the Sermon on the Mount and rejected by the Sanhedrin) and the invitation to the Roman governor through an appeal to truth and justice. Jesus stands before Pilate as He has already stood before the Sanhedrin, to tell them of the action which He expects of them and which will justify the power they exercise, namely, the proclamation of His innocence and of His rank as Messiah. Jesus cannot be faithful to His mission if He refuses this confrontation. If He is to testify that He is the Messiah of Israel and the Truth that enlightens every man, and if He is to show that the kingdom which is not of this world must nevertheless exist on earth as it does in heaven,[24] Jesus must confront those who are responsible for the fate of Israel and those whose responsiblity it is to make justice and truth rule in the world. His death is a political action, intended to remind politicians of the purposes of their power.

Once risen, He seems to be completely outside the political order, just as He is beyond the power of those who put Him to death. He could have demonstrated His victory in a visible way by appearing in Jerusalem, having Himself acknowledged by a deliriously happy people, and overthrowing His enemies. But in so doing He would simply have made a political gesture on the very grounds where the politicians took their stand. He would simply have shown that the law of the stronger still prevails and that men spontaneously go over to the winning side. There was no need for the Son of Man to die in order to prove this self-evident truth! He would simply have left the political order to its natural fate and proved beyond question that there is no hope of politics serving man and the truth.

Instead of that, the risen Jesus sent His disciples to bear witness to His victory before the judges who had condemned Him. By so doing, He tells us that His business is not finished yet. What He requires must still be accomplished, and the supreme objective of political action will always consist in working to prevent the death of the innocent. In setting this goal for the political order, Jesus saves it from its inherent temptation and prevents it from despairing of man.

Chapter 8
Jesus and Things

"Martha, Martha, you are anxious and upset about many things; one thing only is required" (Lk 10:41). "Do not be concerned for your life, what you are to eat, or for your body, what you are to wear.... The unbelievers of this world are always running after these things. Your Father knows that you need such things. Seek out instead his kingship over you, and the rest will follow in turn" (Lk 12:22.30-31). To many people these words of the Gospel sound odd and unreal. To most, they are the airy words of a dream, and incompatible with life as it is, although valid perhaps for a privileged few who are sheltered from the struggles of life. To a minority, they fill the mind with a constant uneasiness: they point to a basic evil that afflicts human existence, but what can be done to change that existence?

Perhaps both the uneasiness and the indifference arise from a hasty reading of the Gospel and from deeply rooted, unexamined prejudices. The Gospel, after all, is interested neither in fantasies nor in mere remorse. It is a call to life, and therefore a call to see things as they really are: to see them as Jesus did.

The World of Things That Surrounded Jesus

Like every other human being, Jesus lived in the midst of

things, and He spoke of the things that made up His world. A list of these things will prove to be of interest to us. The things Jesus spoke of are the things of daily experience: house, door, and window, lamp and lampstand, the bin and the broom, the grain sown and reaped, the coin for merchant or tax collector, bread, eggs, and fish, the garment to be mended, the bottles to be filled with wine, the fatted calf of the rich man and the glass of cold water, the moths and the worms that cannot be gotten rid of, the dirt and dust that constantly collects, the leaven and the kneading-bowl, the salt and the flour, the cloak and the roof.

The outdoor things He speaks of are also everyday things: the weather, the ripening harvest and the weeds, the fish that rises to the surface or stays at the bottom, debts to be paid, quarrels between neighbors, the story of a wedding or a royal reception, the trickery of an unscrupulous manager. Great events and important people are afar off and have little place in ordinary conversation. But discussions of the Law and questions raised by the Scriptures are on everybody's lips.

The world which this list suggests is both broad and limited. It embraces the whole of life and situates life in a context of customs, memories, convictions, and hopes that provide a solid footing and open up vistas. But the circle of things to be dealt with is fairly limited: no oddities from other cultures, no discoveries taking place, no superfluities. Luxury and refinement are not unknown, but they are marginal, something seen from without.

The dominant impression we receive is of an outlook both modest and positive. The things which Jesus had before Him and which He described are those of the simplest Galilean, a man of the people who is not blind to the unusual things He witnesses or the displays of ostentation He may see, but whose main concern is everyday life.

The Gospel of John brings home to us, by contrast, the sheer commonplaceness of the things which fill the Synoptic Gospels. In John we read no longer of things or objects, but of the elements: the wind, the running water, the light, or of human situations: birth and illness, hunger, thirst, sleep and death.

The things involved are pretty much the same as in the Synoptics: bread, fish, vases, perfume. The world is the same, but it is seen in a special light and reveals inexhaustible depths.

This, then, at first glance, is the world of the Gospels. Things in the world have the consistency and importance they would normally have for a villager from Nazareth or a fisherman from Capernaum. We must still ask whether Jesus has scorn and contempt for things. One point, however, is certain: He sees them like everyone else and speaks of them as naturally as the next man.

A World of Manipulated Things

Our impression of consistency becomes even sharper if we notice how these things are presented. Rarely are they described in themselves, as one might describe a landscape or a still life. In almost every instance, things are held in men's hands or controlled by men; in other words, we see not so much mere things as men's actions with them. A woman mixes yeast in the flour; she sweeps her house looking for a lost coin; she puts her pennies in the collection box; she mends a worn garment; she draws water from a well; she lights a lamp and puts it on the stand; she breaks a bottle of perfume. A man observes the evening sky before nightfall and in the morning as he opens his door; he leaves his plow or his net; he builds a house and plans the enlargement of his barns; he sows the seed and calculates the harvest; he separates the wheat and the chaff, the saleable fish and the small fry; he calculates the benefits of a good job or the sum total of his debts.

Never, or almost never, are things in the Gospel inert or described for their own sake; the eye that observes them is not simply curious or distant, the gaze rarely contemplative. Man is always on the scene and always acting. The only instance of a detached vision focused directly on the object as such seems to be Jesus' reflections on the lilies of the field that are arrayed more splendidly than Solomon in his glory (Mt 6:29). When He observes the colors in the sky, He does so in order to find out whether tomorrow's weather will be good or bad. Nothing could be less contemplative, less "artistic," than the way Jesus looks at things.

The point is not that Jesus in distant or absent from the spectacle the world affords. It is rather that His attention never strays from man and his actions. It is a commonplace to contrast the esthetic outlook of the Greeks with their love of colors and spaces, and the dynamic thrust of biblical images with their evocation of movements and feelings. But it would be hard to prove that even in the latter domain Jesus is a master comparable to a Job or an Isaiah; He lives and reacts rather as His people generally do. He is a son of Nazareth and is marked by His childhood and apprenticeship; it was in this context that He gained His knowledge of people and things.

Whatever He sees or speaks of, He views as handled by men and as taken up into human experience. This is why the Gospel is accessible for every period of history; it is why all men are at home with it. For objects change and cultures rise and pass awayl, but the essential actions of eating, dressing, finding shelter, and settling down will always have the same meaning.

Things Used

A sign of Jesus' "positive" outlook on things is the importance He assigns to their use. He sees things as incorporated into man's actions, and He sees the actions themselves as purposeful. The purpose is often mentioned; if it isn't, it is often too evident to need mentioning. A man covers up a treasure he has found so that he may go and buy the field where it is hidden; uses yeast to make the dough rise; lets the weeds grow so as not to ruin the grain in the attempt to dig them out; sorts the fish for the market; sows seed so that it may grow; sweeps the house to find the lost coin; mends a garment in order to wear it; shuts the door so as to have peace in the house—or to pray; kills the fatted calf in order to celebrate the return of the son who has been found; lights the lamp so as to have light to see by.

Nothing could be more trivial than these observations, but

the very accumulation of trivialities gives us pause. Why does Jesus regularly choose His examples from the sphere of the useful, and a very down-to-earth usefulness at that? Where does He get one of His favorite expressions: "Of what use?" Of what use is salt that has lost its savor? Of what use are two eyes and two hands if you end up in hell? Of what use is it to gain the whole world if you lose your true life? Of what use is it to show off your almsgiving and fasting and praying? The showing off becomes your reward, and the reward disappears when the show ends and the spectators go their way.

This utilitarianism disgusts souls who dream of a completely pure religion. They are mistaken, however, since the only benefit Jesus envisages and the only reward He offers is the favorable regard of the Father who sees you and knows the true value of actions and things. The joy Jesus promises His disciples is the joy of discovering in the eyes of the Father as He welcomes them, the unsuspected value of their smallest actions, even of a glass of water given to a passerby. Such joy is the unadulterated joy that springs from love. It does not result from a disinterestedness that is careful to will nothing; it arises from a series of actions that seek to accomplish something. When Jesus asks "Of what use?" He speaks in the light of universal human experience and man's instinctive reactions. For the great majority of men, disinterestedness is only a dream and a luxury, while total disinterestedness will prove completely meaningless to those who seek it. Man's actions must have a purpose, and the actions the Gospel shows us are the basic actions of man in our world.

A world in which nothing is simply given, a world where you must sow in order to reap, light a lamp if you want light, provide oil for the lamp, and have money if you wish to go shopping, a world in which people would not think of wasting things because life is difficult and the economic laws strict—that is the kind of world Jesus knows.

Lost and Found

One sign of the value Jesus attributes to things and the

meaning He finds in man's actions is the place the theme of losing and finding has in His thinking and preaching. The loss of a thing is not unimportant to Him. If a sheep falls into a pit, its owner will of course go and drag it out, even on the sabbath. "Who among you would not do as much?" He asks, showing that it is a natural reaction (Mt 12:11). And from this spontaneous reaction He draws a far-reaching conclusion: "Clearly, good deeds may be performed on the sabbath" (Mt 12:12). Does this mean that seeking what was lost and doing good are one and the same thing?

Even more indicative of Jesus' concern for things that may be lost are the three parables collected by Luke, in which Jesus defends the manner in which He goes out to sinners and welcomes them (Lk 15). There are three parables, but a single lesson—three parables both similar and different. The first, about the lost sheep, is addressed to men: "Who among you, if he has a hundred sheep and loses one of them, does not leave the ninety-nine in the wasteland and follow the lost one until he finds it? And when he finds it, he puts it on his shoulders in jubilation. Once arrived home, he invites friends and neighbors in and says to them, 'Rejoice with me because I have found my lost sheep.' I tell you, there will likewise be . . . joy in heaven . . ." (Lk 15:4-7).

The parable of the coin lost and found is addressed to women, and illustrates the same motif: "What woman . . . does not light a lamp and sweep the house until she has retrieved what was lost? . . . 'Rejoice with me! I have found the silver piece I lost' " (Lk 15:8-10). But the third parable, the one about the son who had been lost and was found, does not begin in the same way: "Who among you . . . ? "What woman . . . ?" The reason for the change is that the father's behavior—his anxiety, his expectation and hope, his forgiveness and joy— is not so natural in a father who has been offended and dishonored.

The originality of Jesus and the Gospel does not consist in playing down the value of things or of the bonds which unite men to their world or to those they hold dear. On the contrary! For, in Jesus' view, the concern we have for persons and things should help us grasp the depth of God's attachment to the world He created and the children whose coming He awaits. There is a profound connection between the overflowing, almost unsuitable joy of the father when He finds his son, and the radical demands of the Sermon on the Mount. For, if there is an element of the murderous even in the insult a man hurls at another, or if adultery begins with the first lustful glance, the reason is not that God has put men into His world with a view to keeping them from touching it or because He feels impelled to assert His own mastery over them. He sets up His prohibitions because His world is a precious and delicate thing and the heart of man is easily touched. But, if we may so put it, the heart of God is even more easily touched; it is in turmoil every time He sees one of His creatures destroying itself: "Not a single sparrow falls to the ground without your Father's consent" (Mt 10:29; literally, "without your Father").

There is a great gulf separating the God of the universe and Lord of the stars and the ages, and the Palestinian peasant forced by his situation to calculate and economize. Yet there is also a greater likeness than we might imagine. The proof of this is the ease with which the Son of God lived in our world, adopted a realistic and undetached outlook, and reflected in His own person the reactions common among those about Him.

"You Are Anxious. . . Do Not Be Concerned"

But what, then, becomes of the clear admonitions: "You are anxious. . . . Do not be concerned" (Lk 10:41; 12:22)? Does Jesus change His attitude to suit audience and milieu? Does He follow a whim of the moment, a passing fancy? Of course not! True, He does not pride Himself on a strict systematic logic, but all His reactions are profoundly consistent. It will be worth our while to uncover the secret of this consistency.

As a matter of fact, there is no great difficulty about getting at it. The prohibition against anxiety is not based on the futility of our efforts or an absence of any value in things. Jesus does not say: "Do not be concerned about what you are to eat, because it's not worth the trouble." No: he gives a very concrete reason: "Your Father knows you need such things" (Lk 12:30). The need is very real, and God takes it seriously. The divine seriousness becomes the basis of Jesus' argument: If God clothes the lilies of the field so splendidly and if he is concerned about the flying sparrow, how can He forget man, who is His child?

A reader may be tempted to falsify the comparison with the birds of the air and the flowers of the field, and then use the falsification to discredit the Sermon on the Mount with its seemingly chimerical outlook. But Jesus does not at all say that a man must live like a plant or follow his instincts like an animal. On the contrary, man as Jesus sees and understands him, is a being who plans his actions and looks forward to the yield from his labor. To be convinced of this we need only note how important the ideas of fruit and harvest are in Jesus' discourses. He speaks of the fruit of the sown field, the vine, the fig tree, and it is always fruit in which the toil, experience, and foresight of man play a determining role. There is nothing in the Gospel to support the dream of a return to nature and a sloughing off of culture.

But, though man must calculate, work, and look ahead he must also remember that he is not alone, but that God sees him, his work, and his calculations. God will not replace man and do the work man should have done, but He does watch what man does and how he sets about it. God, after all, is more interested than anyone else in the creatures He has made. The faith Jesus offers and requires of His disciples takes shape in the conviction that an attentive and concerned Father watches over us. It is a difficult faith, because the truth it asserts is not evident; God's silence is more striking than His attentiveness, and He gives us no sign of His concern. But that is precisely where faith comes in: to trust in God enough not to ask Him for signs; to think Him great enough that He can rely on His creatures. To the man who possesses this faith and confidence, the cares of the world lose nothing of their urgency; the struggles of life are just as brutal as before. Yet life is different now because it has a meaning; because God takes it seriously; and because He comes to His children amid their cares and amid the things that fill their world.

"One Thing Only Is Required"

We have still to come to the decisive words, and they seem calculated to invalidate all that we have been saying: "One thing only is necessary" (Lk 10:42). Exegetes are sometimes unsure how to interpret the words; and the manuscript readings vary, a sure sign that the scribes had their difficulties. Yet, in the perspectives adopted by St. Luke and in the context of his Gospel, the meaning is clear: "The word of Jesus is more important than the temporal things that make us anxious."[1] It is good to think ahead to a meal and to want it to be as good as possible, but when Jesus passes by and speaks in God's name, the most important thing in the world is to listen to Him. This was Mary's choice that day, and it was the better choice.

To deduce from this story the superiority, in principle, of the "contemplative life" over the active life would be to force the text. The meaning is in fact very clear and very precise: When Jesus passes by, when we hear the call of the Gospel and the proclamation of the kingdom, the only thing worthwhile is to stop, listen, and respond. The meaning is thus exactly the same as in "Seek first his kingship over you, his way of holiness" (Mt 6:33) in the Sermon on the Mount. In fact, the perspectives within which this command in Matthew is situated are the same as in Luke: "Stop worrying, then. . . . Your heavenly Father knows all that you need" (Mt 6:31-34).

Seeking the kingdom does not mean assuming that "all these things" are valueless and that the most desirable thing would be to be able to do without them and live instead in a weightless, airy world, free of all cares. The world in which Jesus lived was not suspended between heaven and earth; it was a world in which men made calculations and choices. What Jesus did was to crown all the calculations with a supreme choice and a value that had absolute priority: God and His kingdom. It would be false to say, in God's presence, that the world should simply disappear. The real need is for everything to be ordered, with each thing in its own proper place. In the last analysis, the positive and "utilitarian" outlook of Jesus continues to be in control when He makes everything else secondary by comparison with the kingdom. For, the kingdom is the only thing absolutely necessary; the only thing which if lost is irretrievable.

Obviously, we must distrust simplistic solutions. To say that the kingdom of God is the most important thing or that the Gospel is utilitarian in outlook is in a sense to distort the message of Christ. The message is one of disinterested love, and the only reward offered by the Sermon on the Mount is the discovery that we are always before the eyes of a Father who sees and knows us and waits for us. But in the eyes of God man is astonished to discover the value of his actions and of the things that attracted him or were a burden to him. Only God is necessary and only God can suffice for man. But man learns to approach and find God in things, in the way he deals with them, in the choices he makes among them, in the seriousness with which he uses them, in the distance he is able to put between himself and them. God is radically different from all things, but he gives Himself to us in even the least of them.

Chapter 9

Jesus and Money

"You cannot give yourself to God and money" (Lk 16:13). Jesus' words are categorical and intended to elicit from us a response that is undivided and perfectly clear: We cannot be disciples of Christ and children of God if we live to serve money.

But Jesus is condemning the service of money or the idolatry of money, not money itself. Admittedly, He manifests no sympathy for it, no special curiosity about it. He does not consider it desirable, or regard it as one of the things that makes life worthwhile or establishes a man's true value. The rich draw His attention infinitely less than the poor, and the lot of the rich is a wretched one: "Unhappy you who are rich, for you have your consolation now" (Lk 6:24; the words should be translated in this way, as a lament, not a curse). He expects nothing from the rich who derive their consolation from money, and He has nothing He can give them.

Yet He is not afraid to speak of money, and He speaks of it as something useful that can even be quite valuable at times. He finds it natural that a woman who loses a coin should search the whole house for it, that she should ask her neighbors whether they have seen it, and that she should go out again to tell them she has found it. He does not think it necessarily scandalous that money should be productive and yield an income or that a capital sum can double. The servant who gives his master back ten thousand silver pieces instead of the five thousand he had received (Mt 25:14-21) is not a crook like the fellow who falsifies his accounts (Lk 16:8). He is "an industrious and reliable servant"—in small matters, indeed, but matters for which Jesus has no word of reproach.

We never see Him actually handling money, but there is no reason for thinking that He did not use it like everyone else. The twelve had a common purse, held by Judas, for expenses and almsgiving, and on occasion Jesus ordered purchases made with the money (Jn 12:6; 13:29). He knows the value of the few small coins the poor widow throws into the collection box in the temple (Mk 12:42), as He does of the fortune spent in a moment when Mary of Bethany breaks her bottle of perfume (Jn 12:3-5). In this one gesture of respect and gratitude Mary spends a year's wages, and Judas betrays Jesus for the price of a slave. Jesus lived in a world in which, as in ours, money was used as an index of value. He did not try to escape from the system; He was a victim of its basest aspects, but He also knew the generous ends it could serve.

What is the usefulness of money in His view, then? He gave no direct answer to this question, but His words and behavior make His answer clear enough: Money is intended to be given, and it is good that it should go to those who need it. "Give" is the refrain of the Sermon on the Mount: "Lend without expecting repayment" (Lk 6:35); "Give to all who beg from you" (Lk 6:30); "Give, and it shall be given to you" (Lk 6:38); "Sell your possessions, and give to the poor" (Mt 19:21). The reason why this word bulks so large in Jesus' vocabulary is not that money is evil but that giving is essential. Jesus is a realist: He does not bid us sell so that we may have nothing, but so that the poor may have something to live on. Pope Paul VI's encyclical letter on the development of peoples (*Populorum Progressio*) is based on the Gospel: if there is no sharing and if money is not so used that the greatest possible number of people may profit by the earth's resources, then we will have no Christianity, nothing but a sinful mankind.

The ideal is not an easy one; it is easier for a camel to pass through a needle's eye (Mt 19:24). Though money is meant to serve, it soon makes servants of those who have it. This is why it so easily becomes an idol, a Mammon (Lk 16:9.11.13). It is also why the disciple of Jesus must choose between the service of God and the service of money, just as, back in the time of the pagans and their idols, the chosen people had to choose between the service of the true God and the service of the Baals.

When the pagans sheathed their idols in gold, they thought they were making their cities safer, their country more prosperous, their armies stronger. So too the rich pile up money so as to safeguard themselves against a future they fear. But the more elaborate their defenses, the greater becomes their panic. Yet money is not an evil creature. The wood and gold the pagans used in making idols were things useful and valuable in themselves. But because men are afraid to live and trust themselves to God, and because they need to touch and possess, they shape these noble creatures into ludicrous images of their dreams and anxieties. Money, too, has a certain nobility, for it can be a way of expressing men's trust in one another and a way of making them present to one another despite the distance between them. But for money to be thus nobly used, men must learn to use it for giving, in the image of the true God who is always giving.

Chapter 10

The Agony of Jesus

According to the Gospels, Jesus speaks of His death in two different ways during the period before He must actually face it. He speaks of it as something decisive for Himself and the world, an event that will fulfill God's plan and man's destiny. When He speaks of it thus, He uses the language of the prophets and the apocalyptic visionaries. On a few occasions, when His feelings become too strong and He cannot control them, He cries out, as it were, in words that are an appeal rather than a communication. In these moments we glimpse a secret too burdensome for Him to unload on someone else, but which He would like nonetheless to share with His friends. These two languages—the objective language, on the one hand, of the Scriptures and hard necessity, and the subjective language, on the other, of a living man who is going to His death, already oppressed by all that awaits Him—meet and unite. In this meeting, in the natural mingling of the two, there is revealed to us one of the characteristic traits of the mystery of Jesus Christ. He is heir to the tradition of Israel with its vocabulary, images, and perspectives, and it enables Him to conceive the future that awaits Him, and the meaning of the death He must die; since His heart is vulnerable to all attacks, He is seized and shaken by the coming death, like a man who is defenseless against it. The supreme moment of all history and the center of the whole universe is this agony in the face of death.

The Son of Man Must Be Handed Over and Put To Death

In the Synoptic tradition, the first explicit predictions of the Passion are dated in a precise way: they begin with Peter's confession of faith at Caesarea ((Mt 16:13-23; Mk 8:27-33; Lk 9:18-22). They serve what might be called a pedagogical need, and serve to enlighten and correct the faith of the twelve. It already took a rather exceptional faith to proclaim Jesus the Messiah when one considers His situation. On the evening of the day when the loaves had been multiplied, the disciples shared the enthusiasm of the crowd and their astonishment at the miracle, and were probably among those most eager to make their Master the king Israel was waiting for (Jn 6:15). But Jesus was even quicker in breaking their mood, and He forced them to enter their boat and start rowing (Mk 6:45-48). It was a brutal but salutary way of disillusioning them. After this imposing miracle, which had no sequel, Jesus kept His distance from the crowds and public opinion, even to the extent of leaving Jewish territory. The disciples continued to follow Him, confused in many respects but faithful just the same.

It is this fidelity that Jesus now uses as a springboard. His intention is to convert it into an explicit faith by asking His followers the decisive question: "Who am I in the eyes of the people? Who do you think I am?" The experiment was successful; the answer was correct. In the exiled prophet, in the disconcerting person who possesses such great powers yet is so reluctant to use them, the disciples are able to see not a miraculous, fantastic figure, such as one of the prophets risen from his grave, but the straightforward figure of the Messiah, the Saviour whom God gives His people and the world. The disciples' act of faith is thoroughly real, because in it they commit themselves and all they are to the real person standing before them.

It is a faith still uncertain of itself, still mingled with earthbound dreams. Hardly has it found utterance than Jesus is forced to clarify and deepen it by confronting it with the reality about Himself: "He began to teach them that the Son of Man

had to suffer much" and "be put to death" (Mk 8:31). Moreover, anyone who claims to be His follower "must deny his very
self, take up his cross, and follow in my steps" (Mk 8:35).
Hard words those, but their inflexible demands must be respected and not watered down. But we do not falsify them
if we try to give them their full meaning by weighing each word
and situating the statements in the context in which they were
spoken.

The Son of Man must . . . He is faced with a necessity that
cannot be evaded, an imperative that allows no qualifications.
Jesus is here speaking not theoretically about a duty that must
be done, but concretely about an event that is inevitable. He
is speaking therefore about a future that must come to pass.
What is the source of the necessity? Is there an irresistible fate
at work? A divine decree that cannot be appealed? God is
certainly involved, since in Jesus' eyes all things are possible to
God (Mk 14:36; cf. 9:23) and all necessities are subject to His
will. But nothing says that the imperative Jesus must obey expresses, as such, the will of God. The formula has an impersonal tone: God is present without being an active agent in
the proper sense.

The Son of Man *must be delivered into the hands of men.*
Again the tone is impersonal; the verb is passive, and suffering
is indicated. The subject is a victim who does not act but under-
goes. The active agents are men who lay hold of the victim and
subject Him to all the cruel punishments they can think up. The
verb "delivered" or "handed over," which recurs in the predictions of the Passion and then in the successive moments of the
betrayal by Judas, the arrest of Jesus, and the actions of men in
sending Him from tribunal to tribunal and finally from the
pretorium to death, perhaps echoes the original terror Jesus
felt: the horror of an innocent man as he stands on the edge
of the abyss of hatred, vile treatment, and cruelty into which
he will be thrown. But the word also reflects a long tradition
of biblical prophecy concerning the promises of salvation in
which God undertakes to deliver Israel's enemies into her hands,
as well as the threats in which God says that He will deliver

Israel into the hands of her enemies because of her sins. The images Jesus calls up in the minds of His hearers are those of the experience of complete helplessness, the moment when one is at the mercy of an enemy who has every means at his disposal and will vent his hatred to the utmost; the images of defeat and destruction. He is pointing to something worse than death: utter destruction, limitless failure, complete dishonor. The victory will belong to His enemies.

The Son of Man. Once this subject is introduced, the whole meaning changes. He must indeed be handed over to His enemies and die. But this necessity has its origin in Him and what He is. "Son of Man," as Jesus uses the title, refers indeed to Himself, but it designates first of all the figure whose role He came to play. For "Son of Man" is not directly a way of saying Jesus, the worker of Nazareth who became a prophet and witness to the kingdom of God, but a figure from the world of apocalyptic vision. He is not, strictly speaking, someone hoped for, but the symbolic expression of a hope. In order to point to the coming of the kingdom, a process which they obviously could not describe in advance, the apocalyptic writers created visions, in which the coming of the kingdom is connected with the manifestation in heaven of the Son of Man.

Jesus gives these visions a direct point of reference and a concrete consistency. He does so, not by filling in the details of the vision nor showing their correspondence to coming events, but by identifying the Son of Man with Himself and thus giving this symbolic figure a concrete content: His own life and coming death.

Even before this step is taken by Jesus, the apocalyptic tradition had already linked the figure of the Son of Man to a kind of imperative: The Son of Man *had to* appear on the clouds of heaven. But what we have here is simply the necessity proper to a prophetic statement, that is, a statement which cannot fail to find fulfillment. When Jesus says, however, that the Son of Man *must* suffer, the necessity is not only the prophetic necessity proper to the word of God; it is also heavy with the inevitability we associate with an unavoidable destiny.

That the inevitability of evil and the unavoidable demands of God should coincide is the scandal of the created universe and the scandal of the cross. Can God will this evil? How can we tolerate His willing it for His Messiah, for His own Son?

Enlightenment comes only if we refuse to abandon the very formulating that scandalizes us and if we are willing to confront it directly and at close quarters. If the Son of Man must be handed over to sinners and die because of their hatred, then this "must", which has its origin both in God's will and in the power evil possesses, is due to what the Son of Man is. He is to make His appearance as one victorious in the heavens (to use the language of the apocalypses). If this is to happen and if the victory prophesied is to become a historical reality in the person and work of Jesus, then Jesus must experience the power and horror of sin. Otherwise He would live only at the surface of our humanity, knowing only what is good and light-some in it; He would not know from experience the extent to which brutality, greed, and the will to destroy can deface the image of man. But then He would not be the Son of Man who represents mankind. He would not bring men the only thing capable of saving them from their sins: the proof that they are forgiven, and the evidence that, no matter how far they have fallen, no matter how deeply they have despaired, they are still able to be loved by God and have such value in His eyes that He will hand His Son over to death for them.

This, then, is the mysterious necessity attaching to the cross. It is not the unqualified demand proper to a divine decree in which God imposes His will, nor the irresistible destructive power of evil in the world; it is the necessity by which the de-structive power of sin is met, within the world and its reality, by a power capable of enduring this evil to the bitter end and changing it into forgiveness, reconciliation and love. God is certainly present, as is His will, which cannot allow itself to be scorned; sin is also present, with its deadly consequences. But the law governing our world is not the absolute law of a master who will tolerate no resistance to his orders, nor the inevitability proper to sin which can produce nothing but evil. The law governing our world is the law of the cross. This means it is the law of a God who is unable to bear man being lost through sin and therefore subjects His own Son to the only law He is sure will be fulfilled with total perfection: the law of love.

The Law of the Son of Man

The cross, then, is the law of the Son of Man. It is indeed a law: that is, a strict, inflexible demand. To break it or evade it would be to cause irremediable disaster, since mankind would be abandoned to the power of its own sin and condemned to a definitive and eternal death. The cross is a law which, like all laws, seems to be imposed from without and dictated by a blind indifferent will, or by the nature of things, or by the irremediable malice of man and the basic absurdity of the universe.

At the same time, however, the cross is the law proper to the Son of Man, that is, a law absolutely His own, an exigency deriving from what He is in the depths of His being. Every creature, every man included, comes into the world with its own law that is written in every fiber of its being; that law is the very meaning of its existence and, in man's case, of its personality as well. It is a law which does not originate within the creature itself but comes from outside and is thus a sign that its existence has its source in another, the Creator. Yet the law is the creature's own; it is the form taken by the necessity the creature is under of being itself and of becoming what it is; not to obey that law would mean losing its very being. The same holds for the law which constitutes the Son of Man and makes Jesus be the Son of Man: if He evades it or does not fulfill it perfectly, He ceases to be Himself and loses His very meaning.

Such a hypothesis is improbable, even unthinkable. How could Jesus fail to fulfill His destiny or cease even for a moment to be the witness to the kingdom, the one sent by God, the Son of the Father? These words express the truth proper to the person whom the Gospels describe, and it is a truth that cannot be shammed. Like us, Jesus is subject to a law, caught up in a history and a destiny, dependent on men and events, faced with a task, and exposed to all the risks men must meet. But He lives the law of His being in total lucidity: events come upon Him as they do upon us, but He is never caught by surprise; He is always able to confront them and immediately give them their full significance by making them part of Himself. Nowhere does this perfect mastery show so strikingly as in this law of the cross.

Jesus must indeed be handed over; He must experience the deadly agony of falling into the hands of sin itself and being submerged, defenseless, in the frightful, bottomless abyss of our sins. But He is aware of all this and can foretell it, not by writing a scenario that will be followed point by point, but by living, in His own way and to the bitter end, His own life and the world in which His life is played out. He is daily the witness and victim of man's sin, his power to hate and reject, his capacity to cause suffering and to destroy himself.

From the time of His first miracles, when the Pharisees and Herodians begin plotting to destroy Him (Mk 3:14) and the conspiracy begins to take shape between political authorities and religious leaders that will eventually bring Him to Calvary, He needs neither well-placed informers nor special revelations to tell Him what is going on. His clarity of vision, His sensitivity to all the movements of the human heart, His observation of the people He rubbed shoulders with and the crowds that besieged Him—these enabled Him to know all He had to know. The relentless rejections, the fickleness of the mob, the weakness of the disciples, the perversions of religion, the betrayals of the politicians were familiar to Him from the beginning; He encountered them every day and knew that they would bring Him to His death. What prior knowledge did He have of the details of His death? To judge by His words, probably not very much, but that doesn't matter. He certainly saw them emerge more clearly as the conspiracy relentlessly tightened the net around Him.

A tragic fate? Not really. The Gospels are not tragic, and fate has been vanquished. Yet all the elements are there to make this man the supreme tragic figure: an inevitable destiny, the approach of which is known in advance and announced step by step; the clash of divine law and human nature at its worst, with one individual as the field of conflict. That is what men are, even the greatest of them; such too is the man they call God ... But nothing could be further from the Gospels than such accents of despair. Men remain indeed what they always were, capable of anything. But the vision of them here is not despairing, but forgiving, and the law that governs the world is the law that brings to light the true person of Jesus and the secret of the Son of Man. Mankind must go all the way in its sin, and Jesus must experience that sin in its full horror. He must be seized by it and shaken to His depths by it; He must face it in its worst form. But through it all, He must still be capable of loving man, of embracing Him and rescuing Him from His sin. Then He will be able to give mankind back to His Father, and His mission will be accomplished. Then the Son of Man will be glorified and will reveal the secret which has been responsible for everything: the love the Son receives from the Father and pours out upon the lost human race.

Filled with Sorrow to the Point of Death

All that we have been saying is to be found in the Gospel, either in so many words or equivalently. Jesus said it all to His disciples, at first in a veiled way, because they were not ready for the unvarnished truth and because coming events were still unclear, and then in more and more precise words, as the end drew near and details became clearer. He said it all again, in an unusually solemn yet still very simple way, at His final meal with the disciples.

At the moment when Judas, one of His own, had already sold Him to the chief priests, but before the latter laid hands on Him and when everything could still change, Jesus, with full awareness and full freedom, handed Himself over to death for the sake of His disciples, and placed His body and blood in their hands. He thus gave the proof that the supreme sin, the murder of the Son of Man, would end in His glorification and in the victory of His love and forgiveness. The betrayal and all the vile acts to which it led were required if the secret of Jesus was to be manifested, and the meaning of the law that explains His life was to be revealed, namely, that He loved His enemies infinitely more than they could ever hate Him. God had finally won the victory so precious to Him that for the sake of it He allowed sin to enter the world. God was justified in imposing this law on His Son; Jesus had indeed been capable of being faithful to it to the very end.

The final battle, however, had still to be fought, and it was the most terrible of all. In one sense, everything was over, for not only had Jesus given His word, but He had converted that word into His body that was to be broken and his blood that was to be shed. He could not go back on His word; He could not take back the gift that already contained His death in the concrete form that He expected it: the form of betrayal, denial, hatred, cruelty, fear. He accepted all that when He gave His body; He died then for all His enemies.

At the last moment, however, His strength seems to fail Him; He cannot control His fear, but calls His friends to help Him and begs His Father to spare Him a trial that is too much for Him, a trial He cannot face.

Of all the mysteries of the Son of God made man, His agony in Gethsemani is the most precious to us, but also the most inaccessible. Even His closest disciples did not have the courage to watch Him, but the very avowal of their failure is an incomparable testimony to the event. If the disciples failed, it was because the strength that sustained them and kept them moving forward also suddenly broke down: Jesus was paralyzed. Why? Fear of physical torture, disgust at mankind, helplessness of all His efforts? We must think that all of these came into play, but we must also be convinced that the truth is beyond our power to grasp.

One thing is certain: during these minutes Christ reached the greatest depths of His suffering, was crushed by the heaviest burden. The terrible fatigue that fell upon Him every evening in the cities and the countryside, the despair of the poor, the tears of mothers and innocent children, the disgust with life and the anguished fear of death, in a word all the suffering of mankind—Jesus knew it all at this time and was on the point of succumbing to it. But He held on and got up to meet Judas and His death. He held on because the fearful, revolting reality of it all was the cup the Father was holding out to Him, the law which he had given His Son and which the latter could reject only by ceasing to be the Son.

It is at this point that we find voiced in the Gospels the words Jesus must have constantly been repeating to His Father, like a child to its daddy: "*Abba* . . . let it be as you would have, not as I" (Mk 14:36). At the worst moment of agony, at the blackest hour of the night, Father and Son meet and are united: Jesus goes forward to complete His Passion, exhausted mankind can pursue its journey, and the Father waits for them both.

Part Two
Who Is Jesus?

Chapter 11

Jesus Reveals Himself

Why must we speak of "revelation" when we speak of the Gospels? Why this learned word which so rarely occurs on the lips of Jesus? Why not simply listen to Him speak, let His everyday words sink into our souls, and try to follow His example and respond to His call? Wasn't the Gospel intended for the lowly and the poor? "I bless you, Father, Lord of heaven and of earth, for hiding these things from the learned and the clever" (Mt 11:25 JB).

Why speak of "revelation," then? Perhaps because in the very passage just quoted Jesus goes on to say: "and revealing them to mere children." What Christ brings to the lowly is a revelation, something infinitely valuable, just as valuable as the kingdom promised to the poor. There is no reason, then, for being afraid of the word "revelation," provided we get its meaning straight.

The point of revelation is not to initiate people into a higher kind of technique, a field reserved to specialists, or to explore a mysterious realm of wonder. Revelation is meant for human beings who must bear the burdens of daily life, their trivial and unimportant toil, and the crushing weight of human stupidity and malice. They are to discover the value, the light, and the joy of the Gospel. Revelation means the sudden, happy discovery of something that was already there but hidden, active but not perceptible. It is the discovery that every man has his own technique, that he can make himself heard, that he loves and is loved, that a loving gaze is fixed upon us with passionate concern, and that this gaze is the gaze of God. To receive a revelation is to see one's life transformed.

The revelation that effects the fullest and deepest transformation is the Gospel. The Gospel of Jesus Christ is the most valuable revelation man can receive, for it tells us who Jesus is and what man's life and destiny are. These two things are inseparable and are revealed together. By living our human life to the full, Jesus has revealed to us at one and the same time who we are and who He is.

The Revealer

He who reveals Himself is Jesus of Nazareth. The earliest form of the Gospel is probably the one we see in the outline common to the missionary discourses in Acts (2:14-36; 3:133-26; 4:10-12; 5:30-32; 10:36-43; 13:17-41). These discourses follow the same pattern, and it is one that regularly begins by naming Jesus of Nazareth and summing up His earthly career. In other words, He who reveals Himself made Himself known first of all as a man among others, and it was by observing Him live that those who met Him received His revelation. We must dwell for a moment on this fact.

The important thing is that the name Jesus of Nazareth remains attached to the Divine Person who is proclaimed in Christian preaching, just as the thirty years Jesus lived at Nazareth remained part of His being. We would misunderstand and distort the significance of the years of Nazareth if we saw in them only the paradox of a hidden life or the humiliation of a completely boring existence. But Jesus' life at Nazareth was in no way humiliating for Him! It could not be unless He spent His time dreaming of greatness as men measure greatness. Nor was there anything artificial about it, as though it were a time of testing that He had deliberately accepted or an experiment He was determined to try. No, His life there was the necessary logical consequence of the Incarnation. If Jesus was the Son of God made man, then He had to become a man, and to become a man He had to undergo the long period of apprenticeship of learning that any child must undergo. He had to learn to know the people outside the family circle; He had to learn to speak and listen, to deal with others, to acquire His personal ways and a trade, and to know His neighbors and general milieu.

At Nazareth, then, Jesus passed His apprenticeship: He learned to be a man. This took thirty years, and He needed those thirty years. If He had begun His prophetic ministry five or six years sooner, He would certainly have been the Son of God, but He would not have been the same man, for He would have spoken and reacted as a young fellow of twenty or twenty-five does, and His words would not have sounded the same or had the same significance. The words and gestures of Jesus are those of a man fully mature, and it was the years at Nazareth and the people of Nazareth who gave Him His power and the experience that developed it. It is perfectly true, of course, that a unique personality was assimilating and transforming the substance of this experience; countless Jews around Him had the same experiences but did not become a Jesus of Nazareth. Nonetheless, it was by living that life that He became Himself.

Here was a first revelation of great importance. Those who witnessed Jesus in His years at Nazareth could not grasp their significance at the time, but the evangelists did, and they emphasize it in a style marked by great tact and reserve—the only style suited to recording such a revelation. Luke observes that Jesus grew and developed in the most natural way, but with a perfection and completeness that enabled Him to take His proper place among men (Lk 2:40-52). Mark, who is less given to reflections but probably conveys better the impression made by Jesus, notes the surprise of those who knew Him when they saw Him turn into a prophet: "He is out of his mind" (Mk 3:21). The reaction is very revealing, for it shows that the people of Nazareth did not expect Jesus to have an exceptional career (cf. Mk 6:1-5).

Does this amount to saying that Jesus was changed by his mission? That it made Him a different man? We don't know enough to be able to answer such a question. But we may at least point out how very much the language and style of Jesus are rooted in the natural surroundings of His childhood and youth at Nazareth. Above all, however, there is a most precious conclusion to be drawn from His extraordinary self-effacement at Nazareth. Since these thirty years were needed to form the man Jesus, they were equally needed to reveal who this man is, namely the Son of God. It is the man of Nazareth who will reveal Himself to be God's Son, and He will do it in words and actions learned at Nazareth.

There is thus a direct relation between the mystery of God and a human life that was extremely ordinary and totally devoid of historical significance and earthly ambition. The Son of God could live His unique relation to His Father and His unique love for the Father in the seeming insignificance of a worker's life, in the monotony of very simple ways, and in the narrow compass of a small village. The Son of God did not have to force Himself in order to fit into this framework; He was fully Himself and totally at ease in this situation. This tells us something about the condition of man: that His ordinary actions, trivial doings, and everyday relationships can contain and express in all its infinite fullness the incomparable love that unites the Son to the Father.

His Revelation

What Jesus reveals hardly corresponds, at first sight, to our expectations or to our way of speaking of it. What is our spontaneous reaction? We expect that if Jesus is the Son of God, the first thing He will want to tell us will be precisely this extraordinary fact that is absolutely unique in human history. The reaction is so natural that the evangelists begin their account by telling us, each in his own way, who the person is whose deeds they will narrate. According to Matthew, He is "Jesus Christ, son of David, son of Abraham" (1:1), "king of the Jews" (2:2), and son of the Lord God (2:15). Mark puts everything into one statement: "Here begins the gospel of Jesus

Christ, the Son of God" (1:1). Luke takes a more gradual
approach, first presenting the forerunner and his mission; but
as soon as Mary is told of the birth of Jesus, the latter is immediately called "Son of the Most High" and "Son of God"
(1:32.35). And in all four Gospels the scene of Jesus' baptism
is recorded so that the reader may hear the Father's words to
Jesus: "You are my beloved Son" (Mk 1:11; cf. Mt. 3:17;
Lk 3:22; Jn 1:34). In fact, to convey that truth is the very
purpose of the Gospel and the Christian message (Jn 20:31)
and belief in it is what sends the Apostles on their mission
(1 Thes 1:9-10; Rom 1:4).

The Gospels, then, were evidently written to tell the world
of Jesus, Messiah of Israel and Son of God. But it is no less
evident that Jesus did not go about proclaiming this message.
The fourth Gospel takes a special position in this matter, and
we will have to come back to it, but the three Synoptics, despite evident differences of approach, agree that Jesus was not
preoccupied with proclaiming Himself the Son of God. There
is a clear difference between the message of the Gospels concerning Jesus and the message of Jesus Himself. The difference,
far from disturbing us, should be a source of valuable light, for
it proves that the message of the Gospels is not simply a literal
repetition of Jesus's words but springs from a loving and faith-
inspired meditation on the words and actions of Jesus. The
difference is an effect and a manifestation of the revelation given
by Jesus.

When Jesus came before the public eye and began to traverse
Galilee so that all the children of Israel might hear His word,
Jesus did not speak of Himself. He was not afraid to come
forward and He can hardly be said to have been retiring, but
His words dealt wholly with His message, not with His own
person. The message is the message of the kingdom of God:
God is about to establish a new relationship with mankind.
He is going to intervene in our history and make it His own,
not simply identifying with our hopes and concerns, but making
us share His expectations and hopes, His work and His joy.

This was indeed a revelation, a brilliant light telling us the ultimate meaning of our existence. How can man know God cares for His creature and watches over it with a mother's tenderness and a lover's passion, unless He hears God Himself speaking to him and assuring him? How can sinful man know he is forgiven? How can he be sure there is something good he can make of his life? How can he rejoice at being something in God's eyes and having something to give to God, unless his certainty comes from God Himself?

That is precisely the message of Jesus. It determines His action up and down Palestine; it fills the Sermon on the Mount; it explains His extraordinary behavior to tax collectors and prostitutes and sinners. "The Spirit of the Lord is upon me. . . . He has sent me to bring glad tidings to the poor, to proclaim liberty to captives" (Lk 4:18). "Your Father . . . sees in secret" (Mt 6:4.6.18). "Your Father knows what you need" (Mt 6:8. 32). "Your sins are forgiven" (Mk 2:5; Lk 7:48). "Your faith has been your salvation" (Lk 7:50; 8:48).

The presence of Jesus, His way of acting and living, of speaking of the Father as one who knows what the Father wants and does, and of bringing the Father's forgiveness as though He saw the Father with His own eyes—all that is the revelation of God Himself, of His concern and His presence, His forgiveness and His hope for us. These are things we hardly dare hope for in our wildest dreams, for they seem unimaginable and impossible, but Jesus assures us they are true. He speaks of them as realities He can touch, realities among which He lives; they are experiences which constitute His very being, and He throws the door to them wide open for us.

The Gospel, or Good News, is Jesus' business. He knows the Father's concern for His children, the value He places on their most insignificant actions (even the giving of a glass of water out of kindness), the anguish he feels at seeing them being lost, His fear that they may not return, and His joy when He holds them in His arms again. Knowing all this, Jesus must go out and preach it. This is why He is not satisfied, like John to wait at the Jordan for sinners to come to Him. He must Himself take the road, appearing in Galilee (Mk 1:14) and

going about from village to village (Mk 1:38-39), so that no
one might remain ignorant of the good news. This is also why
His message is a call to joy: "Happy . . . !" (Mt 5:3-10 JB).

But in order to reveal God in this way, as one who deals
not so much with the meaning of man's actions (as did the
prophets who interpreted the future on the basis of the present)
as with what we might call their effect on God and the reactions
they elicit from the heart of God, Jesus must be in a position
to know the heart of God. He must know about God what only
God Himself can know and express. To know it, He must have
it from God by a direct and unlimited communication. Jesus
does not speak of these secrets as if they were astonishing con-
fidences He was privileged to receive. He speaks of them rather
as obvious realities. They contain the secret of His own existence, and they explain the world. In His every action and word
Jesus tells us: This is what God is; this is what the Son is; this
is what the world and mankind are.

How He Reveals Himself

At the same time, however, Jesus hardly ever speaks of Himself, at least as the Synoptic Gospels show Him to us; in the
latter He turns His attention to Himself only after Peter's confession at Caesarea, when He begins to predict His passion. The
approach taken by the Synoptics is very clear and certainly reflects the actual course of events. Mark is systematic about it:
Jesus speaks of Himself in the first person only to refer to His
mission: "Let us move on to the neighboring villages so that I
may proclaim the good news there also" (Mk 1:38). He for-
bids the evil spirits to speak of Him because they know who He
is (Mk 1:24.34; 3:11; 5:7). They know, but they misinterpret
what they know, and their words can only distort men's vision of
the person of Jesus. "Holy One of God" and "Son of God"
point, in the evil spirits' minds, to a privilege Jesus will exploit,
a high title He will profit by, and a justification for His every
ambition.

This was exactly how the tempter thought: "If you are the

Son of God, command these stones to turn into bread.... Thrown yourself down" (Mt 5:3.5)! Jesus must constantly reject this fundamental misinterpretation that would falsify His work and His person. To know Jesus is not to "know who He is" or to be able to put a name on Him or to define Him by a title or function. To know Him means to discover the secret of His being and the source of His life. Of that Jesus hardly ever speaks; instead, He brings His disciples to the point of discovering and expressing it.

The most important event in this respect, as we have seen, is the confession at Caesarea. For the first time Jesus openly asks the key question: "Who am I?" The account of the incident admittedly raises several problems of a literary kind: Peter's answer is not strictly the same in Mark, Matthew, and Luke; Jesus' answer, in Mark and Luke, is one of approval but in the form of a prohibition against speaking of the matter to others, while in Matthew the approval takes the form of a positive strengthening of Peter in preparation for his future mission: "Blest are you, Simon son of John! No mere man has revealed this to you, but my heavenly Father" (Mt 16:17). But, despite these differences, which are due to the special purposes of each evangelist, we have here an event of great importance both for Jesus and for His disciples. It represents the first avowal by men of their faith in Jesus Christ, and the first human experience of His revelation.

The essential point is that this revelation comes from Jesus and yet it is not He, but others, who formulate it. He is certainly responsible for it: without preliminaries, without any external event or outside intervention providing the occasion, He deliberately asks the two questions: "Who do people say I am?" and "Who do you say I am?" The questions are surprising, first of all because no one would think of putting them this way, unless he were playing or were deliberately trying to hide the truth. They are surprising also because no one had any reason for distinguishing between "people" and "you." Could Jesus be somebody other than He was for all who knew Him: Jesus of Nazareth, a carpenter and son of a carpenter, Joseph?

As a matter of fact, however, the double question can have
a meaning, even outside this particular case. It has a meaning
for two people who love one another and are discovering what
they mean to one another. It has a meaning for a person who
is taking on a responsibility and needs to have the fact recognized by others. The question "Who do you take me for?" is
a natural reaction from someone who sees himself misunderstood and wants to remind the others of the true state of affairs.
Thus it is a request that others take seriously the person who
asks it.

In Jesus' mouth, however, the question is not a claim for
recognition by someone who has been misunderstood, nor does
it have the overtones of personal intimacy it has on the lips of
lovers who share a secret that is theirs alone: "What do I mean
to you?" It is a question about His person, but it is asked of
a whole group; it does not concern a role He might have toward
some special individual nor does it relate to a special experience
some individual might have of Him. The answer it expects
is objective and valid for everyone, for it concerns the very
identity of the person who asks it. But, in that case, the question seems to be paradoxical and insoluble. For, if, on the one
hand, Jesus is other than He seems to those around Him, and
if, on the other hand, this other has a mysterious identity which
escapes those around, how may He ask even His faithful companions to penetrate this identity? It is well enough for Him
to ask them to follow Him and not desert Him, but He shouldn't
amuse Himself by testing their capacities for divination! He
should simply tell them the mystery that is beyond their reach
and that they cannot grasp by themselves.

But it is this very paradox that reveals to us what Jesus is.
The paradox is that only He can ask the question, and only His
disciples can answer it; and that the answer can be true only
if it comes from Him but is formulated by them. If the question does not come from Him, it becomes simply an expression
of human stupefaction in the face of something incomprehensible: "Who can this be?" (Mk 4:41). If the answer does not
come from the disciples but is simply given to them by Jesus, it

becomes nothing more than a lesson dictated by a teacher and recorded in the minds and memories of his pupils. Revelation would then be teaching of the kind given in school: a set of correct formulas. Now, in point of fact, Jesus had exceptional ability as a teacher; He could have been an extraordinary theologian and saved His later disciples from immense difficulties of interpretation and from serious errors. But Jesus never addresses Himself to the mind alone; He introduces men to a new life.

This is why, when Peter answers: "You are the Messiah," he is saying something that does not come from himself; he is giving expression to the revelation he has received. But he says it in his own language, and in words which have meaning for him and which he can explain and communicate. He expresses his own experience, but the experience is of the Messiah, that is, the person whom Peter's nation was awaiting. He speaks as an Israelite, and, in a sense, he speaks in the name of Israel. The authorities set over his people—the chief priests, the elders, the teachers of the Law—were unable to recognize the Messiah God had sent them; therefore, Peter takes their place, and the Church begins its birth process in the womb of Israel.

The Son of Man Must Be Handed Over

Jesus has revealed to His disciples the secret of His person; He must now immediately complete the revelation. He must tell them that the Son of Man must confront the hostility of men, not in a victorious battle but in a total defeat. He "must be handed over to them," fall weaponless into their hands, and be reduced to helplessness to the point of dying. But this death and failure are a revelation from God, a revelation of what the Son of Man is. If Jesus had told His apostles: "I am involved in a struggle that will end with my death," He would have left His enemies victorious. He would have shown, in a unique way, that whoever is stronger and crueler wins out, and He would have given mankind good reason to despair. For He would have been telling them that when God enters the world as a lover and giver, He cannot overcome violence and sin, egoism and deceit; all He can do is die. And that in fact is what seems to happen.

But Jesus says something quite different: "The Son of Man is going to be delivered into the hands of men" (Mt 17:22). His attention is focused on the Son of Man and His destiny. He also speaks, of course, of men and their blind hatred, their power to do evil and to destroy. But this power is defeated by the power of God. When the power of men is brought to bear on the Son of Man, it brings to light what He is; it reveals His capacity for love and forgiveness. All the sin that inspires the use of men's power is thereby emptied of its deadly poison and becomes the point of departure for forgiveness, God's victory, and the resurrection.

Jesus Christ reveals both the depths of man's sin and the depths of God's love. He does not come to cover sin over or play down its seriousness or treat it with indulgence and complacency. On the contrary, He sharply denounces it; He confronts men with their responsibilities; He lays bare the wickedness in their hearts and the hypocrisy that undermines all our virtues and corrupts even the best of lives. His denunciations do not have their intended effect. Far from touching men's hearts, the light He brings seems rather to force men deeper into darkness and rejection of God. Has betrayal ever taken a worse form than in Judas who handed His master over for a few coins?

To understand the crimes to which selfishness and fear can lead when exalted as political wisdom, we must look at the meeting of Jesus and Pilate. The behavior of Pilate and the Jewish supreme council shows us where we end when religious pride and national fanaticism manipulate the faith of men. Before the innocent and helpless Jesus there passed in review every human condition and every form of man's sin—and no human being was missing from that parade. He saw the cruelty of His executioners, the vile behavior of the mob, the cowardice of His fleeing disciples, the frightened silence of the honorable people who took refuge in their homes so as not to have to take part in the scene. Such was mankind as gathered in Jerusalem on the eve of Passover; such is mankind today and always. The Lord's Passion reveals mankind's bottomless capacity for evil and destruction.

The Passion also reveals God's depths of forgiveness and, at the same time, the value He puts upon mankind, His creation, and the unfailing hope He places in it. Jesus had to be really handed over and subjected to the power of our sinfulness so that pardon might really be ours. Jesus never had any illusions about us; He never thought, for example, that His sincerity and generosity would be enough to make evil hold back and be silent. Nor did He ever allow His disciples to cultivate illusions of that kind. He told them, rather: the world has hated Me, it will hate you; it has put Me to death, it will destroy you. The power of Jesus Himself does not balance off the power of evil. Sin is not eliminated by showering men with blessings. Jesus certainly did many good deeds; in fact, "he went about doing good works" (Acts 10:38) on every occasion. But He won the victory over sin by experiencing sin in all its bitterness and by giving His life. He conquered by experiencing betrayal and rejection to His last breath and to His final act of forgiveness.

The Revelation of the Father and of the Son

The supreme revelation is the revelation of forgiveness. We speak of forgiveness expressed in words, as recorded by Luke: "Father, forgive them; they do not know what they are doing" (23:34); but perhaps more important is a forgiveness not put into words but shown by the whole attitude of Jesus during His Passion as recorded in the other Gospels. He says not a single word of condemnation or rejection; He gives not a single sign of contempt or even of detachment and withdrawal. In the depths of the horror, when He is most overwhelmed by our sins, Christ remains not only one of us but involved in our sin. He is assaulted by it to the depths of His being, but He continues to look at us as He had before; He continues to call us just as assuringly, to trust in us, and to offer us a share in His future.

Where does he get His unwavering certainty and His power

to communicate it to us? From His Father. And with this we reach the supreme revelation brought by the Passion. The Passion reveals both who Jesus is and what He is for us. He is the Son, and because He is the Son He gives us access to the Father.

From Gethsemani to Jesus' last breath, the secret drama of the Passion goes on, in all the Gospels, between the Father and the Son. Jesus goes to His betrayer so that He may be obedient to the Father and drink the cup the Father holds out to Him. It is the Father, and He alone, whom Jesus invokes when questioned by the high priest, for His appeal is not to a special mission or a charge He had been given (this was the prophets' justification of themselves), but solely to the fact that He is the Son, and to the personal bond that unites Him to God. And this bond is the chief target of the insults His enemies throw at Him as He suffers on the cross: "Save yourself, why don't you? Come down off that cross if you are God's Son!" (Mt 27:40); "Let God rescue him now if he wants to. After all, he claimed, 'I am God's Son'" (Mt 27:43).

Their reasoning seems quite logical. Would any father, no matter how wicked, let his son be put to death if he could intervene and save him? If, then, God who is all-powerful lets Jesus die, it must be that He does not acknowledge Jesus as His son. And if He lets Jesus die as the result of a legal condemnation, He must be saying the judges are right. The judges were not wrong in rejoicing at an outcome they had not expected. The high priests and doctors of the Law had learned to beware of Jesus with His shrewd answers and clear mind, His effective words, and His influence over the crowds. Now, at last, they have succeeded, and God is on their side, for He makes no move against them. Their victory is great, and Jesus Himself seems to acknowledge defeat: "My God, my God, why have you forsaken me?" (Mt 27:46). The evangelist has dared to put this cry of distress from Jesus alongside His enemies' challenges to Him. It is as if Jesus at the end had to admit they were right, as if He had to admit that all His claims were empty.

Yet it is this very cry of despair that reveals the Son. Jesus retracts nothing He had ever claimed; on the contrary, He confirms His former statements that everything in Him depends on God and that if this essential bond is broken, He must die. The real mystery is that He should be able to feel the bond yielding and that He should be able to die. It is a mystery too deep for us. There are two apparently irreconcilable aspects to His words, which are the most daring words in the whole Gospel. On the one hand, they are a cry of distress and give voice to the experience of abandonment and of the unraveling of the bond. On the other hand, He continues to address God as "My God" and to assert the unbreakable bond even at the very moment when it seems to be breaking.

It is probably in the direction of paradox that the evangelists wish to turn our thoughts. They are telling us that the Son of God is capable of experiencing both this certitude and this sense of abandonment. In order for Jesus to hold on to God in the terrible void, and to remain firmly grounded in God even when deprived of every defense, protection, and interior support, He must be joined to God by a bond that is proof against every attack, deeper than any possible contrary experience, and more unyielding than death. When He is exhausted and crushed and can suffer no more, Jesus remains capable of turning even death—a discontinuity at the very heart of His being—into a form of union with God. He can do so because He is the Son and suffers the discontinuity as the Son. Paul's words and the words of the Roman officer who saw Jesus die complement each other: "O death, where is your victory?"

The Resurrection is the manifestation of Christ's victory. It is a public revelation to the world that God declares Jesus to have been right, and that He proclaims Him as His Son and bestows Him, as such, upon men. The Resurrection takes place in the mysterious silence of God. It does not interrupt the course of events; it lets sin pursue its deadly work as before. But it also extends the victory of the Son to all mankind and to history itself.

Chapter 12
The Faith of the Disciples

Meditation on the Gospels makes us aware that the questions Christ asked of His disciples are the very questions put to us by life and by the Lord. The experience of the disciples is constantly repeated across the centuries every time there arises an authentic Christian faith, and each Christian in his turn is called upon to make the same commitment as Jesus' disciples made to their master.

Our intention here is to trace the origin of this commitment; we might speak of its "genesis," using the word in a broad sense, but implying nonetheless a scientific process, a set kind of movement. We shall not be trying to reconstruct the journey of the apostles as they came to believe, nor to establish the stages of their spiritual itinerary. If we speak of origin or genesis, and not of itinerary or development, the reason is that we are concerned with the essential elements of faith that are found in every authentic faith experience, and not with the various forms faith takes in different individuals and circumstances.

The genesis is the work of the Lord Jesus. He it is who causes faith to be born; His presence makes it possible for those who encounter Him to believe or, on the contrary, to refuse to believe. Nothing is more personal than faith, for it involves the depths of our being and the whole of our human existence, yet everything about it is the work of Jesus.

Socrates compared himself to a midwife. He thought he had

the commission, and the skill, to bring confused, infantile minds, that were subject to outside influences and blind impulse, to the certitudes and kinds of behavior proper to a human being. Jesus Christ acted in a similar way. He brought men to a new consciousness—not a purified or mature consciousness, not a stronger or more uncluttered consciousness, but a radically new consciousness: that of being a child of God. Socrates could never have dreamed of such a thing: he was there with the other, keenly attentive, with the strength of his own experience and clarity of vision, but he remained external to the other. Jesus Christ enters the very depths of the consciousness which faith brings; He is at the origin of this newborn being.

The Gospels suggest that we distinguish three essential moments in this genesis. We repeat that they are not three stages in a journey, but three different moments in one and the same genesis of one and the same faith. The faith in question is proposed by the Lord in His Sermon on the Mount; the apostles live it as they accompany Jesus while He moves toward His Passion; it becomes aware of itself under the action of the risen Lord and of the Spirit who is given at Pentecost.

1. The Faith Proposed in the Sermon on the Mount

In choosing to start with the Sermon on the Mount, we are not yielding to sentimentality or tempted by a few brilliant passages that stand out against the background of a more ordinary teaching. We are going instead to the heart of the Gospel, the program proper to the new Law. That the Sermon is to be so regarded is indicated by the location of the discourse and the framework Matthew uses in order to show that the Sermon corresponds to the revelation at Mt. Sinai. But the chief proof is the content of the Sermon, for the Sermon is in effect a compendium of what we might call the strictly evangelical attitudes. Instructions scattered throughout the rest of the Gospel—on forgiveness or prayer, for example—are already gathered up in the Sermon, especially as St. Matthew presents it. Consequently,

in taking the Sermon as our basis we are not making an arbitrary choice of especially telling passages from the teaching
of Jesus. No, we are really getting His essential teaching and
learning from Him what He thinks human life should be in God's
sight. His answer is that human life must be an existence in
faith, or, more accurately, faith in Jesus.

Human Life Lived in Faith

The discourse deals with human life in its most down-to-
earth, everyday reality. It deals with hunger, thirst, tears,
clothing, eating and drinking, quarrels and estrangements between neighbors and friends. It deals with common, demanding,
everyday concerns, with the habitual reality of every home at
every age of history and at every level of human culture.

These things are not to be evaded or played down. Jesus
does not say that man should live like the birds or the flowers,
blindly following the lead of instinct. He knows that man was
made to work, to figure things out, and to look ahead, but He
also tells us that an essential datum we must not forget in our
calculations and projections is the concern God has for us.
God takes care to feed the sparrows and clothe the flowers of
the field: can He fail to be concerned with the most valuable
of His creatures?

When God gave man responsibility for his own life and for
providing by his own labor his food and clothing, He did not
thereby cease being as concerned with man as He is with the
rest of His creation. On the contrary, this concern becomes
greatest when it applies to men. The difference is that God
means to make man share in the great divine concern. God
knows and wills that man should work and take measures to
clothe and feed himself. The parables of Christ are constantly
making this point, the more eloquently as the human reactions
in question are more spontaneous. Jesus takes it for granted
that a housewife who has lost a coin should do everything she
can to find it; or that a vinegrower should go out to see how
the grapes are doing; or that a father who sees his son leave

home should be affected by it for the rest of his life. Jesus does not tell us not to think of these things. He only tells us not to let them become a torment and an obsession, and not to try to carry the burden alone, but to remember that our Father is concerned even before we are, and carries our burden with us.

He also tells us that the Father's concern, which is always greater and more efficacious than that of even the most devoted parents, can take paradoxical forms that shock and scandalize us. God can let men suffer and die; He can let parents watch their children suffer and die. And, the most scandalous thing of all, He can say that those who suffer and weep, and those who are without food and clothing or any source of comfort, are "blest"! How can this be? How can we reconcile God's concern with His apparent indifference, or even His preference and penchant for our sufferings and misfortunes? We shall make no attempt to deal here with the fearful problem posed by the presence of evil in the world, and shall limit ourselves to this one paradox, which has plenty in it to disturb us: How can one and the same discourse, one and the same lesson, tell us that God is attentive to the least of our needs, and yet also show Him capable of letting His creature sink down into bottomless depths of suffering and misfortune?

To this tragic question the Sermon gives an answer that is at once brutal and full of light. The Sermon shows first of all that there is no contradiction between the beatitudes concerning poverty, hunger, and mourning, and Jesus' invitations to filial trust. It is one and the same God who is concerned to feed all His creatures (beginning with man) and who finds His joy in bringing the poor into His kingdom, giving the hungry their fill of His holiness, and filling the wretched with His joy. The same reactions come into play in both cases: the reactions of a Father who wants His creatures to know joy, fulfillment, and beauty.

This God does not love hunger, misfortune, or tears. What He called "blest" are the tears He Himself dries, the nakedness He covers with His own hands, the hunger He comes in person to allay. The reason Jesus calls us to joy is not because there is suffering and evil in the world, but because He comes to put an end to suffering—and comes at the precise point at which the suffering is greatest and the misfortune seemingly insuperable. From one end to the other, the Sermon on the Mount aims at showing us the Father's concern. The present is a time of joy because, in the person of Jesus, the Father's concern is now focused on the deepest and most incurable evil man experiences.

Matthew invites us to shed further light on this revelation by comparing it to God's revelation to Moses at the burning bush that began the liberation of Israel. There too, what God revealed was His concern for the unfortunate: "I have witnessed the affliction of my people in Egypt and have heard their cry of complaint against their slave drivers, so I know well what they are suffering. Therefore I have come down to rescue them from the hands of the Egyptians" (Ex 3:7-8).

All of God's activity and vital energies are focused on His suffering people and on the rescue He is preparing for them. On the Mount Jesus is no longer thinking of one people chosen out of the mass of mankind. He is thinking of all the unfortunate, of all mankind. The liberation He comes to effect is for all of them.

God's Concern, Perceived in Faith

God's concern for us is not something that becomes an evident fact. We have already said that "revelation" does not mean the lifting of a curtain to show an unknown country, a world of light; it means rather a new explanation of our own world; it means that we now see at work in it a mysterious, obscure, and disconcerting action that is at bottom serene and full of light. What Jesus brings us is the revelation of the "mystery," that is, of God's mysterious plan. God takes the world as it is, as man has made it: with its authentic values, but also with the power of evil that is destructively at work in it, with its contagious sinfulness, with its burden of tears and corruption—and He determines to save His creature and bring it to share His joy.

Admittedly, this is not the only possible interpretation of the way things are. There is another that is equally probable; it consists in objecting that God could have disposed things otherwise from the very beginning and that He must therefore be held accountable for the evil He has allowed to happen. The Gospel gives us an instance of these contrary interpretations in the story of the raising of Lazarus. The people present at the tomb with Mary and Martha voice two opposing views when they see Jesus deeply moved and unable to restrain His tears: some are touched by His affection and exclaim, "See how much he loved him!" (Jn 11:36), but others object, "He opened the eyes of that blind man. Why could he not have done something to stop this man from dying?" (v. 37). He could certainly have done something, but He did not wish to. What conclusion are we to draw from that?

Faith, then, is always a choice, and a choice that remains free, despite the weighty good reasons for which we make it. The choice we make is to assert that our life has a meaning; that God is always concerned with men; that we are not lost in a hostile universe; that we have something we are to accomplish in this world, something God takes even more to heart than we do. The choice is one that runs counter to many appearances and many strong arguments. What is it, then, that makes us choose? Why do we believe?

Believing in Jesus

We certainly have the right to ask this question. We do not deny our human condition by asking it, as long as it does not diminish us but invites us, on the contrary, to place our trust in all the good there is in our world. But if we are making a choice, what happens to the certitude of faith? And what religious value can faith thus chosen have? How can it bring us into real contact with God? How is it more than a simple wager, an act in which we are really just refusing to choose and abandoning ourselves instead to chance?

We can avoid a simple wager, and yet not have full clarity.

We can be certain and yet remain in darkness. This is possible because the words of the Gospel, the words of the Sermon on the Mount, are the words of Jesus. Their power and authority stems not from their inner consistency, striking though that is, nor from the salutary effects they may have in us, but from the fact that they are a direct reflection of Jesus' own experience and that His experience is both a genuinely human experience of our world and a genuine, immediate experience of God. There can be no doubt that the words are those of a man who knows what man and human life are. When He speaks of people who can hate and do evil, He speaks from experience. He had enemies from the very first days of His public life, and He knew what hatred and cruelty could make them do. When He speaks of those who hunger and mourn, He is speaking of people He met every day and whom He made no attempt to avoid. The tiresome, the hypocritical, the fickle-minded—He knows them all. He has no illusions about our human nature. He is completely vulnerable and sensitive to all that touches us and all that diminishes us.

He is all this because His attention to us and His concern for us are the attention and concern of God Himself. He sees the loving eyes of God our Father fixed upon us in our distress; He sees the divine will to save us and bring us joy. His miracles prove that His reactions to our wretched state, and the power and mercy He shows, are the reactions and the power and the mercy of God. That is the secret behind the Sermon, and it is the secret of Jesus Himself—that He is true man but also true God.

At this early stage of His ministry Jesus is still far from demanding acknowledgement that He is the only Son of the Father. But His words already elicit from those who really hear him a commitment of faith, because, through the power of minds to communicate and share attitudes, and through the power latent in human movement by which the Son puts Himself in His Father's hands. Jesus lives before our eyes the kind of life His words describe; He lives under the threats and hostility of men and the forces of evil, yet is absolutely certain that His life is in God's hands. Consequently He is able to evoke a commitment of faith from others. That is, He makes it possible for them to commit their lives into their Father's hands, to entrust their human concerns to Him, and to make this act of faith in the light, and as a prolongation, of Jesus' commitment of Himself to God as the Son.

The Sermon on the Mount does much more than give us an accurate description of God and His attitude toward us. It mediates God's concern for us, as experienced by one of us, His Son. At the same time, it shows us mankind's response to God in filial commitment and fraternal communion. When Jesus tells us that God knows all our needs and is attentive to them, He does so with the certainty of one who shares the Father's concern for us and our misfortunes, but He also does it with the authenticity of one who more than others is exposed to our misfortunes and stands open and defenseless to all onslaughts. When Jesus tells us that the Father sees the man who shuts himself up in his room to pray, He is giving us a glimpse of His own experience as a man who must betake Himself to prayer and dispose Himself to speak to God, but also as a man who, being the Son, knows no distance between the Father and Himself.

Jesus lives out before our eyes this perfect intimacy with His Father, this total transparency to the Father, this unqualified certainty that nothing can separate Him from the Father: in short, the secret that constitutes His very Being as the Son and belongs to Him alone. He lives it before our eyes, not in order to display it as a marvelous reality to which we can have no access, but rather in order to invite us to share it. He does not issue the invitation from outside our world, nor does He summon us to enter another world and another kind of existence. No, for He is in our world and shares our existence. When He urges us to entrust ourselves into the hands of God our Father, He is proposing that we reproduce in our lives His way, that is properly His alone, of receiving everything from the Father and of drawing all His nourishment and strength from the Father. He is telling us that His fidelity and joy as the Son can be ours as well.

The Sermon on the Mount thus gives us access to faith by enabling us to share the experience of Jesus Christ. We do not rise above faith, for we continue in our native condition; nor do we have any new consciousness of God or clear evidence of Him. The one we see and grasp is Christ, a man like us, one whose nature and manner of existing we share. But faith makes us really touch God in the person of Jesus Christ; it makes us live our human lives before God. Faith, therefore, is in no sense a blind choice, a noble wager. It is the certainty that in receiving the words of Jesus, we have encountered and found the God and Father of our Lord Jesus Christ.

2. Faith on the Way to the Passion

The Sermon on the Mount already contains the whole of the Gospel. Jesus will add no new elements to the program He set forth at the beginning: that man should receive His life in its entirety from the Father, and live it so as to give joy to the Father and to serve the brethren. But the Sermon is still only a sermon and a program to be carried out. When lived out to the full, the program led the Lord to His passion and resurrection. If we are to live it to the full, we must be personally committed to the Lord and adopt the lifestyle of a disciple.

The public life of Jesus is divided into two major periods: the first, the period of discourses and miracles, shows us Jesus living the Sermon on the Mount and calling men to follow Him. God's salvation and the joy of His kingdom are close; the poor are welcomed, the sick cured, the crowds fed. They feel at times that the kingdom is very near. The multiplication of the loaves brings their expectations to fever pitch. It is the most striking of Jesus' miracles: a whole crowd fed, a sumptuous miracle with everyone sharing its joyous fruits. Has the kingdom now come? Is this the moment for proclaiming Jesus king of Israel? No, Jesus turns on His heel, avoids the enthusiastic throng, sends the apostles out into a storm, and loses Himself, alone, in the night. What has happened?

What has happened is what happens to us so often: a misinterpretation of the Sermon on the Mount and a misinterpretation of Jesus. Men naturally remember what seem to be the idyllic, happy parts of the Sermon: a peaceful life under the eye of God, a world reconciled and kindly, a human race filled with brotherly love, with forgiveness and dedication to others almost instinctive and immediately effective. The Sermon does have some of this in it; it is indeed an invitation to peace and tranquillity. But it speaks of others things that we prefer to forget: the reality of hatred, persecution, sorrow, and tears.

If the Sermon on the Mount is to be verified in every respect, and if man is to be able to go on believing in the Father amid misfortune and even despair, then Jesus must live our life in all its aspects. This means He must have a total experience of our human nature and our sinfulness. He must therefore experience death, and death in its cruelest form; He must experience all the evil men are capable of, and Himself bear the fearsome burden of it. Otherwise, His forgiveness becomes simply a refusal to look at reality; the beatitudes become an illusion; and the Sermon a pipe dream.

Jesus puts a brutal end to the pipe dream for His disciples by getting them away from the enthusiastic crowd after the multiplication of the loaves and forcing them to cross the lake in a storm and without Him. By so doing, He gives them a new understanding of their faith. Faith does not mean simply following Jesus about; it also means doing what He requires when He is not there. This is the faith He will ask them to express formally at Caesarea, as He shows them the difference between amazement and faith: "Who do people say that I am?" (Mk 8:27). The responses betray both uncertainty and a feeling of being in the presence of an extraordinary person: one of the old prophets come back to earth. Unheard of happenings occur, and people stand amazed and paralyzed.

The response of faith, which Jesus elicits from Peter, is precise and categorical: "You are the Messiah," that is, the man God gives us, the Saviour He has in store for His people. In you God speaks; in you we find God; our faith in God is mediated through you. Peter's confession expresses, in the last analysis, the believer's commitment to the man who spoke the Sermon on the Mount.

Jesus immediately seizes upon this commitment and shows what it implies. From this point on, the Gospels tell us, "he began to teach them that the Son of Man had to suffer much, be rejected by the elders, the chief priests, and the scribes, be put to death, and rise three days later" (Mk 8:31). At the same time, He shows that His disciples must obey the law that governs His life: "If a man wishes to come after me, he must deny his very self, take up his cross, and follow in my steps" (Mk 8:34).

Taking this warning seriously does not mean we must refuse all the joys God gives us and live a gloomy life. It means rather that we take seriously the life and death of Jesus; that we unite our life to His and our death to His; that we live and die in faith, in Jesus Christ. For Christ came to live to the full the program He Himself outlines, and, once this program embraces the whole of man's life, it necessarily calls for His death. It is easy to abandon ourselves into the Father's hands while we are still vigorously alive, are supported by our feelings, and have a future before us. Our "abandonment" may even be an illusion. Is it really the Father to whom we are abandoning ourselves?

We will not know the answer to that question, or be able to say what our faith is really worth, until everything around us is taken away, all our supports are withdrawn, and we are left isolated. Then, only God can sustain us; then we will really be grounded and rooted in faith. In a sense, only death can enable us to reach that point; only through death can we reach God in a permanent way. But death, one's own and others', is a man's companion even in the springtime of life. This is why, from Caesarea on, and a good while before His Passion, Christ requires His disciples to take up their cross and enter into the mystery of His death.

The Death of the Son

The death of Jesus reveals to us, at one and the same time, a man completely like us and the beloved only Son of the Father. From the first moment of His earthly life Jesus had been true God and true man, but His death makes clear the full meaning of that statement.

His death is the death of a man: a cruel death amid atrocious suffering, in an atmosphere heavy with hatred, mockery, and blasphemy. It is the death of an exhausted man who cannot carry His cross unaided, a man reduced to silence though He had always spoken so effectively, a man filled with fears and calling on God for help. It is the death of a man at the end of His rope: betrayed by one of His followers, deserted by the others, publicly rejected by His people, executed without pomp, while everyone vies in getting rid of Him. A major purpose of the Passion narratives is to show how all the claims of Jesus are flouted during these hours; how each of the essential ones— the claim to be the Messiah, the king of Israel, the Son of God —is systematically belied by the facts.

As a matter of fact, Jesus had chosen this very moment to proclaim openly what He was. Throughout His life up to then, He had avoided claiming titles which were bound to be misinterpreted. But when He was accused and the high priest formally questioned Him, He answered: "Yes, I am the Messiah; I am the Son of Man who is to come upon the clouds; I am the Son of God" (cf. Lk 22:67-70). But the details chosen by the evangelist show that the outcome of the Passion, in the divinely willed drama that is played out between Jesus and His enemies, was to show the seeming emptiness of His essential titles and of all that He had claimed to be.

The insults showered on Him while a prisoner of the Jewish authorities centered on His supposed prophetic power: they blindfolded Him, slapped Him, and jeered, "Guess who struck you! Play the prophet!" (cf. Mk 14:65) that you claim to be. The crowning with thorns and the caption on the cross show what this "king of Israel" really is, and the insults of the chief priests on Calvary are not silly: "So he is the king of Israel! Let's see him come down from that cross and then we will believe in him. He relied on God; let God rescue him now if he wants to. After all, he claimed, 'I am God's Son'" (Mt 27: 42-43).

A profound logic governs the course of the Passion. It is a logic that is not reducible to the views of the various agents at work there. It is a divine logic that mocks its opponents, but does so for their own salvation, making them play out the ominous game of sin so that they may be saved in the end. God Himself allows man's sin to do its utmost to Jesus; He allows sin to complete its deadly work, so that He may use this awful death and complete failure as the way of showing who and what His Son is.

The point is that only the Son of God was able to remain unshakeably certain of His Father even amid such failure and in the face of such a death; only He could remain unshakably attached to a human race which in its entirety, Jews and Romans, rich and poor, ordinary people and distinguished men, was bent on getting rid of Him. Not a single person in Jerusalem stood up in His defense. That day, Jesus saw the worst our human nature was capable of: cowardice, cruelty, selfishness, hatred. God allowed our sinfulness to vent itself to the full, so that the forgiveness of Jesus might embrace all our sins, even the most monstrous. By dying for His enemies, He committed Himself to them irrevocably; He triumphed over all that separates men, including death, the separation that includes and explains all the others. This conqueror of all divisions is conqueror also of death.

His victory comes from the Father and proves that He is the only Son. Amid the agony of Gethsemani, the abandonment on Calvary, and the implacable vision of sin triumphant, He continues to pray God that He will be done; He continues to call God "Father." For Him to be capable of this, He must be bound to God by an indissoluble link; He must be sustained by a love no wound can weaken. Herein is His defense and protection: He is the Son. Here we see what His divinity really means, the divinity we so often think of as a kind of amulet. It is indeed an armor, but an armor that spares Him nothing of life's hardships or men's cruelties or the blows rained upon Him by sin. It simply transforms all these wounds into testimonies of love and into a revelation of the love that unites the Son to His Father.

This is why the Passion is absolutely necessary if our faith is to have its definitive certainty. The person who hears the Sermon on the Mount and takes it seriously finds faith laying hold of him as he experiences the serene certainty that radiates from Jesus and His words. But as long as Christ has not yet suffered His passion, we do not know how far faith can go. Yet, what kind of faith would it be that set limits, that committed itself up to a certain point but refused to risk all? How far, then, is it possible to live the Sermon and love your enemies? Do the beatitudes remain valid no matter what the depth of deprivation and desolation? We must hear the terrible cry of the crucified Jesus, "I thirst!" before we can believe in the beatitude: "Blest are they who thirst!" The death of Jesus in nakedness and desolation is needed as our guarantee that faith is always possible and that God's fidelity will never fail. God handed over His only Son for our sake and linked us to that Son forever: in His Son Jesus Christ our faith is unshakable.

3. Faith, Easter, and Pentecost

What became of the apostles' faith during the Passion? We know very little about the matter, except that their faith was very much shaken and showed serious weaknesses. That should not surprise us. It was necessary that Jesus die practically alone and that His work appear to have been destroyed. It was also necessary that He complete His self-revelation before men's faith could take on its final form and inner coherence. This means that the Resurrection and Pentecost were both necessary, each contributing something proper to it.

The Resurrection

In one sense, the Resurrection is simply the completion of the Passion, inasmuch as it annihilates death at the very moment of death's victory. Jesus experienced the full horror of death, the crushing burden of suffering it brings with it, and the complete isolation in which it imprisons man in his final moments. Yet death could not touch the bonds that united Jesus to His Father and to men, His brothers. Having inflicted all the evil it could, death's power was exhausted. Jesus rose and was henceforth beyond death's reach. He is no longer subject to the limitations of our world; He is with God and God receives Him completely into His own glory.

In the Resurrection, the humanity of Jesus—our humanity!— is touched by divinity and acquires the infinite dimensions of God. Once Jesus had died while asserting His claim to be the Son, once He had proved his certainty and fidelity to His last breath, once God raised Him up, God did not simply confirm Jesus' claims but took Him in a fully real way into the divine sphere. In this way, God showed that He, the Father, had been the one in full control of Jesus' life and death, and that everything about them, absolutely everything, had been His work and the expression of His will.

Consequently, when Jesus reappeared, in a manner always disconcerting to the apostles, but as the person they could not but recognize as the one they had known in the past, their faith in the risen Lord was not merely the immediate, limited certainty that "It is indeed He. He is all-powerful, and God is with Him." No, the Jesus who rises is the Jesus they had known earlier; it is His whole self that rises and He brings with Him His whole life, all that He had said and done from birth to Passion. The Sermon on the Mount is completely fulfilled in Him, and their progressive commitment, their hesitant, restless faith, becomes utterly assured and strong: "You are the Christ, the Son of the living God." You are He who conquered our death, because You experienced it in all its bitterness. You are He who overcame our weakness, because You take us with You beyond death and beyond our own betrayals.

Pentecost

The experience of Easter, however, is not the whole of Christian experience. Pentecost is needed if the disciples are to make this experience fully and really their own. As long as the Holy Spirit does not enliven and enlighten them from within, they remain mere spectators or passive witnesses of the Resurrection. An extraordinary, indeed unique event has occurred, and they are witnesses to it, but they witness without knowing as yet what it really means for them and the world. There is an immense distance between the attitude of the apostles on Easter and their attitude on Pentecost, for Pentecost and the gift of the Spirit will complete the faith of the disciples and give it its definitive form.

The Resurrection establishes Jesus forever in the attitude of soul in which He died and which expresses His very being: the attitude of one who receives His being and life from the Father and gives it back to Him in its entirety, while also uniting mankind to His sacrifice. "Established forever" does not mean "rendered immobile"! On the contrary, Jesus is now free of all fetters; He has entered the world of freedom and life. But we cannot as yet perceive this world. All that the witnesses to the Resurrection could see was the human being they had known. It is in the risen Jesus that they recognize the Son of God; they know that His Father has raised Him from the dead and brought Him into the glorious joy of God. In short, they see a Jesus who receives His own life, glory, and power from God. While not at all passive, Jesus is simply receptive in relation to God. At the same time, God reveals Himself as the Father and God of Jesus Christ, and as the one who had sent Jesus into the world and has now brought Him back to Himself, since His mission is completed.

The action of Christ in all this may seem to be merely a fragment or moment in the total action of God—a supreme and decisive moment, but nonetheless subordinate and limited. In the eyes of the witnesses to the Resurrection, are God and Jesus two or one? Two persons, of course, but are they one God? How could they be said to be one God? God is the one whom Jesus all His life called "Father," and the Resurrection is the definitive proof of it. But is Jesus, the Son, also God? How could that be?

The question we have just asked is the question we ask today. It is directly prompted by the manner in which we state the mystery of the Trinity, for here we speak of God the Father, God the Son, and God the Holy Spirit. The question was also asked at a very early point in the Church's history, for even in the New Testament Jesus is called God (twice by Paul: Rom 9:5 and Ti 2:13; and four times by John: 1:1; 1:18; 20:28; 1 Jn 5:20). But this is not the way the New Testament usually speaks of Jesus; generally it calls Him Christ or Lord. Could the divinity of Jesus be something the Church discovered only after some years? No, that is impossible. The newborn Church of the apostles and first witnesses to the Resurrection undoubtedly made a number of astonishing discoveries within a few years' time, and she saw the "dimensions" of Christ constantly broaden and deepen. But she could not one day have discovered in Him a divinity she did not know about before. How then did she come to recognize Him as God?

She recognized His divinity on Pentecost, and from Pentecost on she said as much, using language which is not quite ours nor even quite that of St. Paul, but is a related and more concrete version of these. On Pentecost the disciples received the Holy Spirit. This reception did not take the form of a more or less blind and passing enthusiasm. What it brought was a decisive illumination concerning what Jesus was and what they were. The risen Jesus had disappeared from our world, and they did not expect to see Him again until the world came to its end. But the risen Jesus was now present among them: living, speaking, suffering, conquering. The proof of this is that, without seeing Him going on before them, they followed Him, remained united by His word, and reproduced in themselves His actions, including those unique actions which He alone could perform and which brought Him to His death. For, before the very judges who had condemned Him, the apostles came, threatened with the same torments He had suffered and trembling with the same fear He had experienced—and they repeated the claims that had caused His death: He is indeed the king of Israel, the Messiah, the Son of God! A further proof is that they spoke to the Father as Jesus had spoken before them, and, like Jesus, heard Him answer them and share His joy with them.

Such was their experience at Jerusalem. Later, they saw the experience repeated elsewhere: in a pagan officer and his family at Caesarea, and in their most bitter persecutor, Saul the Pharisee, at Damascus. There were no frontiers to hold back the Spirit; He filled the universe. But this Spirit was the Spirit of Jesus Christ, since it was Jesus that was acting in their lives and speaking through them. Jesus was therefore not simply an incomparably special servant of God, a being chosen and cherished by God from among all mankind. Since the Spirit of Jesus is the Spirit of God, since Jesus is at the source of God's action, since He does what God does, since He possesses all the dimensions and depths, the greatness and holiness of God, then Jesus, Son of God, is equal to His Father. He is God as His Father is.

We may sum up in three statements the process which we have seen, by which the faith of the apostles came into existence: Jesus reveals Himself within our human experience as the man who has a complete human experience of God; this experience is authentic only on condition that it is an experience had by God, for God alone can have such a full, certain, and intimate experience of God; and, finally, it follows that in Jesus Christ God has the human experience of God.

We may also sum up in three statements what this faith means in a man's life: In the words and actions of Jesus Christ a man discovers the secret of his own existence, namely, that it comes from God; in the death of Jesus he discovers what he must do with his own life, namely, give it back, in filial love, to his Father; in the Spirit of Jesus Christ he discovers that he is able to receive his life from the Father and give it back to Him, and that he can say to God the words used by a young child and by the dying Son: "*Abba,* Father!"

Chapter 13

Who Is Jesus?
The Word Made Flesh

Who is Jesus? A question of this type can be approached in various ways. In this particular case, moreover, the question has two really different aspects; there are two distinct ways of tackling it and two complementary answers, both of which are required if we are to enter into and understand the mystery of Jesus Christ.

The Ascending Movement: From Man to God

We can take *as our starting point the meeting of a man* living in our world, any representative of our human race, *with the person, Jesus of Nazareth,* who made His appearance among us at a certain point in time. It is a fact that this historical person, this individual, Jesus of Nazareth, has had an extraordinary effect on great numbers of men both during the years He lived on earth and during the centuries that have passed since then; no one before or after Him has had a similar effect. Because they were there when Jesus passed by and because they found their lives focused on, given value, and transformed by their commitment to Him, great numbers of men have asked the question "Who is Jesus Christ?" and have given

154

an answer inspired by faith. Their answer: "Jesus is the Messiah; Jesus is the Savior of the world; Jesus is God." To believe is to acknowledge Jesus as Savior; to believe is to acknowledge that He is God.

This movement that terminates in the acknowledgement of Jesus' divinity is an ascending movement. It begins in a human experience of encounter with the man Jesus, a historical person; in contact with Him and by His action, one acknowledges in faith that this man has done and still does a work of superhuman and even divine dimensions, namely the salvation of the world and the reconciliation of men with God. One is thus led to the discovery that this man is absolutely unique: that He is God. *In this man one has recognized God.* Throughout the Gospels and Acts, as the first disciples of the Lord pursue their relationship with Him, we can see faith being born and awakened; we can see the genesis of the spiritual experience which is the type of our own and which we have explored in detail in the previous chapter.

The Descending Movement: Jesus the Word of God Made Flesh

Alongside these texts which are more historical in character and show the genesis of a faith that consists in acknowledging Jesus the man to be divine, the New Testament contains another series of texts. The latter are equally familiar to Christians and equally precious for their faith, but quite different in character. The former texts move from Jesus the man to Jesus as God and thus reflect the path faith follows as it is awakened. The other texts, which we shall be studying in this chapter, follow a descending path. They move from God to man and describe what might be called *the process by which God becomes man.*

Two Series of Texts

In order to see the difference between the two viewpoints and the two kinds of texts, let us read, side by side, two texts—

both of which are very important in the New Testament. One is the preaching of the Gospel by Peter on Pentecost, as narrated in the Acts of the Apostles (2:22-36); the other is the Prologue of St. John's Gospel, the passage that used to be the "Last Gospel" at Mass.

The text in Acts follows the movement of Jesus' human life with its successive phases: the period of success and miracles, then the period of opposition culminating in the triumph of His enemies, the trial and His death, and finally the Resurrection and Ascension. But the description of Jesus' life in this passage is not written from outside, as it were, nor is it limited simply to external events. It is an account inspired by faith and it shows the invisible reality of the events and the driving force behind the miracles—the will to redeem the world; and behind the Resurrection—the ascension of Jesus to His divine condition where He possesses the omnipotent Spirit.

The Prologue of St. John follows an order which is exactly the opposite of the first. It starts with the beginning of all things, that is, with God, and contemplates the Word of God as He exists in the intimacy and as it were in the privacy of the Godhead; it describes His invisible action in the creation of the world and the history of mankind; and finally it shows Him taking a human nature and becoming incarnate, coming to dwell among us and make visible the mysterious glory of the invisible God.

Peter's sermon moves from earth to God, from time to eternity, from flesh to Spirit. *St. John's Prologue moves from eternity to time,* from God's world to man's world, from the glory of the Son to the witness given by the disciples.

In this difference of viewpoints there is something more than a simple difference of starting points: heaven vs. earth, the beginning of all things vs. the time of Jesus' life on earth. There is more even than a difference of movement: the descent of the Word into the world vs. the ascent of Jesus to the bosom of the Father. There is also a difference in the way the person Jesus is presented.

In the sermon in Acts, the preacher starts with what happened on earth when a certain Jesus of Nazareth appeared in Palestine. He proclaims that this Jesus is now risen and lives in a glorious splendor that is divine, but does not say a word about what this Jesus was before He appeared on earth, that is, about the existence in God of a divine being who became Jesus of Nazareth. John, on the other hand, writes his Prologue in order to make it clear that the Jesus whose history he is about to relate has as it were a prehistory; that the history has a prologue that is not literary but historical, or, more exactly, eternal and outside of time, in the world of God. Acts tells us of the mystery of Jesus' exaltation above every creation, while John describes the mystery of the Incarnation of the Word who became man and received the name Jesus.

The contrast between these two ways of presenting the mystery of the Incarnation summons us to an effort at understanding. The effort will be a modest one, very much aware of its limits; but it will be made with the assurance that one of the greatest acts of homage we can pay to God is reverently and gratefully to make our own the marvelous glimpses He gives us of His mystery. With the New Testament texts as our guide, then, we shall try to approach the mystery of the Incarnation from three complementary points of view. Since the contrast we have already seen is due chiefly to the different aspects the mystery presents according to the position in *time* which the observer takes, we shall ourselves take up successively *three different standpoints in time.* The result will be three visions that are not opposed to one another, but are distinct and complementary. We shall view the mystery of the Word made flesh:

1. As it was revealed to the disciples *after the Resurrection of Jesus* and as it exists today for us;
2. As it existed *before the human life of Jesus;*
3. As it worked itself out *during the time of Jesus' human life.*

The order to be followed—starting from the end, then going back to the beginning, and finally ending in the middle—may be disconcerting. I do not adopt it in order to rouse curiosity, but because it reflects the path the early Church followed when she had to find a way of expressing, completely and coherently, the mystery by which she was living and which she was to proclaim to the world. Moreover, if we end with the time of Jesus' earthly life, one reason is that during this time the mystery was not only most completely hidden from us but was also active in the most decisive way. For this was the time when the Word made flesh worked our salvation, the time when the Son of God redeemed the world.

1. After the Resurrection

When the man Jesus rises from the dead He does not become God—He was already God—but He enters into the divine condition.

We begin with the Resurrection and Ascension. We need not ask whether these two events were really distinct in time, as were the disciples' first experience of the risen Christ and their later certainty that they would not see Him again before His final return. The central fact for the disciples is that when Jesus rose He entered a new condition in a world that till now has been closed to Him. We call this world "heaven" and mean by it a world inaccessible to us, a world of light, perfect purity, and joy; in short, the world of God. The New Testament authors, writing in an age when men delighted to imagine the wonders of that world (while knowing perfectly well that they were simply exercising their imaginations), see Christ ascending straight to the apex of this world, "high above the heavens" (Eph 4:10), "above every other name" (Phil 2:9), above every creature no matter how noble and pure, above the angels themselves, and taking His place "at the right hand of the Majesty in heaven" (Heb 1:3), at that supreme point where God dwells and from which He directs the universe.

Where did the Lord's disciples get their certainty? We should not think of these men as naive. They make no claim to have seen Jesus ascend into heaven, for heaven is precisely what the eye of man cannot perceive. The cloud at the Ascension, in Acts, is not an ordinary cloud but a divine phenomenon that hides God's world from ours. The certainty of the disciples concerning Christ's ascent is based on two experiences: the experience of the Resurrection and the experience of the Spirit.

The Resurrection

After the Resurrection, the disciples *saw Jesus alive, but appearing and disappearing at will.* He was free, immortal, invulnerable. This was a sign, and it acquired its full significance when they remembered that this man now living had been put to death for having claimed to be the Son of God and God's equal. Since God had raised Him up, He must have been thereby confirming the truth of Jesus' startling claim.

Pentecost

To this external experience of the risen Lord there was added another experience, that of Pentecost, and this was decisive. On Pentecost the disciples were filled with the Spirit of God, and that Spirit came to them from Jesus. He put Jesus' words on their lips; He gave them the courage and confidence of Jesus in their confrontations with men; He sent them on their way to the ends of the world in order to preach the mystery of Jesus. But if they were thus seized by God's Spirit and if that Spirit is Jesus' Spirit too, then Jesus must possess God's Spirit and be able to pour Him out on every creature. Yet who save God could possibly thus dispose of God's Spirit? For the Spirit of God is by definition the Spirit who can belong to no one but God.

In a similar way, our spirit as men is that which is absolutely personal in us, and no one can take it from us. We, however, are radically incapable of giving our own spirit to someone else. *Only God,* a God who is three Persons, *can give His Spirit;* only He can be Himself over against Himself. *This unique and mysterious giving* takes place in the disciples of Jesus and is repeated in all who commit themselves to Jesus in faith. *Here is the proof that Jesus is He who gives God's Spirit* and that He has received from God not only all power over the world and its elements, even over life and death, but also power over God Himself and over the Spirit. *Therefore, He is God, equal to God and equal to God's Spirit.*

God Has Made Him Lord

The oldest texts of the New Testament, especially those in the Acts of the Apostles, also show us the thrilling surprise the disciples of Jesus felt when they realized that the man with whom they had lived, eaten, and drunk and whom they had seen suffering and trembling with fear of death, was now on the level of God and possessed divine rank. They express this passage from one world to another in extremely simple language which later reflection will improve on but never eliminate, since it expresses an essential aspect of the mystery. In his sermon on Pentecost St. Peter says that "God has made both Lord and Messiah" this Jesus of Nazareth whom men had put to death (Acts 2:36). And St. Paul distinguishes between the time when the Son of God appeared, "descended from David according to the flesh," and the time when the Resurrection established Him in His power as Son of God and in the power proper to the Holy Spirit (Rom 1:3-4). *By His Resurrection, then, Jesus acquired a power which He had hitherto not had at His disposal.* We can give this power various names, but they are all ways of designating the Holy Spirit: its origin in God or eternal life, and its effect in men.

God Has Made Us His Children

There is a perfect correspondence between two movements or transformations: the movement which brought the risen Jesus into the world of God and into His Father's glory, and the movement by which God initiates us into the secrets of

His love and the mystery of the three Persons. At the moment when He whom St. Paul calls "the first-born of the dead" (Col 1:17) escaped from the power of death and was set by God over all creation, all who believe in Him were also reconciled with God and enabled to appear before God as "holy, free of reproach and blame" (Col 1:22). They became God's children and share His life; and this is already eternal life.

This correspondence between the Lord's Ascension and our admission into the love of the three Persons should enable us to give the mystery of the Ascension its full meaning. The Ascension is not a physical event, but neither is it something limited to Jesus. *For the risen Jesus there are no more limitations.* A man of our race, born at a certain point in time and subject to all the conditions proper to our human nature, has triumphed over death and thereby acquired the incalculable dimensions of the universe itself and the inexhaustible boundless fulness of God. *Being filled with God, He now fills all things.* Of course, we can gain but a very inadequate idea of this transformation even if we think of it on the model of the richest transformations known to us: for example, the changed vision of the world an inventor of genius has at the moment he becomes aware of his discovery, or the triumphant fulness experienced by two beings who fall in love with each other. They are valid yet almost insubstantial as images of the triumphant joy of Christ when He is received by His Father and given possession of all creation.

Jesus Was Already God

The change which gave Jesus entry into God's world must be seen as vast indeed. A man passes from earth to heaven, indeed to the highest heights of heaven; a mortal being enters eternal life; a defenseless victim of every cruelty men can dream up experiences the joy of God Himself. *For Jesus,* in His human heart and flesh, *this is a totally new experience,* as it will be for us, when He comes to raise us from the dead.

However, though the experience is new for the man Jesus,

Jesus Himself, that is, He who in this man says "I" and "me," is not a newcomer to God's world. *As God He is at home.* During the whole time that He *lived as a man before rising as God,* He was already God. Before all ages, He existed as God.

There, precisely, is the mystery. It is here that we meet it for the first time. The same being who is God from all eternity is also a man born in time and later brought into God. But, before tackling the core of this mystery, and in order to prepare ourselves to do so, we shall first attempt to shed some light on our path by asking how the disciples of Jesus became aware of this truth.

No One Becomes God

Their certainty is based on a fundamental principle which is not explicitly formulated in the New Testament. It did not have to be, for it was too obvious: no one becomes God. Paul-Louis Couchoud has worked out a historical thesis that cannot in fact be sustained, but he defends it with a penetration that is authentically religious in its inspiration. His thesis is that Jesus never existed, because Jews would not have agreed to divinize a man. Here are some of Couchoud's very provocative remarks.

> Who are the men that, in the course of history, we see becoming gods? In polytheistic cultures, apotheoses are possible and shock no one. It is possible to cross the frontier dividing men from gods. . . . The Roman emperors were declared divine after their death. . . . At the time Paul was at Ephesus, "the greatest of the gods" landed there: Claudius the stutterer, with bobbing head and slobbering lips, who had been transformed into a god by the will of the senate. . . . "I feel myself becoming a god," jeered the dying Vespasian. . . .
>
> Who would want to compare these cases with that of the God whom St. Paul proclaimed? In a monotheistic religion, a man does not become God by promotion. A man

is either God to begin with or he remains a mere man for good. There can be no apotheosis.[1]

The point is made with admirable clarity, and is profoundly true. Within Judaism it was impossible to conceive of a man becoming God. The apostles, therefore, did indeed recognize God in Jesus; they did indeed recognize Him from the way He died and rose; they did indeed regard His Resurrection and Ascension as the moment when God brought Him into the realm of glory. But never did they say that at this point Jesus became God. In his sermon on Pentecost Peter says that "God has made [Him] both Lord and Messiah," because before His death Jesus had not taken possession of His power as Lord and His function as Savior. *But Peter does not say that God made Jesus God.*

Jesus Acted As God

But it was not this fundamental principle, solid though it is, that convinced Jesus' disciples that their Master was God even during His mortal life. Their conviction was not a conclusion reached by reasoning, but arose from seeing what He had said and done. They became clearly conscious of it only later on, after the Resurrection, but what they realized after the Resurrection was that *the divine traits of the risen Jesus were already to be found in the mortal man.* He already *possessed God's Spirit* when He spoke with authority; He already possessed the supremely accurate vision of God Himself when He laid hearts bare, or forgave sins and converted tax collectors and prostitutes, or when with an infallible word He determined the destiny of those He called to follow Him. *He was already on God's level* when He commanded the wind and the sea without being obliged first to pray to God, or when He described, as though He had it before His eyes, the attentive concern of the Father as He hears the secret prayers of His children, and the Father's joy as He receives back His prodigal sons. *He already possessed eternal life,* since He could with a word, and simply because

He wanted to, restore life to Lazarus or the little son of the widow of Naim. *He was already God when He died,* since God raised Him up to prove that He had rightly claimed to be God's Son, even though all creatures, and even the Father Himself, seemed to have abandoned Him. If the risen Jesus is the Son of God, and if the one who rose was the same who had been crucified, then Jesus of Nazareth is God: He has been God since His birth, God since the moment He was conceived.

What Was Jesus Before His Conception?

Here we are again faced with the mystery that is beyond our grasp and which we must nonetheless try, not indeed to explain, but to define and situate as exactly as we can. Did Jesus exist before being conceived by the Holy Spirit in the womb of the Virgin Mary? Yes, and no. No, the *man* did not exist before being conceived: a man exists only once He has been conceived, and Jesus would not be really a man if His human reality had existed before His conception. Jesus was not yet a man before Mary's "Yes" to God's invitation.

However, He who was to be named Jesus, He who was to be born of the Virgin Mary and to die under Pontius Pilate, did already exist, because He is God and God cannot begin to exist. This is why we must add that, though the man did not exist as yet, Jesus did however already exist. For, the man born of the Virgin, and the Son of God born of the Father before all ages, are not two, but one; they are the same person. This raises the problem of Christ's preexistence, and brings us to the second part of our chapter.

2. Before the Incarnation

Before the Word took flesh, the man Jesus did not exist as yet, but the Word was already the Christ.

This statement contains two truths we must try to grasp

clearly. First, we must get rid of an illusion created by our imagination. Then, we must appreciate the data supplied by the Gospels.

No Human Preexistence of Jesus

Before His conception, as we have seen, there was no man Jesus in the world. The human nature of Jesus is a creature of God, and it had a beginning.

That would seem to be a very simple truth, and one we need not insist on. In fact, when we think of Christ, we have a good deal of trouble in sticking to this seemingly obvious truth. We find it hard to draw the inevitable conclusions it contains. From the fact that Jesus is the same person both before and after His Incarnation, we spontaneously conclude to a *three-period outline* of His existence: one period before the Incarnation, in eternity; a second covering His earthly life from conception to Resurrection-Ascension; and a third comprising His return to eternity. The influence of this outline constantly distorts the vision supplied by the Gospels, because *we imagine the first period to be like the other two,* and especially like the third. We think of the man Jesus as remembering the first period of His existence, the period when He was in God, with the Father.

Such a view inevitably prevents us from taking seriously the human nature of Jesus. His life was indeed filled with trials, but from the moment He came on earth He already knew—He had always known!—the suffering that awaited Him, and also the joy He would again have with His Father. For Him, therefore, everything was quite different from what it is for us. When a man is God (we tell ourselves) He can endure anything. Anything that can happen to God can only be accidental—painful, even fatal perhaps, but always provisory and indeed already wiped out, as it were, because completely foreseen. After all, Jesus had experienced the divine glory; He knew He would have this experience again after a few moments of testing. How could His whole life fail to be colored and transfigured by this deathless memory, this presence always close to Him?

The error in this kind of reasoning, which is so common with us, is that it always supposes Jesus to have the memory of an earlier and supremely happy existence. *But Jesus cannot remember such an existence because He never experienced it.* A man remembers what He experiences in His human nature and in His life as a man. He cannot remember what is not part of His human experience, because His memories can only date back to His conception and His appearance in our world. Since Jesus is truly a man, He cannot remember the divine existence of the Word; He cannot remember His own eternal existence as the Word of God. This is not to say that Jesus the man did not know Himself to be the Son of God. It means simply that His knowledge of this fact did not prevent Him from living His human life as we live ours, that is, experiencing from day to day what human life is, and discovering, as that life went on, the joys and sufferings that can fill it.

Preexistence of the Word, Preexistence of Christ

Jesus did exist, however, before coming into the world, for He is the Son of God, and the Son of God from all eternity comes forth from the Father and returns to the Father. Here again, we are capable of a reasoning process that is correct and that is constantly repeated in the Church's tradition. But before reasoning things out, the Church first listens to her Lord as He speaks to her, and *Jesus undoubtedly speaks to His disciples of His preexistence.* He says He has come into the world (Mk 10:45; Lk 12:49; Jn 8:14; 10:10) to search out what was lost, to spread a fire upon the earth, and to give life. He says He comes from above, and not from the earth as we do. He says that He has seen the Father, whom no man in the world has ever seen (Jn 6:46), and that in His works He simply repeats what He has seen and heard when He was with the Father (Jn 8:26-38). When His enemies grow furious because He speaks of Abraham's joy at seeing His day—"You are not yet fifty! How can you have seen Abraham?"—He calmly tells them "I solemnly declare it: before Abraham came to be, I AM"

(Jn 8:57-58).

These statements are too categorical to be evaded. It is clear that He who comes before the Jewish people and is called Jesus of Nazareth existed before coming into the world. But we may not conclude from this that His prior existence was that of a man. No, it was the existence of God's Son. Jesus' very manner of speaking is significant. *When He speaks of Abraham, He uses the past tense* and speaks about a man who lived at a certain point in time and whose existence had a beginning: "Before Abraham came to be." But when He speaks of Himself, He uses the present tense: "I AM." Even though the time when He speaks is that of Pilate and Herod, it is the same Jesus who is present: Jesus, the Son of God.

Jesus also expresses His preexistence in somewhat different but no less clear language, when *He speaks of His mission* and says *He has been sent.* In the Gospel of John texts to this effect are quite numerous. Those in the Synoptic Gospels will probably strike us more, just because the vocabulary being used does not occur very often there. The clearest statement is to be found in the parable of the murderous vineyard workers, in which Jesus, shortly before His death, tells His enemies, in almost so many words, the meaning of the event that is about to occur. The owner of the vineyard is anxious to get his share of what he expects to be a fine harvest from an excellent vineyard on which he has expended a great deal of care. He has sent his servants to take delivery of the expected wine. The vineyard was the house of Israel, and God expected it to yield an incomparable wine. He had sent His servants the prophets, hoping they would persuade the tenants and bring back the product He desired. But one after another the prophets were mistreated and sometimes murdered. Finally, at his wits' end, the owner turns to the only one left: "He still had one to send—the son whom he loved. He sent him to them as a last resort" (Mk 12:6).

A parable obviously does not yield unqualified conclusions. From the story Jesus tells, one point, however, is clear: before Jesus, the prophets were already messengers of God; but that was unanimously accepted in Israel. What makes Jesus' statement about His mission special is that His mission is of another order than that of the prophets. They were servants; He is the Son. The prophets came one after another; but God keeps Jesus always with Him, and, once He has sent Jesus, He has no one else to send and nothing more to give. We might say that *God stakes everything when He sends His only Son.*

Will God lose the game? It would seem so, since the only Son will be put to death as the prophets before Him had been. But, He will die because He loves and, consequently, will make His enemies His friends and His friends the children of His own Father. He will also enable God to *taste at last the fruit of His vineyard: the special taste of a human life* that is entirely dedicated to love of the Father and the Father's children. For, the Son, though different from the prophets and having another origin than they, has shared their lot and their life; the same blood runs in His veins as in theirs. Thus, when the Father receives the Son, He tastes not only the love given Him by His Son (a taste He has known from eternity) but also the new and matchless savor this love has when it is the love of a human heart.

In the Beginning Was the Word

Since the Word existed before becoming the man called Jesus of Nazareth, Christians who meditate on their Lord are naturally led to ask: *What was this Lord doing before He became a man?* The question is inevitably an inadequate one; it does not put things properly and tends to lead the questioner astray. How can we speak of God doing something before the Incarnation as though He existed in time? Our vocabulary is inevitably deficient.

At the same time, the question is not wholly misleading. The very words of Jesus were an invitation to ask this kind of question. When He spoke of His mission, when He spoke of His being present to Abraham and the prophets, when He also spoke of coming after them to continue their work and accomplish what they were unable to accomplish, He was suggesting that *when these other men spoke and acted, their work was already His.* Jesus came to fulfill the Law and the prophets, but His manner of fulfilling them was unique and unparalleled. He does not make a distinction between elements of the Scripture to be preserved and others to be abandoned, but goes straight to the essential point, and, standing at this center, sheds light on all the avenues that lead through the whole. Though "he had no teacher" (Jn 7:15), He is at home in the forest of the Scriptures and effortlessly reveals their divine depths.

Once He was converted, *St. Paul,* the Pharisee who burned with zeal for the Law (Phil 3:5), discovered that this Jesus, whom He had regarded with horror as the destroyer of Israel's religious tradition, was on the contrary the heir to it, because He had founded it. The message of the prophets was already His Good News (Rom 1:2), and the Law was given to Israel so that when the time was ripe God might be able to send His Son, "born of a woman, born under the law . . . so that we might receive our status as adopted sons" (Gal 4:4-5).

The *Gospel of John* gives us the final word on the subject. If Jesus is at home at the very heart of the Scriptures, if *He is the heir to the Scriptures,* the only one the Scriptures really speak of and the one for whose sake they exist, the reason is that *He is the one who speaks in the Scriptures.* Jesus Christ is the Word of God: the Word that gave Israel existence among the nations, the Word that guided her to her destiny, the Word that directs the history of all peoples, the Word that created the world. *What was He doing before He came into the world? He was doing the things the Scriptures tell of: doing them and telling of them.* He was creating heaven and earth, and telling the story of that creation; He was choosing Abraham and Moses, and telling them what He was going to do with them. He is the Word of God that creates, and creates by speaking. He was there when the universe came into existence, and the universe came into existence because He spoke. *As He existed before coming into the world, so He existed before the world itself came to be.*

The biblical tradition itself enabled John to discover the permanent, creative presence of Christ. But because He had seen the Lord and knew that the Lord has come "to gather into one all the dispersed children of God" (Jn 11:52), John is able to plumb the ultimate depths of that tradition. John sees in Jesus the *Dabar* (Hebrew: Word) that finds expression in the Scriptures, but He gives Him a new name: *Logos* (Greek: Word). The *Logos* is still the Word that God speaks in order to create the world and direct history. But since the world is not just the world of the chosen people and since the history is that of all mankind, John chooses a new term for this Word. It was a word foreign to the tradition of his fathers, a Greek word familiar to all those men of the ancient world who endeavor to reflect on the world and man's destiny in it.

In choosing the term *Logos* and substituting it for the older term, St. John is not saying that all the wisdom and reflective thought to be found in the world are the Logos and therefore already Christ. Man's wisdom and reflective thought are human realities, and have their value as well as their weakness and deficiencies. The point is rather that if Christ Jesus is the Word of God and the world is His work, then the action of the pre-existent Christ is not limited to the history of Israel. Every man who comes into the world is enlightened by Him and touched by His action. From the very beginning of the world Christ is the Wisdom of God, and this Wisdom is offered to every man. The Word has something to say to every human heart.

3. The Word Becomes Flesh

The Decisive Period

We come finally to *the period of Christ's life on earth,* the period when, in the man Jesus, God showed Himself as He really is. *This is the decisive period,* for in it God gives the supreme proof of His love by giving His own Son. It is the period in which men, confronted with the Person of Jesus and with His life and death, become aware from hearing and seeing Him, that they must do the thing which will shape their whole existence: believe in God. This period provides the starting point for what we called, at the beginning of this chapter, the first movement, the one in which we look at Jesus and ask who He is. Before focusing on this movement, we wanted to *situate this decisive period* between the eternity of the Word in the bosom of the Father and the eternity of Jesus Christ risen. We have done so in order to be sure that *when we turn our attention to the mortal man Jesus, we would forget nothing of the riches of His divinity.* Let us now, therefore, look at Jesus living among us, and try to grasp the fact that *His every action is the self-expression of God's Word.*

The Illusion of Jesus' Two Existences

As we read the Gospel and contemplate the life of Jesus, we are always in danger of succumbing to what might be called an optical illusion. We believe that Jesus Christ is the Son of God and that His being a man leaves His divinity untouched—and both of these statements are true. Therefore, we tend to think, Jesus lived on two levels, on two separate storeys, as it were, one above the other, with no communication between them. On the lower storey He lived His life as a man like us, bore the heat and burden of the day, ran into hatred, relaxed among His friends, and died alone. We have no doubt that this life was fully real; in fact, it is with deep feelings that we perceive the indisputable signs that this was a man, fully authentic and exemplary. But then we go on to say that the picture is incomplete: that we have to add the upper storey, which changes everything. For, if Jesus is God, then at the level of His divinity, He lives a life that is necessarily blessed, invulnerable, filled with the serene and changeless light in which the three Persons dwell beyond the clouds where no storms can touch Them.

We are here at the very heart of the mystery, and therefore must aim at being as accurate in our understanding as we can.

This manner of imagining a two-storey existence is a serious illusion, even though in its own way it states an important truth. The truth is that Christ the man does not cease to be God; that He is always united to His Father in a total closeness and in absolute certainty; that He sees Himself being loved by the Father and returning that love in an immediacy of relationship of which no creature can even dream, yet which God intends us to reach in His Son. That immediate relationship we must call "vision," for that is the word Jesus uses in speaking of it.

The illusion begins when we turn this vision, this relationship between the Son and the Father into a higher-level duplicate of His existence as a man; when we make a storey of the same kind as the lower, earthly storey, distinguished from the latter only by its scope, its peace, and its light. Then we are imagining God after the model of man, and reducing the love of the three Persons for one another to a kind of spiritual consolation.

God's Actions: Living a Human Life

We imagine that if we are to preserve Christ's divinity we must rope off at least a small area of tranquillity, a sort of park that is shut off from human life with its ugliness and degradation. Such is our optical illusion, although in the last analysis it is an illusion fostered by our self-centeredness. In point of fact, *the divinity and the humanity in Jesus do not form two storeys set one above the other.* His human life and His intimacy with the Father are not two spheres set side by side and closed off from each other. They are rather two concentric regions that are in communication with each other (if we wish to use images—and how can we avoid doing so?). Or *they are two dimensions interior each to the other.* Jesus lives His divine life as a man; He lives His intimate life with His Father, making it the wellspring and innermost secret area of His life with us. Direct communication with the Father in the Spirit is not in Jesus a higher existence, but is the source of His life as a man.

All this is taught us by both St. Paul and St. John. When John writes: "The Word was made flesh," he is not merely say-

ing that there was the eternal Word, then there was Christ, a
man in whom the Word dwelt. *The important word is "became"
or "was made."* The Word *became* flesh, and what He did at
the moment when He took our human nature to Himself, He
never ceases doing—during His earthly life before His death,
and during the ages after the Resurrection. Between the eternal
Word and the Word made flesh, there is something far different
than a mere succession in time: there is the divine action by
which the Word becomes man. He does not cease to be the
Word, for the Word does not turn into something else; rather
He is permanently becoming a man, that is, *at each moment He
causes His human nature to exist.* In Jesus is to be found our
human nature in its fullest form, with every element of our
flesh and spirit. But there is not a single element, not a single
action or feeling, that is not the self-expression of the Son of
God. *In Jesus, the Son of God lives our human life.*

The Whole Divinity in the Whole Humanity

We must add that the Son of God lives our human life *to the
full.* Jesus has not kept in reserve a sort of divine area that is
not connected with His humanity, an area into which He might
withdraw from our concerns and our sins. We see Him with-
drawing into the solitary places to pray, but this is not in order
to get away from us; on the contrary, He thus withdraws at
decisive moments when our fate is in the balance: when, for
example, he must elicit the faith of Peter and the other disciples.

What the Gospels show us, Paul explains to us. Christ Jesus
"emptied himself" (Phil 2:7) so as to make our condition His
own. Just as John in describing the Incarnation shows us the
Word originating the process whereby the man Jesus came into
the world (the Word *became,* made Himself, flesh), so Paul, in
an even more explicit way, shows us *the activity of the Son of
God* as He "empties himself." He uses this language because,
in an even more brutal fashion than John, He will go on to
show Jesus reaching the depths of abasement, accepting "even
death, death on a cross!" He wants us to realize that this ter-

rible death did not come to Jesus as a sort of tragic accident or unavoidable fate, but was the expression of a divine choice. The extreme misfortune and distress Jesus experienced did, of course, descend upon Him from without; they were something He had to undergo. His Passion meant passivity on His part, since He was the victim of men's sins, and God does not will evil and sin. But God can indeed actively take upon Himself the burden of men's sins and experience the darkest moments of our human condition and the depths to which we have fallen. This is why *the Son of God brings into play all His divine power and love to make Himself the last and least of men:* a slave hanging on a cross.

We Have Seen His Glory

This is also why we see, by faith, in this tortured man an incomprehensible miracle of divine power and the supreme revelation of God's glory. Never before or since did God reap such a harvest from our human race; never before or since did the Son of God accomplish a work of such amplitude and so integrally expressive of a love divine in its quality.

Let us, therefore, not attempt to look for the divinity of Jesus outside His humanity, off in some nonexistent height between heaven and earth. Let us rather fix our eyes on the man and contemplate Him with humility and care. He reveals God to us.

Chapter 14

We Have Seen His Glory

Because John had seen the glory of the only Son, he felt bound to gather up all his precious memories of Him and to record his experience of Jesus, on which he was constantly meditating. He felt bound to write his Gospel and dedicate it to all those who, down the centuries, would believe in Jesus Christ. And because Paul saw the Lord on the road to Damascus, he felt bound to preach to all nations. Because Peter and his companions saw Jesus alive and among them again, they felt bound to say so before the tribunal and the very judges who had put Jesus to death a few weeks before.

Why this need to go out and tell what they had seen? To tell strangers a story in which they had had no part and which meant nothing to them? Whence the strange idea of going out and disturbing so many people about an event so remote from them? Why is it that Christians cannot renounce speaking of the Lord and setting Him before other men?

If it is true that Jesus is risen and that His Resurrection is but the first-fruits of a general resurrection, then understandably we must tell all men this marvelous news that so closely concerns them. But, once the news has been broadcast and the necessary information given, may we not simply trust in the inner power, the explosive force, of the news itself? That kind of news should not take long in making its way around the world. Why then does this news take so long? Why does it have to be preached anew each day? Why is it so difficult to convince people of it?

The answer is that we are not dealing simply with an event and a piece of news. Therefore it is not enough merely to publish a report of it. The event is inseparable from a person, and the person is discovered only by meeting Him. Men do not rise from the dead because there is a precedent for rising or because Jesus has broken a path which now lies open behind Him, but because He lays hold of them and involves them in His own Resurrection. He is both the event and the person: "I am the resurrection" (Jn 11:25). The only way to experience His life is to believe in Him.

Throughout the Scriptures, from the opening of Genesis to the visions of the Apocalypse, we find the same movement, the same balancing between two poles. There are events which seem to cut across the lives of men, burdening them to the point of crushing them or sweeping them along on a wave of jubilation: victories and disasters, births and deaths. On the other hand, we can glimpse through the events a mysterious, fascinating face; the face of one who guides events without seeming to and who is attentively present even though He seems absent and far away; the face of a God who hides as though He feared being recognized, yet who never ceases to call to us and to be on the watch for those who know how to find Him.

The Burning Bush

"Come no nearer! Remove the sandals from your feet, for the place where you stand is holy ground" (Ex 3:5). The first experience of God is often that of discovering that He was there without our realizing it. When Jacob awakes at Bethel he cries out: "Truly, the Lord is in this spot, although I did not know it!" (Gn 28:16). Later, as he returns to his own country, he discovers at the ford of the Jabbok the name of the mysterious adversary with whom he had had to struggle all night long: "I have seen God face to face, yet my life has been spared" (Gn 32:31). Abraham had had the same experience before him: in the three travelers whom he saw standing at the terebinth of Mamre (Gn 18:1) and received so generously, he discovered Yahweh, "the judge of all the world" (Gn 18:25), for whom nothing is so marvelous that He cannot do it (Gn 18:14).

Later, when God intervened on Mt. Moriah and stayed Abraham's hand as he was about to slay Isaac, He did so in order to tell Abraham that He, God, had seen all of Abraham's anguish and now knew that His servant was both faithful to his Lord and filled with love for his son: "I know now how devoted you are to God, since you did not withhold from me your own beloved son" (Gn 22:12). Yahweh respects both fear of the Lord and a father's love for his son; both alike are precious to Him.

In any life, God does not begin to act only at the moment when He manifests His presence. On the contrary, He often leaves no traces of Himself at the moment when He first really begins to act in us and our lives. Moses was an exile, hunted by Pharaoh's police, suspect and rejected by his fellow Israelites, a fugitive hiding in the desert, and forced to hire himself out to a foreigner. That was the time when God suddenly revealed Himself. A moment of dazzling light, but the flame that leaped up from the bush not only lit up the heavens and transfigured the desert out to the horizon; it also shed a brilliant light on Moses' life and its vicissitudes. His people's misfortunes, the tyrannical rule of the Egyptians, his own helplessness and exile in the empty desert—all that was apparently failure and absurdity. And now to learn that God Himself had been attentive to it all! "I have witnessed the affliction of my people in Egypt and have heard their cry of complaint . . . I know well what they are suffering. Therefore I have come to rescue them" (Ex 3:7-8).

Here was a disconcerting revelation indeed. For Moses must believe that God does not will this injustice and misfortune, since He is now intervening to put an end to it; yet He must

also believe that God has allowed His people to suffer all this
to the point of being crushed by it and losing even the taste
and instinct for freedom. Such a paradox cannot be resolved
or explained; it can only find justification through the faith to
which it gives rise. Because of the words he hears and the striking tone of God's voice, Moses cannot doubt God's generosity
or the sincerity of His reactions. And because Moses is thus
certain, he can accept God's long delay and see in it a further
proof of God's generosity. That is how Paul understood the
delay; explaining to the pagans why "in past ages he [God] let
the Gentiles go their way" (Acts 14:16), he says: "They were
to seek God, yes to grope for him and perhaps eventually to
find him" (Acts 17:27).

God left man to his freedom and his quest, to his struggle for
wisdom and his disastrous follies; He left him to act as he
wished, for better or for worse, left him free to do evil or do
good, build up or tear down. God acted thus, however, not
because He lacked interest in man or because He was afraid
of taking sides; rather, He was taking His creatures very seriously indeed and respecting their innate resources to act for
themselves. At the same time, He is clear and categorical about
what He wants to do with men: to save and rescue them (Ex
3:8). His decision and the course to which He commits Himself shed a new light on the past in its entirety: God had always
been there, infinitely attentive but also infinitely circumspect.
He cannot intervene in a violent way; the only acknowledgement He wants is the acknowledgement of faith. This is why
He needs a man to serve Him; this is why He chooses Moses.

Only a human being, able to sympathize and believe, to want
and to wait, is capable of understanding and bearing witness
that God can take the initiative and entrust Himself to His
creature, that He can wait for a response from His creature
and count on that creature's faith. This is the first of the revelations made at Horeb. It comes not through the bush, which of
itself could not reveal God. It comes through the faith which
can understand that God can want His people's salvation and
yet not give it to them ready-made, and that this God can

commission Moses to save His people and yet not give him the means of doing it. "The cry of the Israelites has reached me. . . . Come now! I will send you" (Ex 3:9-10). The words prove the authenticity of the revelation and point to its inexhaustible depths. The account as such is certainly from a later time and follows a traditional form so that we cannot reconstruct the original scene. But the experience attested in the account is beyond doubt, and is strictly in keeping with the most genuine kind of faith. To discover what God is is also to discover that He is with us in the future, in what does not yet exist and never will exist unless we enter into it with Him, just as He was with us in the past, at the very source of our being before we came to be.

This God is not just one more face in the gallery of divine beings. He is not distinguished from these others by being greater or more majestic, by acting on a larger scale or making a greater noise on earth. On the contrary, He makes Himself known through the echo He creates in men's hearts, and through the meaning life takes on for those who give themselves to Him. For them, as for everyone else, including Israel in Egypt, life is a puzzling mixture of suffering and hope, distant goal and struggle, dreams and harsh toil. But for those who believe, for Moses who hears God speaking to Him, the chaos of life becomes a place of presence and a promise of meeting.

Someone with Us

If Moses was to believe that silent events and an obscure future were really penetrated by an intention and a will, he had to be certain that he was in fact dealing with someone real. The biblical account shows him therefore asking the logical question: "What is your name?" (cf. Ex 3:13). No one can bear witness and give an account of his own faith, unless he can refer to someone whose existence is independent of subjective experience, someone capable of making his reality accessible to others.

The answer Moses gets is beyond question an answer that

comes from a person, someone who gives evidence of a real personality and a special way of communicating Himself and summoning man to action and communication. "I am who I am" or "I am he who is" (Ex 3:14): however the divine statement is translated, it is strongly marked by reserve and distance. This is characteristic of a God, of course, but it is also characteristic of any person; we can understand it only on the basis of our own experience as persons. Doesn't each of us, along with every man who comes into the world, have days when he must say to those who ask him about himself; "I am who I am"? Nothing is more pliant and impressionable than the heart of a child that is moved by every impulse and is open to every invitation. And yet nothing is less penetrable, nothing more resistant and sharply delineated than a human personality: it is what it is, and no one can enter into it by violence. The human person is a mystery, and the mystery only grows deeper, the closer we draw near to it.

But, when the person is a human being, there is a large element of opaqueness and inertia in the mystery. If we are what we are, it is because we are ourselves and no one else. But it is also because life, birth, heredity, past experiences, conscious and unconscious memories all leave their mark upon us and shape a personal physiognomy whose characteristics are daily intensified and hardened. Being what they are is for most men a limitation and a destiny they must accept, rather than a source of power and energy. The voice which speaks to Moses betrays neither weakness nor any attrition from passing time. In one and the same breath it says both "I am" and "I am with you" (Ex 3:12-14). Precisely because God is what He is and because no pressure or opposition can threaten Him or even touch Him, His very being is a guarantee of His presence and protection. Moses need not know the future that awaits him or the adventures that lie ahead. It is enough for him to receive God's promise and to be sure of always finding God near him. For, the One who will be with him will be ever the same: unshaken and unshakable.

This divine power is accompanied by deep sensitivity. The

God who defines Himself by His stability and holds the future in
His hands because He knows He does not have any need of it,
is also attentive and vulnerable; He is touched by man's cry of
distress, and revolted by injustice. When He chooses Moses,
He opens His heart to him, makes known His decisions, and
allows Moses to share His reactions. For this God, revelation
does not mean offering a program and a plan of action; it
means, first and foremost, letting His heart speak: "I have witnessed . . . I have heard. . . . I have come." Moses' faith rests,
at bottom, on one certainty: the God who speaks thus, the God
who feels so deeply the scandalous state of the world and reveals His feelings to others, the God who thus pledges His divine
power, is a God who can never fail us.

Such is the face revealed to Moses, the manifestation on
which the whole faith of Israel depends. It is an invisible manifestation: neither in the burning bush nor later in the hollow
of the rock where God stations Moses to protect Him while the
divine glory is passing by (Ex 33:22) does Moses really see
God's face. So too, when Isaiah, overwhelmed, cries out: "My
eyes have seen the King, the Lord of hosts!" all he can actually
describe is the train of a royal garment filling the sanctuary (Is
6:2-5). But the fact that the face remains invisible does not
prevent the Old Testament from asserting that Moses saw the
Lord and that this is the highest of all experiences and the greatest thing man can hope for. Why? Because at this moment
God and Moses really were face to face (Ex 33:11), and no
third party mediated between them. God really communicated
Himself to His servant and opened His heart to Him.

"I Tell You What I Have Seen in the Father's Presence"

There seems to be a vast gulf between the Sermon on the
Mount and the great assertions of Jesus in the fourth Gospel.
When the crowds came to see and hear Him, Jesus spoke to
them very simply of their daily lives and concerns, disputes between neighbors, meetings and reconciliations. But to the
teachers of the Law of Jerusalem He tried to give some insight

into His person, His relations with His Father, the light that was in Him, the Presence that was always with Him. Thus we seem to be in two different worlds, dealing with two radically different kinds of experience.

And yet the two languages and the two approaches are in fact saying the same thing and giving voice to the same basic experience. The language of the fourth Gospel is more explicit and plunges more directly into the mystery, but it draws its coherence and authenticity from the seemingly quite simple words of Jesus of Galilee. When the latter says, as though enunciating something obvious, that men should not worry about food or clothing because their heavenly Father knows their needs (Mt 6:31-32); when He assures them that the Father sees in secret and treasures men's most selfless actions (Mt 6:4.6.18); or when He says that the poor, the sorrowing, and the hungry are "blest," He is not appealing to universal experience or stating truths anyone can verify for himself in everyday life. Rather, He is speaking of His own experience and inviting men to verify the truth by becoming His disciples.

Jesus is indeed speaking of everyday life and everyday cares. But He shows the Father attentive and concerned with life at its most ordinary, because He Himself experiences the abiding joy of living in the Father's presence and responding to Him. He sees the Father and hears Him saying: "You are my beloved Son," and He has come to enable men to share His experience and His joy. The joyous experience is His own, but He is among us so that we too may have it. He is sole witness to the manifestation of the Father, for on Him alone do the heavens open and the Spirit descend, and He alone hears the heavenly voice. But He accepts the vision and the words so that He may share them with us. They are His secret, and no one can take it from Him. But He lievs it in the midst of men, as one entirely immersed in their life, because His secret is the secret of their lives as well. A lost secret and a light that has been extinguished—but a secret that will change our lives, and a light for which our eyes were made.

In all the words and actions of Jesus we find the same strange commingling, which is both unique and complex. He is always speaking of things that seem self-evident, of elementary attitudes, of actions so infinitely simple that there seem to be no alternatives to them. It is as though we were face to face with the very reality of life. A woman turns her house upside down to find the coin that slipped from her purse; a man takes his donkey to the watering-trough; a father discovers that God is like him; adults are requested to look carefully at children; the rich are asked to give. Isn't that what life is all about? Need we do more than follow its lead?

Yet nothing is more difficult or more contrary to our instincts. The miracle wrought by the Gospel is to effect a conversion more difficult than having a camel pass through the eye of a needle. The light of the Gospel shows us that life is simple, but also that Jesus alone can give the life-giving water. The Gospel shows us what was already there; it leaves everything as it was, but it also gives all things their proper emphasis and reveals their true depths, just as the dawning light makes us see the world with new eyes.

Here then is the mission of the Church; here is what the Christian is called to bear witness to. Church and Christian must make the light of Christ shine out; they have a secret to reveal, a new experience to share with men. But the whole purpose of the secret is to illuminate everyday existence and the lives of all mankind.

The Glory of God on the Face of Christ

The secret resides in what Jesus says but even more in the way He says it, in the certainty with which He says it, and in what the words presuppose and manifest. How does Jesus know that the Father treasures the actions of His children and that He is deeply concerned with the poor who have nothing? The Father's attitude is not evident to anyone who looks at our world, nor can it be deduced by reflection on the nature of God. And so Jesus does not appeal to observation or reflection; He simply says what He Himself sees. But does He see things as they really are? Is it true that the poor are blest and that God is attentive to all our needs? It is true for Jesus. He sees that it is so. He experiences it; and He makes others experience it wherever He goes. He is telling us of things not as they now are but as they are coming in the kingdom which is imminent. We need only open our door and let God's rule in; then we too will experience the reality of things. Jesus knows and sees how things really are, but He cannot make others see it unless they believe in His word and follow Him.

The most astonishing thing about Jesus is that everything most deeply personal and individual about Him is also the expression and revelation of Another, the Father. This is clear in every line of the Sermon on the Mount; it is clear from the very way He tells us—without feeling any need of further explanation—what the Father wants, what the Father does, and what the Father expects of us. It is clear, even more startlingly, from the way He deals with sinners. With them He is entirely Himself. Nowhere do we see more clearly His independence of human conventions, His receptivity and tenderness, His clarity of vision, His freedom, and His gift of reading hearts. No prophet ever acted as He acts. They had all been ready to receive repentant sinners, and John even lived among them. But even John waits for them to come and gather around him, while Jesus goes out to sinners, looks for them in their own surroundings, accepts their invitations, and eats and drinks with them (Mk 2:15-16). Such is the mission of the Son of Man, and such the way of life He adopts in our world.

Such an attitude gives rise to scandal, and Jesus must justify Himself. He does so, as usual, through a series of parables: the money-lender and his two debtors (Lk 7:41-43), the physician and the sick (Mk 2:17), the sheep lost and found, the coin lost and found, the son lost and found (Lk 15). Now, these parables are immediately understandable and profoundly true in what they say of men, but they are also deeply paradoxical. The last characteristic is especially clear in the series of parables about things lost and found. Nothing is more natural than the housewife's disturbance at finding her money gone and her joy at recovering it. The action of the shepherd in abandoning the ninety-nine sheep to go after the missing one is of the same kind, and just as understandable, even if less frequent. But what father is in fact able so completely to forget the offense committed against him, to live solely in hope of finding his son, and of receiving him with such joy? And yet the father of the parable is man as he does not exist yet, but as he is coming and being called into existence by Jesus.

The reason Jesus can describe man in this fashion is because He has His eyes fixed on God. In God alone does He find man as He describes Him. Nothing proves better the depths of what we might call (though in a somewhat different sense than St. Paul) the "humanness of God." Nothing better illustrates how, when Jesus is most deeply and spontaneously Himself, He is also the expression and echo of God. If He goes out to sinners, He does so both because His heart urges Him to it and because He is filled with awareness of His mission. He forgives because it is His immediate reaction to do so, but also because He experiences a divine event: God's forgiveness. In other words, in Him there is no gap between life and mission, between the individual and the messenger. His identity is not that which is deliberately willed by the envoy who dedicates himself wholly to his mission and consecrates his life to it as did John the Baptist, the friend of the Bridegroom. It is rather the spontaneous, radical identity proper to someone who is Himself only insofar as He comes from another and who does the actions of God because He is among us precisely in order to tell us how God acts.

This then is the glory proper to Jesus, and this the manifestation of God in Jesus. The glory is His alone, and yet it is entirely the Father's gift to Him. God alone can forgive sins, but Jesus can also forgive because He knows exactly how the Father acts, and because in forgiving He expresses exactly the Father's mind. The glory is the glory proper to the only Son (Jn 1:14); for if Jesus is to be wholly Himself while yet being the perfect manifestation of God, if He is to be, spontaneously and in every fiber of His being, exactly what the Father is, He must be, even in His humanity, the Son and nothing else. To see Him is to see the Father (Jn 14:9): not as though Jesus were a double or the reproduction of a photograph, but in the sense that He is completely filled with the Father's loving presence, so that when we see and hear Him the face of the invisible God is manifested to us.

This revelation once again confronts us with the paradox of Christian mission. Only Christ can make the Father's face known to us, because He alone has seen it. Like Jesus Himself, the Christian who has come to know the Father cannot but tell others of what he has seen. Yet what he goes forth to tell others existed before he ever came on the scene. For, wherever there is an uncalculating human heart, wherever a man knows the joy of pardoning and welcoming an enemy, the tender love of the Father of Jesus Christ is present and active. And yet, the closer men are to that source of tender love, the more need they have of Jesus if they are to be faithful to that love and become conscious of its origin.

Chapter 15

Christ and the Holy Spirit

Jesus was filled with the Holy Spirit (Lk 4:1); Jesus says very little about the Holy Spirit. Both of these facts are evident from the Gospels, but they are not easy to correlate precisely. Yet both must be kept before us if we wish to penetrate the mystery of the Holy Spirit and His relation to Jesus Christ.

Jesus rarely speaks of the Holy Spirit, and, when He does, He does not necessarily give the words "Holy Spirit" a different meaning from what they might have in the Old Testament. He says that David, in composing the Psalms, was "inspired by the Holy Spirit" (Mk 12:36). "Blasphemy against the Holy Spirit," a sin that will never be forgiven, is an offense directly against God (Mk 3:29) and the most serious a man can commit; it is an attack on God, a rejection of Him at the very moment when He gives Himself most fully as the holy God. But Jesus does not say in what this commitment on God's part consists, nor does He give any new characterization of the Holy Spirit. God "will give the Holy Spirit to those who ask him," says St. Luke (11:13), but this is probably Luke's effort to concretize Matthew's vaguer words "good things" (7:11). It is highly probable, then, that Jesus did not emphasize the role and personality of the Holy Spirit until the end of His life, in the farewell discourses,

The farewell discourses, whether in the synoptic form of the teachings given facing the temple that was doomed to be destroyed, or in the Johannine form of the conversations after the Supper, seem to have been the occasion on which Jesus revealed the special mission of the Holy Spirit. Mark's account here is by far the most natural: Jesus knows He will soon die and that His disciples must live on in this world in fidelity to His work and His name; He knows they will have to face the same opposition that was His own lot; when He Himself has left them, the Holy Spirit will be there to bear witness to Him (Mk 13:9-13). Applying a method he frequently uses, Matthew constructs a great missionary discourse by putting together two distinct instructions that were separate in time. One of these dealt with the temporary mission of the disciples during the Galilean period of Jesus' ministry; the other dealt with their mission after Jesus' death. The climate in which the disciples will work is quite different in each: on their first mission they may run into some opposition; on the second they will be persecuted. When, therefore, Mt 10:17-22 mentions the Spirit, it does so because the evangelist has mingled two different perspectives which are clearly distinguished in Mark and Luke.[1]

The Gospel of John presents data very like those of the Synoptics. In John, too, the special role of the Holy Spirit emerges only in the last days of Jesus' life, in the discourse after the Supper, and the role is the same as that described in Mark: the Spirit is the witness to Jesus in time of persecution (Jn 15:26; 16:18-11). Apart from this explicit teaching, which is more developed than in the Synoptics but running along the same lines, the statements about the Holy Spirit in the fourth Gospel are of two kinds. Some clearly express the Church's experience of the Spirit, but they are offered as reflections of the evangelist (cf. 7:39: "He was referring to the Spirit. . . . There was, of course, no Spirit as yet, since Jesus had not yet been glorified"). Others are put on the lips of Jesus and always presuppose, explicitly or implicitly, the opposition between flesh and spirit (Jn 3:5-8; 4:23-24; 6:63). A new birth, a new worship given to God, a new power resident in the words of Jesus

—in short, a new experience is foretold and promised. The source of it is the Holy Spirit, but the new reality is prophesied rather than experienced. It is promised for a time that is still in the future, and the Spirit is still, as in the Old Testament tradition, the gift proper to the eschatological age.[2]

From these convergent facts we may justly infer that, at least up to the time when Jesus was telling His disciples of the future that awaited them, He did not seem to give the Holy Spirit a special role. Rather, He locates the Spirit in His usual place in the biblical and prophetic tradition: at the center of God's action, as the highest manifestation of His power and as the principle of creative newness by contrast with fleshly weakness and creaturely helplessness. But none of these characteristics is completely new. The thing that strikes us most is the casual character of what Jesus has to say of the Spirit. It is as if He had no choice but to mention the Spirit when speaking of such matters as these.

This reserve becomes all the more noteworthy when we bear in mind another basic datum of the Gospels: Jesus' own possession of the Holy Spirit. Jesus is filled with the Holy Spirit. This fact is not repeatedly mentioned by the Gospels, and consequently we might think of it as something secondary. Yet the emphasis put on it shows it rather to be something essential.

The baptism of Jesus has considerable importance in the Gospel traditions. It is recorded precisely in order to show that all of Jesus' activity has its source in the permanent presence of the Spirit within Him. Speaking in the house of Cornelius at Caesarea, Peter sets up a continuity between the divine anointing Jesus received immediately after His baptism by John, His salutary ministry to the sick and possessed, and the power of the Holy Spirit: "You know what has been reported all over Judea about Jesus of Nazareth, beginning in Galilee with the baptism John preached; of the way God anointed him with the Holy Spirit and power. He went about doing good works and healing all who were in the grip of the devil" (Acts 10:37-38).[3] In all four Gospels the baptism inaugurates the public ministry of Jesus and is its starting point. The man who comes looking for

John and the man who comes up out of the Jordan are one and the same person, and the experience He has had there has not changed Him, for He knows what He is doing when He asks for baptism, and is not surprised by an alien power. Nonetheless, His whole future activity now depends on what He has just experienced. And what He has just experienced is the Spirit.

The Spirit at the Baptism

The Gospel accounts of the baptism of Jesus pose some difficult problems. The accounts were evidently written long after the event. They suppose the practice of baptism in the Christian community, and they describe a personal experience of Jesus, along with His prayer, the vision He saw, and the words He heard, even though there is no evidence that these details have their origin in anything He told the disciples at the time or later. The only witness who seems to have grasped something of what was going on was John the Baptist: "I saw the Spirit descend like a dove from the sky, and it came to rest on him" (Jn 1:32). But John does not claim to have heard the conversation between Father and Son. Besides, at the time the dialogue would have been unintelligible to any other human being; it would acquire meaning only after the Resurrection of Jesus when the secret of His life and person was made known.

Yet, despite these difficulties, there remains a fact impossible to deny because it could not have been invented: Jesus went looking for John the Baptist and asked for baptism at his hands, and it was at the moment of His baptism that He entered upon His mission. It would be rash to think we can see further than the Gospels into the motive for His action. The most we can do is to situate His action in its context. When Jesus wishes to perform a decisive religious action, He does not go to Jerusalem and become a student of the priests and teachers of the Law, nor does He go up to the temple. Instead, He goes looking for the prophet and mingles with the people who had come from all over the land and from every social class to hear the prophet's words, receive his baptism, and then wait for God to manifest His power in the world and come to fulfill His promises. Jesus joins this crowd; with it He listens to God's word and shares the crowd's expectation. At the moment when He does what everyone around Him has done or will do, when He goes down into the water and receives baptism, He also receives from on high an entirely unique experience: God speaks to Him and fills Him with His Spirit.

In the presentation by the evangelists, which is clear even though schematic, certain points are clear. The account does not describe Jesus' experience in terms of its psychological content; the vision of the heavens being opened and of the being who descends from heaven "like a dove" is in the style of the apocalypse (cf. Ez 1:.5.27-28; Rv 4:1; 5:6; 19:11). It does not give us direct knowledge of Jesus' consciousness at the moment, but rather presupposes this and relates an event which Jesus consciously experienced. The account itself is significant. It resembles the scenes of prophetic calling in the Old Testament, as well as God's presentation to men of the king or the servant He has chosen (Ps 2:7; Is 42:1; 49:6). Yet it is not simply identical with either one of these. Those whom God called to be prophets felt the call addressed to them by an alien voice that turned their lives topsy-turvy; they already had a trade and a family, responsibilities and friendships, and now God suddenly snatched them away from all that and sent them about His work. The divine declarations, on the other hand, were focused less on the person of the servant or chosen king than on the public to whom God was presenting them; the interior experience of the one sent is not mentioned at all. The contrast between such episodes and the baptism is therefore quite clear-cut. In the baptism, Jesus Himself is the addressee of the divine words, and, if we are invited to contemplate the event, it is that we may see Jesus receiving the Father's word and the gift of the Spirit. His experience is not directly described, but it is nonetheless the focus of attention and the central factor in the whole scene.

In a number of ways the scene resembles those found in the apocalypses. Jesus is like such seers as Ezekiel, Daniel, and the heroes of the apocryphal apocalypses: Baruch, Esdras, Enoch.

Yet there is an immense distance between Jesus and these others. Ezekiel, Daniel, and John himself on Patmos are given leave to be spectators viewing a world that is alien to them; they are overwhelmed and paralyzed by terror or ecstasy; they see unfolding before them scenes which remain incomprehensible until an interpreter explains them (Dan 7:16; 8:17; Rev 17:7). Jesus too sees the heavens opened and the Spirit descending like a dove. He is not in heaven and communicates with it only through visions and words, but He is Himself the addressee of the words and the vision. He is in a position of equality with the one who speaks to Him, and the Holy Spirit brings Him nothing but a consciousness of what He already is: "You are my beloved Son. On you my favor rests" (Mk 1:11).[4] The scene is one of mission; this fact indicates its proper place in the Gospel and connects it with the temptation that will follow immediately, as Jesus moves forward under the impulse of the Spirit (Mk 1:12-13). But the real mission of Jesus cannot be reduced to certain actions He must perform; His real mission is to be the Son, the Father's beloved, in the world of men.

A noteworthy aspect of the episode is that, while we are told nothing of the consciousness of Jesus, the Father's attitude is clearly expressed. It is as though Jesus' only reason for being there was to enable the Father to give voice to His love and joy. When God told Israel centuries ago that He was certain of having a servant on whom He could rely completely, His proclamation of this servant's coming was always accompanied by an assurance of the joy He would derive from Him (Is 42:1; 49:8; cf. 53:10). Today the promise is fulfilled; the Servant has come, and God makes known to Him the divine joy.

All this is accomplished by the Spirit. It is He who links heaven and Jesus; it is His activity that unites them. We might say that the only action specifically His is to communicate to Jesus the words and the joy of the Father.

The Spirit in the Public Life of Jesus

We might almost say that after the baptism of Jesus the Holy

Spirit disappears from the Gospel narrative. And in fact He appears with all His power in only two further scenes: the temptation in the desert and Jesus' assertion of His mission in the synagogue at Nazareth (Lk 4:16-21). Both of these episodes, which form part of the inaugural stage of Jesus' ministry, are concerned with the person of Jesus as manifested in His actions. The temptation of Jesus by the devil is aimed at discovering the identity of Jesus: "If you are the Son of God..." (Mt 4:3.6).[5] And the words of Isaiah on which Jesus comments in the synagogue relate both to what He has come to do ("to bring glad tidings to the poor...") and to what He is ("The Spirit of the Lord is upon me").

These two episodes at the beginning of Jesus' ministry explain, in fact, everything that follows. If Jesus is capable of confronting the evil spirits and "healing all who were in the grip of the devil" (Acts 10:38), it is because by the power of God's Spirit Jesus has stood up to Satan. If He brings God's grace and forgiveness, His light and freedom everywhere He goes, the reason is that the Spirit of the Lord rests upon Him. The presence and power of the Spirit are the hidden source of His every action, and the very secret of His being.

If, then, this presence is noted later on only by Luke and only at the moment when Jesus voices His jubilant thanksgiving to the Father for having revealed His secrets to the little ones (Lk 10:21), this does not argue either the absence of the Spirit or the indifference of the evangelists. Their silence means, on the contrary, that the Spirit is fully at home in Jesus and need not prepare Him for use as a divine instrument by making a different man of Him, transforming His mind, or converting His heart. Being simply Himself and constantly receiving the Spirit in His fulness are one and the same thing for Jesus. The Spirit does not come to Him from outside, but is, as it were, the very source of Jesus' spontaneous action, so much so that we cannot even imagine what Jesus would be without the Spirit. In fact, Jesus would not be Jesus without the Spirit!

All this is enough to explain why the evangelists are silent about the action of the Spirit in Jesus. But there is another silence we must explain: Jesus' own silence about the Spirit when He speaks to His disciples. They, after all, are not the equals of the Spirit; they must call upon Him, learn to recognize Him when He comes, and open their hearts to His action. Why, then, does Jesus say nothing about the Spirit until the last moment, and speak of Him only when He Himself is about to leave His disciples?

His silence is not very difficult to understand. It is due both to the ever concrete character of His teaching and to the mystery of His own person. Jesus never describes or defines or speaks in a detached analytic way about the deepest secrets of God: the union of the Father and the Son, and the reality of the Spirit. And yet who could be more capable than He of doing so and providing a clearer analysis of a more accurate and suggestive description? What a theologian Jesus could have been, and how many errors He would have spared his disciples! But Jesus speaks only of what is part of His life; moreover, there is but one experience of which He speaks to men: the expereince they have had or the experience He promises them they will have. Thus, when He speaks to the disciples of the imminent coming of the Spirit, He tells them they have already experienced the Spirit, and He relates His promise to that experience: "I will ask the Father and He will give you another Paraclete ... you can recognize him because he remains with you and will be within you" (Jn 14:16-17).

If, therefore, Jesus does not speak of the Spirit to His disciples as long as He Himself is with them, the ultimate reason is surely that their experience of the Spirit is inseparable from their experience of Jesus Himself. How could they distinguish in His actions between what comes from Him and what comes from the Spirit, since He is Himself only insofar as He receives the gift and power of the Spirit? How could they distinguish between their response to the power they felt in Jesus and the truth of His word, and their response to God who bestows this power upon Him and speaks through His mouth?

The inability thus to distinguish is inherent in faith—the faith no prophet claimed for himself, but which Jesus considers as the only proper response to what He does: "Lord . . . you have the words of eternal life. We have come to believe; we are convinced that you are God's holy one" (Jn 6:68-69). If the disciples are to be able to perceive the Spirit as distinct from Jesus, Jesus Himself must first disappear from their midst; His bodily absence will enable them to understand that another is able, not to repeat or reproduce Him, but to make Him dwell in their hearts. They must first see Him leave them in death and then live again beyond death; they must see Him die and rise again.

The disciples do, however, have a prophetic foretaste during the mortal life of Jesus of the experience that will come to them only after the Resurrection. For, they have been given to understand that their faith in Jesus does not derive solely from Jesus Himself. Peter's confession of faith at Caesarea, as recounted by Matthew, becomes the basis for this understanding. When Peter puts into words what Jesus really is, Jesus replies by telling Him that this truth and Peter's faith come from the Father: "No mere man has revealed this to you, but my heavenly Father" (Mt 16:17). What is surprising here is that Jesus says nothing of the Spirit, although it would have been an apt moment for speaking of the Spirit's action. But He prefers to speak only of Him who gives the Spirit and everything else: the Father. The Spirit, after all, is a gift, and all gifts are from the Father. The whole aim of Jesus' dealings with His disciples is to teach them to know and find the Father. When the Spirit is given He will be able to make men recognize Him (Jn 7:39; 14:17).

The Spirit and the Risen Jesus

"There was, of course, no Spirit as yet, since Jesus had not yet been glorified" (Jn 7:39). John's words are seemingly naive, and yet they say exactly what he wants to say: there is no Spirit, because the Spirit, being as elusive and intangible as the wind (Jn 3:8) can be perceived only through His effects. These effects are interior: the Spirit of God acts in the spirit of man

(Rom 8:16; Eph 4:23). And yet, via man's spirit He transforms the whole man, body included, and even touches the whole of creation. Even while He was still a mortal man and subject to suffering, Jesus was able, by the power of the Spirit and through the mediation of His body, His actions, His words, and His living presence, to heal the sick and to free the devil's victims. The Spirit effected a direct and harmonious relation between Jesus and the natural world. The Resurrection meant the full flowering of that relationship, for the Resurrection is both a transfiguration of nature and a revelation of the Spirit.

The Christ who rises from the dead is the Christ of old, with His style and gestures, with the same approach to men and things. He is to be found where He was found before: walking the roads, sitting at table and eating, watching the nets and the catch. But now even the actions most concerned with matter are only transparent signs of another presence and of a power that embraces the world. The road to Emmaus winds across the whole face of the earth; the Lord's table is set for all mankind; the Lord can converse with every man in his own tongue. Such is the risen body that is transfigured by the Spirit. Such is Christ, now that He is "made Son of God in power according to the spirit of holiness, by his resurrection from the dead" (Rom 1:4).

His visible actions are only signs now. They tell us that we are confronted with Jesus, with His bodily human self. The Spirit gives the human nature of Jesus its power to communicate and influence. But it is also the Spirit that is communicated and makes of the second Adam "a life-giving spirit" (1 Cor 15:45). The proof that the risen Christ possesses the Spirit fully is that He pours out the Spirit even on men who never met Him, Jesus, provided only that they believe in him (Acts 2:33-38).

The first activities in which the Church engaged (according to the Acts of the Apostles) are evidence both of the Spirit's power at work in the disciples and of the source from which the Spirit comes, namely, the person of Jesus. The actions of the apostles and first believers are actions of which they, as men, were radically incapable: having a faith strong enough to order a paralytic to stand and walk (Acts 3:6) or to confront the mob in the temple (Acts 4:11-24) and the threats of the Sanhedrin (4:19-20), and loving one another enough to pool all their possessions and to be one in heart and mind (Acts 4:32). All that Jesus had tried to make His disciples understand experientially while He was with them, all that He had been able to elicit from them only by His authority and the force of His personality, all the elements in them that had not been able to stand up to the test of Jesus' Passion—all this is easily accomplished now that He has disappeared from their midst while remaining present through the Spirit He communicates. The whole of His Gospel, which was a summons and a teaching and a path trod in the footsteps of Jesus, now becomes through the Spirit's power an experiential reality in the disciples; it becomes a power that goes out from them and draws men irresistibly.

Baptism and Confirmation

Perhaps the difference between the period before His death when Jesus initiated His disciples and the later period of expansion and growing freedom can shed some light on the difference between Baptism and Confirmation. As long as we persist in defining each of the two sacraments solely in terms of the rite, that is, a momentary action that is instantaneously efficacious, and pay no attention either to the human process through which the believer passes or to the experience of Jesus in the Gospel, we shall find ourselves in an impasse, unable to isolate an effect proper to Confirmation that is not already produced by Baptism. If, on the other hand, we bear in mind that Baptism and Confirmation together constitute Christian initiation and that to say this initiation is a sacrament is to say it is the work of Christ, then we shall gain a greater understanding by noting the two periods of initiation through which Jesus led His disciples.

The first period was during His mortal life. It was a slow, gradual initiation; we might even call it methodical and pedagogical. During it the Spirit was already present to rouse the commitment of faith, as, for example, at Caesarea. But the primal experience was of the Master's presence, the meaning of His words, and the attitudes and behavior He wanted them to learn. May we no regard this period as the equivalent of baptismal initiation? In the latter, the Church, we might say, knows what she is doing and how she moves forward. She can pass judgment on dispositions, test faith, establish stages, provide a course of teaching, and propose formulas, creeds, and professions of faith. This period of initiation is absolutely necessary, for through it the Church receives and in turn passes on the Gospel from generation to generation. In it the Church is both teacher and disciple: she teaches what Jesus has taught her (cf. Mt 28:19); she hands on the Gospel and listens to it. She moves here in the realm of the word, of examples, of the visible and audible. The Gospel is not her own, nor is the initiation her own; that is why it is a sacrament, an action of Christ. At the same time, however, the initiation is accomplished only through her: she does the baptizing.

But the Church does not give the Holy Spirit, nor does she confirm as she baptizes. Rather, she calls upon the Holy Spirit, and the gesture of imposing hands is not a rite of communicating powers, but a symbol of invocation and prayer. In Acts 6:6; 8:15; and 13:3, the imposition of hands accompanies a prayer asking that God would bestow His gift on those the Church designates. The imposition of hands does not bestow the Spirit any more than the action of baptizing does; rather, Peter and Paul impose hands, and the Spirit comes (8:17; 19:6).

Just as baptism is a sacrament because, via the tradition of the Church, Jesus initiates men into His Gospel, so the imposition of hands is a sacrament because it calls down on the baptized the Spirit whom Jesus pours out, and because there is no Spirit apart from the risen Jesus. And just as the initiation Jesus gives is complete only on Pentecost when the Spirit leads men to act spontaneously in the ways Jesus had patiently taught them, so also Christian initiation must be crowned by the expectation and experience of the Spirit if it is to be anything more than teaching and instruction and if it is to provide Christtians with anything more than milk (1 Cor 3:2). A Church that would dispense with Confirmation would show that she is not interested in the Holy Spirit and that she has no purpose but to conscript soldiers and keep them docile. She would be rejecting the very Gospel she thinks she is passing on.

Part Three
Abiding Realities

Chapter 16

Jesus Christ, Priest and Prophet

Jesus Christ is a priest, a prophet, and a king. These three predications are traditional in Christology, and there is a temptation to make of them three distinct and complementary titles, expressing three distinct and parallel dignities. Yet if we take the various dignities of Christ as our starting point, we will almost inevitably be led to interpret the three titles by human standards; and if we make the three parallel to each other, we are likely to miss the special sense they have when applied to Jesus. This becomes clear if we compare Jesus as priest with Jesus as prophet. For not only is Jesus not a priest in the evident sense that He is a prophet (since a priest and a prophet are two different roles), but also He is not a prophet in the same way that He is a priest. These differences are not at all secondary, but are due to the very nature of prophecy and priesthood.

Jesus Lives Like a Prophet

Since He was not born into a priestly family, Jesus evidently could not lead the life of a priest, which meant serving in the temple at regular intervals, spaced though these were so as to make possible the practice of any regular trade that did not render a man unclean. Another career, however, was open to Jesus if He felt Himself drawn to the study of the Law and motivated by a desire to penetrate more deeply into the religious tradition of His people: He could become a disciple of the scribes. The scribes, or "teachers of the Law," were recruited from all classes of society, from the great priestly families to those consisting of unskilled laborers (the great Hillel, for example, was a simple day laborer). In the time of Jesus, the scribes constituted an intellectual aristocracy and enjoyed considerable prestige. As official interpreters of the Law and the oral tradition, they were regarded as the successors of the prophets and were respected by the people. "To what shall we compar the prophet and the scribe? To two messengers of one and the same king" (Palestinian Talmud). In the Palestine of that time, the tombs of the prophets and the tombs of the rabbis were the focus of the same legends and objects of a similar veneration. The Talmud even gives the scribes a higher place than the prophets in certain respects: the prophets must provide credentials to back up their message, whereas if a scribe received official ordination after long years of apprenticeship, he is authorized henceforth to promulgate his personal views.

Jesus does not follow this path. When He went on pilgrimage with His parents at the age of twelve, He was fascinated by the temple at Jerusalem and the teaching of the scribes. Yet when He leaves Nazareth as an adult in order to obey His calling, He seeks out a prophet, John the Baptist. Now, after several centuries of silence, God's word is heard once more, in the words and actions of John. We have no basis for reconstructing the motives Jesus has in making His choice. All we can say is that He prefers John's austerity, His powerful words and the movement of the crowds who seek John, over Jerusalem, the religious capital of Israel, with its temple, its liturgy, and its theological schools. The Spirit is present in the prophet, rousing ordinary people, soldiers, and sinners—and that is where Jesus wants to be. He becomes part of the crowd and has John baptize Him; this event, according to the testimony of the Gospels, is the beginning of His mission.

That mission clearly is the mission of a prophet, with its words received from God, the presence of the Spirit, Jesus' independence of the authorities, His calling of disciples, His miracles that bear witness to His power. True enough, there is much about Him to surprise and disconcert His fellow men, yet the category of prophet remains the most suitable one into which to put Him. He is a prophet who in a sense falls outside the category, and yet He is a prophet or at least a man who claims to be one. Friends and enemise alike speak of Him in the same way "A great prophet has risen among us," say the people of Naim when they see Jesus restoring to his mother a young man being carried off for burial (Lk 7:16). "If this man were a prophet, he would know who and what sort of woman this is that touches him," thinks Simon the Pharisee as he watches Jesus welcoming the sinful woman (Lk 7:39).

When Jesus becomes so well known that Herod begins to be uneasy and has inquires made about Him, the opinions gathered are divergent but they agree on one point: the man may be John the Baptist risen from the dead or Elijah returned to earth or the new Moses, the great prophet of the final age—but in any event, Jesus is considered to be a prophet (Mk 6:14-16). Later, as the end draws near and Jesus enters Jerusalem amid acclamations and manifestations of Messianic joy, the whole city is deeply stirred, and everybody is asking: "Who is this?" The answer comes: "This is the prophet Jesus from Nazareth in Galilee" (Mt 21:10-11). The jubilant reply is matched, a few days later, by the insults of the Sanhedrin and the guards: "Play the prophet for us, Messiah! Who struck you?" (Mt 26:68).

The perspective is not quite the same in all these texts; the perspective in Matthew is not identical with that in Mark or Luke. Yet all three evangelists bear witness to one incontrovertible fact, namely, that Jesus' contemporaries regarded Him as a prophet. In daily life and in everyday contacts, when people met Him or engaged Him in conversation, they called Him "Rabbi," which was the honorary title given to the scribes. This was a testimony to the competence of a man who had never gone to the rabbinic schools yet handled Scripture like a master

(Jn 7:15). But if He was the equal of the greatest teachers as far as knowledge of the Scripture went, He had something about Him that transcended their discipline. The power that resided in His words and actions (Mk 1:22-27) could only have come from on high, and was the mark of a prophet.

Jesus Himself induced men to think of Him thus, for He put Himself forward as a prophet. After having been baptized by John, He adopted John's way of life and began to baptize in the same fashion: welcoming those who came to Him, immersing them in water, and probably preaching a message quite similar to that of John (Jn 3:22-23). To be sure, the fourth Gospel later insists that it was not Jesus, but only His disciples, who did the baptizing (Jn 4:2). The comment is important in that it emphasizes that this baptism was not yet the baptism proper to Jesus and given in His name so as to make men Christians. But this does not change the fact stated in the third chapter of John's Gospel: that Jesus' first ministry was in imitation of John.

When John was arrested for having publicly denounced in true prophetic style the king's scandalous behavior (Mk 6:17), Jesus gave up the life of a prophet-baptist (Mk 1:14; Jn 4:1-3) and adopted a new style. He now went from village to village in Galilee, proclaiming everywhere the imminent coming of God's kingdom. Instead of remaining in one place and drawing the crowds through His words and activity as a baptizer, He lived on the move, looking for the sick and the infirm and going to visit sinners and tax collectors. The prophet thus turned into an evangelist or direct witness to the event He proclaims and the Good News He brings. The change was a considerable one, as we shall see, and created an original lifestyle, but the lifestyle was still that of a prophet.

Thus, when He meets with disbelief from the people of Nazareth, Jesus explains their reaction in terms of the usual reaction a prophet elicits from those close to Him. "No prophet is without honor except in his native place, among his own kindred, and in his own house" (Mk 6:4). Thus too, realizing that His enemies are determined to destroy Him, He explains His behavior and His destiny in the light of what happened to the prophets: "I must proceed on course today, tomorrow, and the day after, since no prophet can be allowed to die anywhere except in Jerusalem" (Lk 13:33). Again, on the very eve of His death, He confronts the authorities at Jerusalem—"the chief priests, the scribes, and the elders" (Mk 11:27)—with their responsibility by telling them the parable of the murderous tenant farmers (Mk 12:1-12), in which, after first sending the servants, who evidently represent the Old Testament prophets, the father finally sends "the son whom he loved." The crime which the authorities are ready to commit makes them "the sons of the prophets' murderers" (Mt 23:31). The evidence, then, is solid and clear: Jesus regards Himself as belonging to the line of the prophets, and their example helps Him explain the reactions He arouses and the destiny that awaits Him.

Jesus Speaks As a Prophet

Jesus' language is another thing that relates Him to the prophets. Despite their varied gifts and forceful, highly individual personalities, the prophets of Israel were alike in having the same basic views and similar callings. In addition, they deliberately placed themselves within a clearly outlined tradition, preached certain types of messages, and shared immediately recognizable ways of speaking. One of these last that is very easy to spot is the sentence of condemnation (which we met earlier in this book).

For example, Elijah says to Ahab who has just had Naboth murdered so that he might take his vineyard: "After murdering, do you also take possession? For this, the Lord says: In the place where the dogs licked up the blood of Naboth, the dogs shall lick up your blood, too" (1 Kgs 21:19). And Nathan says to David who has just gotten rid of Uriah so that he might take Uriah's wife, Bathsheba: "You have cut down Uriah the Hittite with the sword; you took his wife as your own, and him you killed with the sword of the Ammonites . . . Now, therefore, the sword shall never depart from your house. . . . Thus says the

Lord: .... 'I will take your wives while you live to see it, and will give them to your neighbor' " (2 Sm 12:9-11).

Everything is said in three short steps: the sin committed, which human justice cannot punish; God's judgment and its logic, "therefore"; and the punishment, which is the deadly fruit of sin.

Jesus adopts the same style and procedure more than once. For example, to the Pharisees, who claim Jesus has power over demons because He is helped by Beelzebul, prince of demons, He replies: "If I expel demons with Beelzebul's help, by whose help do your people expel them? Let them be the ones to judge you. . . . That, I assure you, is why every sin, every blasphemy, will be forgiven men, but blasphemy against the Spirit will not be forgiven" (Mt 12:27-31). To the authorities in Jerusalem, who have determined to destroy Him, He proposes the parable of the murderous tenant farmers and then says: "For this reason, I tell you, the kingdom of God will be taken away from you and given to a nation that will yield a rich harvest" (Mt 21:43). And to the scribes and Pharisees: "Woe to you scribes and Pharisees, you frauds! You erect tombs for the prophets and decorate the monuments of the saints. You say, 'Had we lived in our forefathers' time we would not have joined them in shedding the prophets' blood.' Thus you show that you are the sons of the prophets' murderers. Now it is your turn: fill up the vessel measured out by your forefathers. . . . For this reason I shall send you prophets and wise men and scribes. Some you will kill and crucify . . . until retribution overtakes you for all the blood of the just ones shed on earth, from the blood of holy Abel to the blood of Zechariah son of Barachiah"(Mt 23:29-35).

This language is highly significant. Jesus uses it, we may say, when He has exhausted His other resources and when the Good News meets with rejection. But it is not the word of the Good News that condemns. Jesus' own word is the Gospel, and the Gospel is meant not to condemn but to proclaim salvation (cf. Jn 3:17; 12:47). And in fact, in the three instances quoted, condemnation is pronounced not by Jesus Himself, but by the disciples of the Pharisees (Mt 12:27), by those who listen to His parable and give the right response to His question (Mt 21:41), and by the contemporaries of Jesus who condemn themselves by raising monuments to the martyred prophets (Mt 23:31).

And yet the word of Jesus Himself has a function even at this moment of condemnation. Its function is to reveal the contradiction in which the sinner places Himself, so as to show, with a divine clarity, its deadly logic and fatal outcome. In this sense, Jesus stands fully in the line of the prophets. The word of the prophets was powerful not for magically lifting the veil that hides the future, but for bringing to light the necessary connection between the sins they witnessed and the terrible future to which these sins were leading. Amos did not have to be a prophet to see that Samaria's prosperity was threatened and that the armies of Assyria would bring terror in their wake. His prophetic function was to see this situation as the occasion for God to bring home to men how seriously meant His requirements were and how carefully He watched over His work and His people.

Close though He is to the prophets, the language of Jesus is distinguished by a very important trait. The prophets constantly repeat, almost as a refrain, "Thus says Yahweh," or "Oracle of the Lord," to show that they are simply messengers and that the word really comes from another. These references to God are never missing when the prophets pronounce a condemnation. Jesus, however, though using the general prophetic formulas, omits all mention of God's word; in fact, instead of appealing to God, He explicitly says that His words are His own: "I assure you" (Mt 12:31); "I tell you" (Mt 21:43). The statement which terminates the "Woes" against the Pharisees is identical in form with divine statements in the Old Testament: "I shall send you prophets . . ." (Mt 23:34; cf. 2 Kgs 12:11: "I will bring evil upon you . . ."). This manner of using a traditional formula and taking the prophet's words to His own account shows that Jesus was conscious of being a prophet and more than a prophet, and of speaking God's words in His own name.

Jesus, Prophet of His Own Work

The reason why Jesus can claim for Himself the authority proper to the word of God is that He is on an equal footing with the God who sends Him and fully up to the mission He has been given. This twofold equality, which relates to His past or origin and to His future or destiny, gives His prophetic calling and His prophetic action their unique characteristics.

The Gospels present the baptism of Jesus as the equivalent of the scenes in which the prophets received their call. Jesus too hears God speaking to Him, and the divine words become the starting point of His public ministry; henceforth He belongs neither to His family nor to the village where He had spent His life, but to His mission alone. We must observe, however, that the scene of the baptism is quite different from the classical scenes of prophetic calling, since the heavenly word does not effect a sudden change of personality nor does it arouse any emotion, disturbance, or fear in the one called; it is as though this man were already living on the new level.

Above all, the divine message does not prescribe any action that Jesus is to perform. It simply tells Jesus what He is: "You are my beloved Son. On you my favor rests" (Mk 1:11). These words are enough; Jesus has only to hear them and He will be faithful to His calling. His mission is to be the Son, in other words, to be just what He is. To live among men as the Son is to reveal the Father, to show what the Father is, how important He is, and what His will is. In Jesus, existence and mission, person and calling, coincide completely. Jeremiah and the Servant of Yahweh and John the Baptist had indeed been consecrated prophets while still in their mothers' wombs (Jer 1:5; Is 49:1-5; Lk 1:15), which meant that they could not evade their mission and that God had indissolubly bound together their vocation and their very being. But the bond was superimposed upon their being; they had to acknowledge and accept it, often at the cost of severe interior suffering. We find nothing comparable in Jesus, for He is unintelligible to Himself except as standing in the presence of God, as Son born of the Father, and as receiving from the Spirit the joyous certainty of what He is by His very nature.

The joy is an abiding joy, but the one who receives and experiences it is a man. Jesus is the Son and cannot but be the Son, but He must show men what the Father is, and this He can do only through His human life. He must live, work, speak, communicate with men, and share to the full the human condition in life and in death. Jesus' vocation necessarily embraces His existence and His mission, His work and the future that lies before him. And here again we perceive the prophetic side of Jesus and the unparalleled way in which He is a prophet.

Since He is the Son and cannot be separated from the Father, Jesus lives in a state of complete certainty (Jn 8:29). He knows that His work will succeed because it is God's work. But this certainty does not protect Him against surprises and suffering; it does not affect the weakness and the greatness of His human nature. He possesses the prophetic gift in a uniquely full measure, but He also has the authentic human consciousness which the gift supposes. Consequently, we find paradoxically coexisting in Him a complete certainty about the future of His mission and a real, unfeigned ignorance about His course of action and about the future of the group of disciples He will leave behind Him in the world.

The paradox is an inescapable one. If Jesus does not know that His action affects the entire universe and saves all of mankind, He cannot give His life for men; He can only turn His death into a great gesture of generosity. On the other hand, if He sees the future unfolding before His mind like a film, He no longer is truly part of our world, but exists outside of human time. More accurately, He would be living totally outside reality, since this filmed version of the future exists only in our imagination which cannot conceive the future except as already brought into existence, that is, as past. In Bergson's words, "time is a process of discovery or it is nothing." A false conception of God's creative knowledge can lead us to misconceive the dignity of man. As Hans Urs von Balthasar writes:

> Jesus was genuinely a man, and it is an inalienable part
> of man's nobility that He can and must freely plan His
> existence for a future which he does not yet know. . . . To
> deprive Jesus of the same opportunity and to have Him
> move toward a goal known in advance and distant only in
> time, would be to deprive Him of His dignity as a man.[1]

The behavior of Jesus in the Gospel bears witness that He, like every other human being, is affected by the events that He experiences and that force themselves upon Him with their brute reality, even though He may have foreseen and predicted them. More than this, He Himself expressly declares that He is ignorant of such important matters as the date of His return and the end of time: "As to the exact day or hour, no one knows it, neither the angels in heaven nor even the Son, but only the Father" (Mk 13:32). And yet the day in question is supremely *His* day, since, if He is to come as Son of Man and put an end to the history of the world, He must here and now be the Messiah who will die in order to carry out God's plan for the world. But can we justify such a paradox as this: that though He knows He will die for all men, He does not know what the future holds for mankind?

In any case the fact that Jesus is a prophet sheds some light on the paradox. As one who is a prophet, and a prophet by His own authority, who has prophetic knowledge of His own work and action, Jesus knows the importance of His actions and the meaning of His life and death. He knows that He brings to men the forgiveness of the Father, the gift of the Spirit, and the coming of the kingdom. He knows that the gift will cost Him a cruel death and the triumph of His implacable enemies: "The Son of Man is going to be delivered into the hands of men" (Mk 9:31). He also knows that this death will bring Him a divine victory of inexhaustible scope: "You will see the Son of Man seated at the right hand of the Power and coming with the clouds of heaven" (Mk 14:62).

When He predicts His death, Jesus does not seem to be drawing on an extraordinary capacity for foreknowledge. His death, after all, could be readily foreseen; He Himself is utterly clear-sighted, and He is able to look into men's hearts and discover the secrets they think are hidden. What is properly prophetic about His prediction is not so much the event itself as it is the event as God plans and wills it. That is really what Jesus is saying: that by dying, and by dying this particular death, He will fulfill the plan which God has for His Messiah and has made known to us through the figure of the Son of Man. The emphasis is on the "must" and indicates a recognition of the meaning and value proper to the necessity which the prophetic act establishes. In what might seem to be merely a monstrous crime or the inevitable consequence of man's sinfulness, Jesus' prophetic vision sees the will of the Father who transforms a death in which man's sinfulness is supremely manifested, into a supreme gift of love and forgiveness.

Of the events which are to follow His death Jesus never speaks except as a prophet; that is, He states them as certain, but never describes them. He foretells His own Resurrection in two ways, each borrowed from Israelite tradition: in continuity with the apocalypses and Daniel He foretells the heavenly triumph of the Son of Man (Mk 14:62), and in continuity with the prophet Zechariah He tells His disciples, as He enters upon His Passion, that the flock scattered by His death will come after Him into Galilee and be reunited (Mk 14:27-28). These are unhesitating prophecies, yet they are sufficiently vague to prevent men from expecting a detailed kind of fulfillment and thus hindering their faith. If the prediction of the Resurrection had taken the form of setting up a rendezvous, it would have been an invitation not to faith but to curiosity: Will He come or won't He?

A further prophecy of Jesus relates to the future of His disciples and is given in the so-called eschatological discourse (Mk 13). Jesus is certain that after His departure His disciples will continue to be gathered in His name; that their lot will be like His; that they must face hostility and persecution; that they will be tempted to forget and deny Him. But no detailed description is given of these events which are stated both in the apocalyptic guise of cosmic upheavals and as the natural consequence of being followers of Jesus. Here we have a proof that Jesus was not transported into the future, but spoke from the place in space and time in which He found Himself, and made use both of His personal experience and the language of the apocalypses.

The only specific event foretold seems to be the destruction of Jerusalem (Mk 13:14-20). Yet even here no details are given; any "details" indicated are borrowed from earlier descriptions, especially in the Book of Daniel. But this indifference to factual detail does not make the event any the less certain; it simply tells us what the true gift of the prophet was. Jesus does not claim to describe the future either of Jerusalem or of His own community, but He does speak categorically on two points: the permanence of the community of His disciples to the end of times, and the destruction of Jerusalem.

He can speak with such certainty here because these two points are an essential part of His mission. If He is the Messiah and if Jerusalem refuses to acknowledge Him, then the holy city's fate is already determined. Jerusalem was called into existence so that it might be the city of the Messiah and that it might prepare for Him and await Him. To fail in its vocation cannot but be utter catastrophe for it. At the same time, the catastrophe is not to wipe out the community of Jesus: they "must flee" (Mk 13:14), for they have a future before them. They will experience wars, famines, natural disasters, the hostility of men; they will find themselves in the same situation as their master, but they have nothing to fear, for these storms are a sign of coming peace as surely as the new leaves on the fig tree point to the summer that is approaching (Mk 13:28-29).

In the last analysis, the originality of Jesus as a prophet is not to be found in His language, which resembles very much that of His predecessors, especially the authors of the apocalypses. Nor is it to be found in the number or accuracy of His predictions, or in the power of His imagery or the intensity with which He speaks. It is to be found in His focusing of everything on a single central point: the kingdom of God and the death and return of the Son of Man. It is to be found in the way this central reality is verified in the person of Jesus Himself. In the person of Jesus the kingdom is already here; in the life and death of Jesus the Son of Man's coming is fulfilled. The prophetic certainty Jesus possesses is due to His consciousness of His own mission; just as His mission, because it is that of the Messiah, embraces the entire world, so His prophetic vision embraces the future of the world to the end of time. When all is said and done, Jesus utters but a single prophecy, but it involves His life and His death, and to it the whole Christian hope is linked: "Amen! Come, Lord Jesus!" (Rv 22:20).

Is Jesus a Priest?

Everything about Jesus—His actions, His speech, His way of life—shows Him to be a prophet. He wished men to see Him as a prophet and He played the part of a prophet to the end. On the other hand, He never did anything to incite men to call Him a priest. It was true enough, of course, that the Jewish priesthood was the hereditary possession of the tribe of Levi and the families descended from Aaron, so that Jesus could not possibly come forward as a priest. But neither did any word or gesture of His suggest that He wished to take the place of the priests or even to prepare the way for a new and hitherto unknown type of priesthood.

He gives the impression of being almost indifferent to the priests: He is severely critical of the scribes and Pharisees, whose hypocrisy He publicly castigates, but He says nothing of the priests or their behavior. And yet it is they, and especially the representatives of the great priestly families, who have authority over the temple and are responsible for the abuses which stir Jesus to violent intervention. This intervention, however,

far from linking Jesus with the priesthood and making Him a
priestly figure, puts Him in a typically prophetic tradition, that
of Amos and Jeremiah (Am 7:10-17; Jer 7:1-15; 26:1-15).

Nor do the disciples of Jesus think of calling Him a priest.
The Letter to the Hebrews is in this respect a complete innova-
tion; its basis for assigning Jesus the title of high priest is not
any known tradition but a piece of carefully worked out specu-
lation. In other words, the description of Jesus as a priest is
undoubtedly the result of reflection within the Church and of theological thought. The theology is undoubtedly profound, legitimate, and rich in implications. It furthers our understanding
of the mystery of Christ; it constitutes an indispensable stage
in the development of a Christian thinking based on the relation between Christ and the Jewish Scriptures. But does all that
justify our saying that Jesus is priest as well as prophet? No,
certainly not. Shall we conclude, then, that the title of priest as
applied to Jesus is valid only for a theology that is relatively
peripheral to the New Testament as a whole and that we should
use it only with very careful restrictions?

It is our view that we should indeed be careful in the use we
make of the title and the meaning we give it. But it would be
wrong to regard it, on that account, as something secondary. No,
the title of priest tells us something extremely important, so
important that without it the title of prophet iself would be
emptied of its specific content.

When the Letter to the Hebrews emphasizes the high priesthood of Jesus, it does not do so in order to add another honor-
ific title to the list but to give expression to the work He has
done and continues to do. This work is the completion of His
humanity that is achieved through His passion and death, and
at the same time it is the power He obtains, through His passion and death, of transforming men and making them new
beings, sons of the Father. Albert Vanhoye writes accurately
in His commentary on the early chapters of the Letter to the
Hebrews:

The human nature Christ took to Himself was not radically different from ours, but was a true human nature of flesh and blood . . . "in the likeness of sinful flesh" (Rom 8:3). This does not mean, of course, that there was ever in Jesus the least complicity with sin. . . . But His human nature did experience the effects of sin: it was weak (cf. 2 Cor 13:4), subject to suffering, and doomed to death. While in such a state, it could not be enthroned in heaven, since "flesh and blood cannot inherit the kingdom of God" (1 Cor 15:50). The human nature of Christ, being like ours, had to be "perfected" in a process of radical transformation. It has to pass from a fleshly type of existence to a completely spiritual type of existence. Such a passage evidently involved far more than simply progress in virtue; it involved a complete remaking of His nature. That is why He had to die.[2]

This transformation was not, however, limited to the person of Jesus and is meant for all men. The same author goes on to say:

If we want to state fully the vocation of man, we may not speak simply of a road he must traverse; we must speak also of an interior transformation he must undergo. Men must indeed advance toward God and draw near to Him in His glory. But they cannot draw near to Him as they are. If they are to advance, they need a "pioneer in the order of salvation," someone to break ground and cut a path for them by submitting Himself to the transforming action of God . . . . Mediation between God and men was not perfectly established by the simple fact of the Incarnation. If men were to be able to reach God, it was not enough for the Son of God to become one of them. If the impossible had happened and Jesus had remained permanently in His earthly state, He would by that very fact have put distance between Himself and God since an opposition existed between human nature in its earthly state and the holiness of God, and it had to be overcome by a dramatic series of events. In other words, it was not enough for the Son of God to have assumed human nature; He also had to transform it. Only Christ could be the perfect mediator, but what made Him such was the transformation effected in him for the sake of all men, or, in other words, the redemption.[3]

We have cited these lengthy texts from one of the most capable specialists in the Letter to the Hebrews, because, without in any way challenging the priesthood of Christ or detracting from the rich treasures contained in the title, Albert Vanhoye shows us that for the author of the Letter, Christ's priesthood was not of the cultic order nor exercised in a liturgical act, but was of the existential order and exercised in the human reality of Jesus' death. Here we have the explanation of why Jesus never used the vocabulary of priesthood to interpret His work; it would have led to all sorts of misunderstandings. It would have suggested that the climax of His mission was a solemn liturgical act, whereas in fact it consisted in giving His life for His brothers.

In the effort to express this reality which is the very stuff of human existence, it is not out of place to use the language of ritual and priesthood; in fact, this language is a solid complement to the language of the word and prophecy. The notion of priesthood supposes certain ideas—ritual, myth, sacred times and places, etc.—and brings them into play in various ways and widely differing degrees of depth. It suggests a whole approach to the world, and a radical way of organizing the human universe. It implies a system of values and modes of behavior. In fact, the notion of priesthood and all it involves seems to be a permanent category of mankind and religion. When the Letter to the Hebrews uses the vocabulary of priest, sacrifice, and temple in order to interpret the coming and action of Christ, its aim is to show the radical character of that coming and action. The person and action of Christ are the very basis of the Christian existence that is meant for every human being; they are a creative source. To say that Jesus is a priest is not to limit Him to a marginal area of life, but to proclaim that He transforms the very existence of the human race; that He penetrates to its very heart; that He creates a new universe.

Jesus, Priest and Prophet at the Last Supper

The proof that priesthood and prophecy are not opposed but united in Jesus is the Supper and the Eucharist. The Eucharist is a priestly action; Jesus performs it in the course of a Passover meal, uses the sacrificial language of the body broken and the blood shed, and makes it an action to be repeated, the starting point of a new age, and the focus of the gathering of mankind. All this is signified by the ritual of the Supper, the time (Passover), the place of the traditional meal, the actions determined by custom, and the original words which gave the actions a new and heretofore unknown value. All this was also willed by Jesus who at the Supper solemnly inaugurates the new covenant. All this, finally, is of a priestly nature and makes of Jesus a priest and the founder of the kingdom of God.

But this priesthood is wholly new. The ritual words do not refer back to some originating event or to a mysterious world that encloses our visible world. The words belong to our world and to the historical existence of a man born within our human time, an existence that can be accurately pinpointed in space and time. The Eucharistic words are not derived from any ritual; while pronounced in the course of a meal the actions of which were carefully regulated by tradition, the Eucharistic words are a human event of the here and now. They express the decision by which Jesus surrenders Himself to death for the sake of His friends. There is, in short, a complete coincidence of the new rite and simple, everyday human life. A guiltless man is betrayed to death by a coalition of hatred, grudges, and fear; a friend gives his life for his own and bids them farewell. The two faces of our human nature, the two currents which stir in every life: hatred and love, rejection and self-gift, are present to an intense degree in this room, and Jesus experiences them and bears the burden they impose. The mystery is that the experience of a human being, of a Jew from Nazareth living in the reign of Tiberias, can be a priestly action and a creative event. If it really is and if Jesus shows that He is aware of it, then He is a priest.

But He is also a prophet, and indeed the prophet of His own work. The action of the Supper is in continuity with those actions of the prophets whereby they brought out the irrevocable character of the event they were foretelling, the destruction or the restoration of Jerusalem. At the Supper Jesus performs that kind of action, but in this case prediction and event coincide, and coincide in Himself. To break bread and to hand Himself over to death are not two distinct things, for the word of Christ is efficacious, and when He says "This is my body given for you," He effectively gives His life at that moment, so much so that when Judas comes to make Him captive, He will but execute the Master's own word.

Thus the mystery of Jesus Christ is to be located at the point where the two lines meet: prophecy and priesthood. As priest, Jesus bears the burden of, and lives out, the event that founds the new human race. As prophet, He sees the event coming, predicts it, and gives it expression in words at the moment when He brings it to pass.

Chapter 17

Jesus, Word of God

"The Bible is the word of God": what are we saying when we keep using these words as though they were obvious and raised no questions? It is true enough that God speaks in the Bible, but He does it so readily that the very readiness makes us suspicious. "Word of God! Word of God!" the prophets keep saying. But, without questioning their sincerity or denying the value of their message or detracting from the quality and authenticity of their experience, we may ask: Are we to take their statements literally?

Will you say: "Their words do not originate with them"? But neither do the words of the poets or of those great inspired figures who have set mankind on new paths: a Socrates, a Buddha, a Karl Marx. Neither did they speak in their own name. They spoke rather in the name of a truth which dwelt in them and forced itself upon them. We are disposed today to listen to prophets and obey them, because we despair so much of our present world. Why should not God speak through the mouths of our modern prophets as much as He did through the mouths of Jeremiah or Amos?

There is another noteworthy fact. While the prophets are constantly and explicitly referring to the "Word of God!" the authors of the historical books and the Wisdom literature are not at all concerned with doing so. They write in order to perpetuate the memory of events as it has reached them or to bear witness to it, or to pass on their own experience to others. But nowhere do they claim that their writings are the word of God. Why, then, do we put them on the same level as Moses and the prophets? Why make the Bible in its entirety the word of God and solemnly proclaim it as such to the Christian community?

The New Testament poses the same questions as the Old. If the Gospel merits being accepted as the word of God because Jesus claims to speak in His Father's name, by what right should this privilege be extended to the Letters of Paul or James? It is perfectly clear that it is men who speak in these writings: men indeed of deep faith in Christ, but also men who manifest in every line their limitations as well as their gifts. Besides, after listening to Jesus, how can we say of any other man that he brings us the word of God?

God Speaks Through Things

There may be a satisfactory answer to these questions. In a certain fashion God speaks through things:

> *The heavens declare the glory of God,*
> *and the firmament proclaims his handiwork . . .*
> *Not a word nor a discourse*
> *whose voice is not heard;*
> *Through all the earth their voice resounds,*
> *and to the ends of the world, their message (Ps 19:2-5).*

What makes these verses valuable is not only their poetic power, but their universal truth. All over the world, once man reaches a certain level of development, he becomes sensitive to the mysteriousness of the world and a call that goes forth from the things that make up the world; he begins to look for the intentions behind events and for a meaning of his existence. And even if he does not succeed in finding a meaning, even if his quest is in vain and ends in a negation or rejection of God, what he is really rejecting is the way in which God speaks and keeps silence. If the so-called atheist does in fact reject God, he does not deny His existence as he might deny that an island exists on the map; he rejects God because he does not find Him communicating Himself in the way in which he expects God to communicate Himself. The God whom the atheist rejects is a God who speaks, but the atheist rejects Him because He speaks in the way He does.

Whether He is accepted or rejected, God does speak in one fashion or another, and the world itself is one of the ways in which He speaks. But where does this bring us? If we say that God "speaks," is this itself not just a manner of speaking? We are asserting a presence different from that of material objects; we glimpse an intention, a meaning for the world. We dream perhaps of communication with a Someone, and we try to assign a voice to the mute universe. But who really speaks in all this? Is God really speaking, or do we hear the echo of our own desire? It seems clear that mankind cannot convince itself it is alone in the universe, but how is it to discern among all the voices that are but man speaking to himself? Among all the "divine words" men have collected down the centuries, by what right do we call only some of them "word of God"? And what is the legitimacy of the statement which the Christian faith regards as basic: "In Jesus Christ God speaks to us"?

In Jesus Christ God Speaks to Us

Rather than try to compare this article of faith with other more or less similar statements found in other religions, it will be more profitable for us to see how, according to the New Testament, God speaks to us in Jesus Christ. We must consider how Jesus acts and presents Himself to men, how He speaks, and how He is heard.

The most striking thing about Jesus' speech is that even His most spontaneous and personal statements are at the same time the statements of another whom He calls His Father. He never stops insisting on this in the Gospel of John: "My doctrine is not my own; it comes from him who sent me" (Jn 7:16); "I only tell the world what I have heard from him, the truthful One who sent me" (8:26); "I have not spoken on my own; no, the Father who sent me has commanded me what to say and how to speak" (12:49). According to these declarations, it might seem that Jesus is simply a mouthpiece and must pass on, verbatim, the message entrusted to Him; yet we would be ill at ease with such an automation.

In fact, however, we need only listen to Jesus, whether in the Synoptics or in John, and we immediately perceive that He is no automaton but speaks naturally and indeed in an inimitable way. Words spring from Him in response to events and meetings with others; there is no artifice, no affectation. There are no discourses learned by heart in advance, no wearisome repetitions, no mechanical methods. Jesus does, of course, on every occasion bring His audience around to His sole preoccupation, the kingdom of God. But He does so because this is the inclination of His heart and being, not because He is afraid of failing to repeat words another has ordered Him to repeat.

The point at which the words of Jesus and the words given Him by His Father most evidently coincide is, of course, the forgiveness of sins. When it comes to sinners, Jesus, we might say, cannot stay put; He must take to the road and go out to meet them. In this respect, He is quite unlike John the Baptist. John drew sinners to him; he did not reject them but welcomed them and sent them away changed. But he stayed put on the bank of the Jordan, close to the water he needed for his baptism (Jn 3:23). Jesus lets nothing hold Him back: He must move and preach the Gospel elsewhere, too (Mk 1:38). For this Gospel is the good news of God's forgiveness, and it is news that concerns all who need that forgiveness. If Jesus takes to the road, He does so because He is the bearer of a message that can come only from God. Who but God can decide that sins are forgiven (Mk 2:7)? Who is able to stop the accusation man is constantly leveling at himself: "I have sinned"? Only He who searches the heart and soul (Ps 7:10; Jer 12:20) can make pure water flow from the corrupt spring within us.

Yet this is precisely what Jesus does. He dares to say, in a perfectly tranquil way: Your sins are forgiven (Mk 2:5; Lk

7:48). We do not understand His action at all if we think of simply the effect of a power He has received. It is true that "the Son of Man has authority on earth to forgive sins" (Mt 9:7), but this authority cannot be that of a totally free hand which allows Him to act as He wishes. We must take with full seriousness such Johannine formulas as "The Son cannot do anything by himself" (Jn 5:9). If Jesus can forgive sins, it is because with an unmediated certitude and by a direct communication (which John calls a "seeing") He knows that God is in the act of forgiving.

The forgiveness of sins can be accomplished only by speaking to the one who is being forgiven. Thereby we eliminate the ambiguity of which we spoke at the beginning of the chapter: How can we know whether God speaks if we do not apply to Him a language made for ourselves? If a man is to know that he is forgiven, he must have someone there before him who knows his sin and can communicate the certainty that this sin is indeed forgiven; that sin, far from being wiped out by mythological fiction, has become an indissoluble bond and the starting point of a new intimacy between forgiver and sinner. The keenest remorse, the most intense effort at purification, and the most inflexible will to change one's life will never add up to forgiveness; it must be received and heard. We must hear forgiveness spoken. That is why Jesus' forgiveness always finds expression in words that are both personal and public, words in which the entire mission of Jesus is brought to bear: "Your sins are forgiven, your faith has saved you, go and sin no more."

Because forgiveness necessarily takes the form of words spoken by a man in the language of men, while being at the same time the expression of an action done by God, the forgiveness Jesus gives is the sure sign that God is speaking to men. We no longer are listening to the mysterious language of nature and its beauty, that we can decipher only with hesitation. Rather, we hear words that seem incomprehensible and unimaginable, yet are to be taken literally; and that transform man's life and the world at large.

Now, the whole life of Jesus is the expression of these words of forgiveness. From His baptism by John, wherein Jesus comes to mingle with the crowd of sinners seeking pardon, to His last words on the cross when He asks His Father to "forgive them, they do not know what they are doing" (Lk 23:34), Christ is constantly bringing to men the forgiveness of God. The purpose of the entire Gospel is "to announce a year of favor from the Lord" (Lk 4:19) and the deliverance of the oppressed. What this passage refers to is not simply words of consolation and encouragement or an object of growing hope; it refers to a concrete and radically new event that is linked to the presence of a single individual, Jesus.

The presence of forgiveness and Jesus also turn the Sermon on the Mount into an authentic word of God. If the Sermon were simply a more profound interpretation of the Law of Sinai, a more radical interpretation of the decalogue, we might have to suspend judgment. Perhaps an extraordinary man would be capable of pushing the logic of the Law to its ultimate conclusions. The "golden rule"—"Treat others the way you would have them treat you" (Mt 7:12)—was not discovered by Jesus; it was known to the world of antiquity. What makes of the Sermon the word of God is not its perfection or its inimitable accents, but the fact that it is inseparable from the person and action of Jesus. The Sermon springs from the event we sum up as the "Gospel," and that is why it begins with the beatitudes. The beatitudes have meaning and value only because Jesus has come into the world to bring God's forgiveness.

If, however, the forgiveness is real, it creates a decisive relationship and becomes a point of departure. The new law is not only the perfecting of the old, but the expression of a new situation determined by the coming of Jesus and the forgiveness of God: "Go and sin no more. You have experienced the Father; now you know what kind of attention he bestows on his children; you have met him and you know he expects something of you." God's forgiveness is a word from Him, because it means that He is present, and obliges us to receive Him. The Sermon on the Mount is God's word because it obliges us to meet and return His gaze.

Replying to God Who Speaks

The sign that God is speaking is that man responds to Him.
It is not a directly visible sign. Just as God may often seem
to be speaking, without our being able to know what He says,
so a man may imagine that he is responding to God when in
fact he is simply following his own desires or taking refuge in
his own dreams. Here, once again, the coming of Jesus dispels
the dreams and confronts us with reality. In bringing forgiveness, He brings a real word from God. But by that same word
He makes it possible for us really to respond to God. Thus
God's word is real because it is efficacious and produces its
effect. When heard, it elicits its own response.

An important scene in the Gospel, and one to which we have
often referred in this book, shows the efficaciousness of God's
word as spoken through Jesus. The scene is that of Peter's confession of faith at Caesarea. Even in the shortest version of it
(Mk 8:27-30), it has three distinct stages: Jesus' question:
"Who am I?"—Peter's reply: "You are the Christ"—Jesus'
confirmation of his reply, in the form of a prohibition: "Do not
speak of this to anyone." The three stages make up an extraordinarily powerful whole.

Jesus asks the question, and the question is both surprising
and natural. Natural, because it echoes the spontaneous reactions of men who are faced with the actions and behavior of
Jesus: "What does this mean?" (Mk 1:27); "Who can forgive
sins?" (Mk 2:7); "Who can this be?" (Mk 4:41). Surprising,
because we are astonished that Jesus should ask such a question.
Either the identity of Jesus is easy to establish, and men need
only inquire and they will learn [He is Jesus of Nazareth, "the
carpenter, the son of Mary, a brother of James and Joseph and
Judas and Simon" (Mk 6:3) or His identity is a mystery].
But if He Himself does not reveal it, how are others to find it
out? Yet Jesus is not posing riddles.

His question is a perfectly serious one. Jesus makes this
quite clear by distinguishing between what other people say
and what His disciples say. For, in fact, there are two answers

to His question. The one given by other people is not mini-
mizing; it is simply superficial. It puts Jesus into the category
of the miraculous—of dead men returning to life, of unexplain-
able events at which men are present, passive and entranced.
The answer given by the disciples removes Jesus from this artificial world. It tells us what Jesus is for Himself and what He
is for the disciples. The Messiah is not a personage of the past
who has been transported to the realm of myth. He is the one
whom God has promised to His people. No one can anticipate
and draw a portrait of Him; each person creates an image of
Him reflecting his own hopes and dreams.

When Peter says that Jesus is the Messiah, he is saying that
the man standing here before him—in all His concrete reality,
His forceful words, His limited means, His modest results, His
great heart, His unshakeable firmness, His problem of winning
others—is the Messiah God is today giving to Israel. Peter
thus states what Jesus means to the Jewish people and what
He means to God who sends Him. Peter sees in Jesus the fulfillment of God's promise, and joins in a single act of faith
God who sends His Messiah, and Jesus who is sent.

Jesus' question, therefore, was a real question; that is, the
answer was not given in advance. In order to answer as he
did, Peter had to act in a truly free way, rejecting some quite
valid reasons to the contrary and opening himself to the invitation God was addressing to Him. There were reasons, after
all, which seemed to prove that Jesus could not be the Messiah:
His obscure birth, His failure, His refusal to force Himself upon
men. But Peter overcame the difficulties and, at Caesarea, made
the first act of faith to be made by the Church: he confessed
who Jesus was and, by proclaiming Him to be Messiah, committed himself to Him. For, since God was sending the Messiah to save Israel, to acknowledge the Messiah meant a commitment to be His disciple.

Now, this act of faith is in the form of words. More accurately, it is an exchange of words, and the scene shows us
exactly the interaction of the two speakers. To start with, there
are Jesus' words, that is, His question; the sign that there is in-

deed a "word" here, that is, a verbal communication, is that the question leads to an answer. The question Jesus asks looks beyond the few words used in formulating it. It supposes a whole past in the form of all the experiences the disciples had thus far had of Jesus: miracles, teaching, daily contact. This extensive experience, itself a succession of statements, is now condensed into one short set of words. This is proof that all these earlier "words" (verbal or non-verbal) had not been mere discourses or verbal developments intended to convince or impress, but invitations and questions—in other words, the start of a dialogue.

Jesus' real question elicits from Peter a real answer, and the answer involves the very life of the disciple. Here we have the decisive sign. Jesus' word is indeed the word of God because it moves Peter and sets him on the path of dedicated union with God. And the answer really is Peter's own; that is, it does not voice the consent of someone who has been convinced by better arguments or seduced by his feelings. Jesus, though a master of words, makes no use here of the manipulative possibilities at His command; He simply asks His question, and the only answer He wants is an answer inspired by faith. And because Peter does answer in faith, he puts his whole self into his answer. It expresses more than his hopes as a Jew, more than his deep attachment to Jesus, more even than the gift of his fidelity. Peter realizes that he has heard an authentic "word," and that this word requires an answer. The answer is what changes him from Cephas to Peter.

Yet, even though the answer comes into existence in Peter and is formulated by him, at the same time it is given to him by another source. The text is most explicit in Matthew's telling of the story: "Blest are you, Simon son of John! No mere man has revealed this to you, but my heavenly Father" (Mt 16:17). Jesus is not referring to an extraordinary revelation. Quite the contrary, for if Peter had had an unusual experience of some kind, he would himself have realized that it came from God. Precisely because he had no such experience but everything happened through the mediation of his daily experience, he might think that he had made his discovery on his own. Jesus must therefore bring him to the recognition that God was at work.

The action of God, however, does not somehow lessen Peter's action but, on the contrary, gives it its real value. Peter's words now become, in a literal sense, the word of God. This on two grounds: because his answer was elicited by Jesus' question, and because as formulated by Peter it was due to the inspiration of the Father who was secretly at work in Peter. In such a situation we have the very essence of what "word of God" means. God's word is not primarily a discourse to an audience, the verbalization of logical thought, or the projection of a great dream. It may also be those things, but it is first and foremost exchange and communication, invitation and response. God gives us His word in Jesus Christ so that it may be absorbed and eaten.

The Word of the Two Testaments

We can now understand why the two parts of the New Testament are both the word of God. In the Gospels Jesus speaks, in the apostolic letters Peter and his fellows reply. But Jesus' own word, as transmitted in the Gospels, is already a word that has been assimilated in faith and interpreted and translated; Jesus spoke Aramaic, and all the Gospels are in Greek. Conversely, all the words of Peter, Paul, or James are simply developments (adapted to different situations and experiences) of the original confession of faith that first established the relationship between God, Jesus, and believers: "You are the Messiah." At every point we have the same word and the same response: Jesus Christ.

We can also understand better now how the Old Testament too is the word of God. It is essentially such because of the Christian confession as Peter uttered it at Caesarea: "You are the Messiah." In thus confessing Jesus, Peter identified Him with the promise that sums up all of Israel's Scriptures. To make this identification, Peter had to recognize the same word of God in the form of expectation in the Scriptures and in the form of fulfillment in Jesus. There had of course been a long process of preparation leading up to Peter's discovery. The role of God's word in the Scriptures—Law, prophets, and Wisdom literature—had been so constantly and consciously asserted that it could not be forgotten. Yet, so long as the Word of God had not become flesh, so long as His Word had not elicited the response of faith from men in this world, and so long as His Word had not been spoken in our language and life, it would always be possible to think that Israel's history and spiritual odyssey was but one expression of man's religious yearnings and that the divine "words" which it possessed in such fulness were in fact only the highest witness to man's spiritual potential. That God did in fact speak through Israel's Scriptures and still speaks through them to all His children is something we have come to know for sure through Peter's confession of faith in Jesus Christ, the Word made flesh.

Chapter 18

Disciples of a Free Jesus

Does the Gospel make me free? The only worthwhile answer is: Look and see! Look at the lives of those who claim to follow the Gospel, and see whether or not they are the lives of free men. You can, of course, ask the question of these people, and they will surely give you an answer, but you have the right to distrust the answer. It is easy, after all, for men to think themselves free when in fact they are the victims of habit, or the dream or illusion of freedom. The surest way to know whether or not the Gospel makes men free is to look at the lives of those who base their existence on the Gospel.

There are such people among us today, and we can question and observe them. But there are others, twenty centuries back and apparently a world away from us. Their testimony is, however, irreplaceable, because they were the first to experience the Gospel and because they are proof that the experience was for them the experience of freedom. We refer, of course, to the authors of the New Testament, the men to whom we owe the Gospels and Letters, the men of the first Christian generation, the apostles and disciples of the Lord.

We may say indeed that they too might have fooled themselves and thought themselves free when in fact they were

232

forcibly led by a higher power. But one thing at least is sure: we can watch them live, for they made no effort to hide. They tell us quite simply of their experience, and while they may be deceiving themselves as they speak, the way they speak and react will surely not long deceive those who watch and listen. Jesus and His disciples after Him never lived behind a veil of mystery; they did not live private lives, but preferred to frequent the places where men gathered: the temple courts at Jerusalem, the synagogues, the public squares. They exposed their true selves everywhere, and in writing they wrote for people who wanted to read them. They wrote to tell what they believed; they opened themselves to others. And the picture they give of themselves is the picture of free men.

Before Their Judges

A man shows whether he be free or slave when he is in chains, threatened by violence, and gripped by fear. The men of whom we speak experienced these things, and often. Frequently we find them arrested and hauled before judges. The life of Jesus Himself is climaxed by an arrest, a double trial (before Caiphas and the Jewish court, and before Pilate and the Roman court), condemnation and execution. His experience was the event that dominated the lives of the apostles, according to the account of Acts. Peter, John, the Twelve, Stephen, Paul, Silas, and so many others whose names are unknown to us experienced in turn the same accusations, the same threats.

The clearest example is Peter. For having invoked the name of Jesus over a sick man and having publicly proclaimed that Jesus is risen, Peter is arrested and brought before the supreme council of the Jewish people. The council, made of the leaders in the priestly aristocracy, is the same one that sent Jesus to His death. On that night of condemnation Peter had tried to follow Jesus but had ended up denying Him publicly, while His Master was still in the very building and even though he, Peter, had just sworn fidelity. Now Peter is no longer in the courtyard but face to face with the very men who had condemned Jesus, and he knows that the same condemnation threatens him. The judges who question him feel themselves in a far stronger position now than they had been on Holy Thursday night. They had sent Jesus to His death because He claimed to come directly from God and to be God's very Son. Well, events had punished the blasphemer: Jesus died and God did not interfere; therefore, God was on the side of Jesus' judges.

Peter now challenges this interpretation which seemed so clear to everyone else; he claims that God had indeed been with Jesus and had proved it by raising Him from the dead. But Peter can give no tangible proof of this Resurrection; he can only state his own unquestioning faith: We saw Him, and He sends us to tell you. We are not more courageous or stronger today than the night we deserted our Master; all our strength comes from Him.

To dare brave human justice in this fashion and to overcome his fear, Peter must have been a free man.

Before Public Opinion

Freedom in the face of fear and danger is a tremendous thing and does honor to human nature. Greater still, and rarer, is the freedom of the man who dares think and speak out against the accepted wisdom of those around him. Today, when free thought is often just a name of a new conformism, we have difficulty in imagining the freedom of spirit that gave birth to Christianity. The Acts of the Apostles furnish us with striking testimonies to it.

Telling the Jerusalem authorities that Jesus was risen certainly took extraordinary courage, but we might possibly explain it by the deep impression Jesus had made on His disciples and the need they felt of showing their fidelity to Him. It would thus be a magnificent act of noble courage. But Peter goes further.

Facing this assembly of important people who ran everything in Jerusalem, Peter even tells them what their duty is: They must disown their past actions and commit themselves to Jesus. These men are the official, qualified representatives of the Jewish tradition, men formed by the observance of the Law and the detailed, eager study of the Scriptures. Now a few uninstructed, uneducated, inexperienced provincials from Galilee tell them that all the Israelite Scriptures have now been fulfilled and have thus manifested their full meaning—all the Jewish hopes, all the centuries of history, the whole proud spiritual heritage that was in fact unparalleled and knew itself to be religiously and morally superior to the rest of the world. Peter neither rejects nor plays down this great tradition; he simply says that in the person of Jesus it has found its full meaning and supreme embodiment, and that if these men wish to be faithful to their heritage, they must believe in this Messiah whom God has given to them.

Peter's bold action is an extraordinary manifestation of intellectual and religious freedom and the first example of Christian freedom over and against State and society. The Jewish world which the disciples of Jesus confront is not a corrupt pagan society. It has a magnificent understanding of the true God; it fosters authentic human values; it elicits a splendid fidelity. Yet, says Peter and his companions, it must be converted and recognize in Jesus Christ God's true face and in His message the only way which leads to God.

Free in the Spirit

In order thus to challenge the opinions and deepest convictions of their compatriots, the followers of the Gospel need far more than their own courage and convictions; they need the freedom which is the Holy Spirit's gift. This freedom is an experience both given and needing to be undergone. It is the experience of being able to act in ways of which they know they are radically incapable, of being able to resist under intolerable conditions, of being able to find ways of reaching the goal in situations to which there is no answer.

They can do all this because the Spirit is with them, that Spirit who is Himself Another and produces in them the words and actions of Another. He is the Spirit who is in very truth the Spirit, that is, the force that transforms them. The Spirit is not an alien presence; He does not replace our action with His, but on the contrary enables us to be masters of our own lives. He enables us to see and will and choose, but it is we who do the seeing and willing and choosing. In the presence of the high priest it is indeed Peter who speaks, with his Galilean accent, his provincial awkwardness, and his burning memory of his own weakness. He is not manipulated from outside nor does he simply repeat a lesson learned; he is not in a state of visionary exaltation, nor is his will alienated like that of a deranged person. No, he is a witness, and appeals to his own personal experience and the experience of those whom he addresses. He cannot escape from the reality of the men and events around him. Yet in the midst of his reality he bears witness to a radical transformation, for he acts as he has never acted before. Another dwells in him, and he has become a man in the face of other men. The Spirit dwells in him and he is free.

We Must

Peter is free so that he may obey. One of the most frequent words in the New Testament is "must." "We must obey God rather than men," Peter tells the high priest who has forbidden him to preach the Gospel of Jesus. But how can he be free if he must obey all these "musts"?

The best explanation is to look at Jesus. He is the first to speak in this fashion, and he does it frequently. Does this mean He is not free? On the contrary: He often speaks of a "must" precisely in order to assert His freedom with regard to a custom, an outlook, a principle currently accepted, or even a categorical law. "I must be about my Father's business," He tells His parents who have been searching for Him for three days. "We must fulfill all of God's demands," He tells John when the latter refuses to baptize Him. Despite the sabbath, He "must" cure a woman who has been sick for eighteen years. The father of the prodigal son "must" set convention aside and celebrate a

feast as the expression of his joy. Despite the lack of understanding on the part of His people and scandal given to His
disciples, Jesus "must" suffer and be rejected by His own.

In all these instances, then, a stricter law has been imposed
than the best grounded human judgments and the most sacred
practices of men. It is a law which leaves Jesus free in the face
of God's own Law, especially the law of the sabbath. But is
"freedom" still freedom when one acts freely in the name of
a law?

Is Jesus Free?

Freedom is an essential quality of Jesus and His activity. It
is not the freedom of someone who stands on the periphery of
everyday life and the usual ways of men, nor the freedom of
someone who challenges the law and declares war on it. Jesus
is neither an outsider nor a revolutionary; He does not resist
the law on principle, but normally lives within its framework.
He gives no evidence of being under constraint with regard to
the law, nor is He preoccupied with defining the law more precisely or justifying it or extending its scope. It seems to be for
Him a basic fact of life, something taken for granted. He is at
ease with it.

Yet He does not hesitate to abandon the law—not for the
pleasure of doing so nor on principle, but because He is faced
with a more urgent imperative. He must cure; He must save;
He must forgive.

Here we have the secret of His freedom: this inflexible demand He cannot evade. He is free, because it is not a demand
imposed from outside, but comes from the very depths of His
being; it is direct and spontaneous. He would not be Himself
any longer if He were to evade it. He cannot keep Himself
from curing the sick person who asks Him for a cure; He cannot keep Himself from the company of sinners and prostitutes.
He speaks indeed of a law or commandment given to Him. But
it is not a law written in His nature or temperament; He does
not act as He does because that is the way He is made and He

cannot act otherwise. If this were the case, He would be a slave.

The law comes to Him because He is not alone—Another always dwells in Him. He cannot live for a moment without the eyes of that Other being fixed on Him; He cannot live without the love with which His Father embraces Him. He is at every moment completely free because He never takes His eyes from His Father and because with every breath He opens Himself to the Father's love.

This is the source of His complete availability, His capacity for responding instantly and unreservedly to all whom He meets. This is why He has no need of elaborate plans. It is we who need plans and projects lest we be baffled and paralyzed by events as they come. Jesus can simply let men and events come upon Him; He will always be Himself, He will always give Himself to any comer. No one will be able to push Him around, lead Him astray, or impress Him.

Not that He is insensitive: on the contrary! The faith of the Roman officer, the generosity of the poor widow touch Him deeply. But neither fear of Herod nor the policy of Caesar will hold Him back for a single moment from the path He is following.

You Will Be Free

Himself free in regard to everyone, Jesus invites us all to be likewise free. He invites us to share His experience. The striking thing is that the invitation should be issued in the form of a law, the most demanding of all laws. The Sermon on the Mount is a series of imperatives more rigorous than the articles of the Decalogue: "You have heard the commandment imposed on your forefathers, 'You shall not commit murder; every murderer shall be liable to judgment.' What I say to you is: everyone who grows angry with his brother shall be liable to judgement" (Mt 5:21-22); "Should anyone press you into service for one mile, go with him two miles" (Mt 5:41).

The demands of the Sermon are absolute and practically unlimited. The man who adopts the principle of giving two hours of his time to someone who asks for one, or of depriving himself of necessities for the sake of someone who asks for what he has to spare, soon finds out he no longer belongs to himself and is being devoured. Where, then, is his freedom? It is not enough to say that the man has willed all this, for is it sure he would have willed it if he had foreseen it all?

And yet the true follower of the Gospel is free even in the most serious consequences of the choice he has made. He remains free because he is constantly choosing. The Gospel is always radical, calling constantly for a decisive choice and allowing no half measures. But its yoke is light. The obsession with perfection and the fear of failing to make an extra effort are not freedom but neither are they the Gospel. On the contrary, they sum up the attitude which Jesus condemns in the Pharisees, who always want to do more because they think themselves better than other people.

The Gospel makes men free because it concentrates all laws in the one great commandment: You shall love. You shall love others as you love God: putting your heart into it, making their concerns your own, seeking to be one with your brothers. You shall love God with the same seriousness and practicality you show when you must cure a sick person or save a life.

The Christian's troubles are never over. The person who commits himself to the Gospel always has more to do and endure; the suffering of men and the burden of sin weigh on him more heavily each day. Yet as he advances, he experiences freedom. Not in the form of proud, bitter satisfaction: "I wanted this," but in the form of a presence in his life and a voice that murmurs almost imperceptibly: "When you were young, you fastened your belt and went about as you pleased. Now another fastens your belt and leads you where you did not want to go." Wherever you are, you are sure that you reached this point because of Him: you are free.

Notes

NOTES TO CHAPTER 1

[1] *Dialogue des Carmélites* (Paris: Seuil, 1949), p. 136.

[2] Mt 26:63-66; Mk 14:60-64; Lk 22:66-71. John's Gospel does not record the appearance of Jesus before the Sanhedrin, but the whole of his Gospel shows that Jesus challenges men to adhere to Him through faith and that this faith consists in acknowledging Him as the Christ (1:41-45; 4:26; 9:22; 11:27), the Son of Man (3:14; 9:35), and the only Son of God (3:18.36; 5:23; 6:40; 10:36-38).

[3] Jn 1:11. "His own" probably means here the Jewish people. But there is a real analogy between Christ's relationship to His people and His relationship to mankind as a whole. In both cases He is not only a gift given by God from on high but also the fruit of the earth and the human race.

[4] Georges Bernanos, *Joy*, translated by Louise Varèse (New York: Pantheon, 1946), p. 236.

[5] Origen, *In Ezechielem homiliae* VI, 6; quoted in Henri de Lubac, *Histoire et esprit. L'intelligence de l'Ecriture d'après Origène* (Paris: Aubier, 1950), p. 241. Cf. Henri Crouzel, "La passion de l'Impassible," in *L'homme devant Dieu* (*Mélanges Henri de Lubac*) (Paris: Aubier, 1964), 1:269-79.

NOTES TO CHAPTER 2

[1] A sign of the link, which is essential to prophetic knowledge, between the future and the decisions men make in the present is the typical prophetic formula used in proclaiming future events: "Because you have committed such and such a sin—says the Lord—such and such will happen to you." The connection between the act done and its consequences is a necessary one, and yet everything

can still turn out differently if the sinner converts: that is the message the prophet brings.

[2] Hans Urs von Balthasar, *La foi du Christ* (Foi vivante 76; Paris: Aubier, 1968), p. 181.

[3] Maurice Blondel gave a good deal of thought to this mystery, which he felt to be the very heart of Christianity. "The essential distinction and de facto separation, which holds for every human being in this life, between the deeper personality and the awareness of the self at any given moment, allow ... a good deal of room for all that has been said or assumed about the 'growth' of our Lord. The growth did not affect His basic certainty of His divine sonship ... and His universal redemptive mission ... yet it was a real growth ... It left Him in a state of genuine becoming; He was not prefectly one with Himself but was subjected to the very real trials of obscurity and the effort to overcome it ... as long as He was in this present state of subjection and suffering" (in *Au coeur de la crise moderniste*, edited by René Marlé [Paris: Aubier, 1960], p. 245). Cf. Jean Mouroux, "Maurice Blondel et la conscience du Christ," in *L'homme devant Dieu* (*Mélanges Henri de Lubac*), 3:185-207.

NOTES TO CHAPTER 3

[1] It is not only in Hebrew and Aramaic that the word "brothers" is used both for brothers born of the same mother or father and for all the more or less close cousins in the family group. Such language is used in many parts of the world, wherever the clan is the real family unit.

NOTES TO CHAPTER 7

[1] Two small books by specialists, intended for a wider public, were recently published almost simultaneously, with similar titles and on the same subject: Oscar Cullmann, *Jesus and the Revolutionaries* (New York: Harper, 1970) and Martin Hengel, *War Jesus Revolutionär?* (Stuttgart: Calwer, 1970). The authors come to similar conclusions: Jesus was condemned by Pilate for political reasons, namely, the fear of an uprising against the authority of Rome, but there is no basis for regarding Jesus as an adherent, or even a sympathizer, of the Zealots.

[2] Cf. Josef Blinzler. *The Trial of Jesus*, translated by Isabel and Florence McHugh (Westminster, Md.: Newman, 1959). Cf. Pierre Benoit, "Le procès de Jésus selon J. Blinzler et P. Démann," in his *Exégèse et théologie* 1 (Paris: Cerf, 1961), pp. 312-315. We know

H. van der Kwaak, *Het Proces van Jezus* (Assen: Van Gorcum, 1969), only through the laudatory review by Pierre Benoit in *Revue biblique* 78 (1971), pp. 133-134.

[3] In his *Vom Zwecke Jesu und seiner Jünger*, published by Gotthold Ephraim Lessing among the *Wolfenbüttel Fragments*, part 7 (Braunschweig, 1778).

[4] Karl Kautsky, *Foundations of Christianity*, translated by Henry F. Mens (New York: Russell and Russell, 1953), pp. 309-316.

[5] Julius Wellhausen, *Einleitung in die drei ersten Evangelien* (2nd ed., 1926).

[6] Robert Eisler, *Jesus basileus ou basileusas* (2 vols.; Heidelberg: C. Winter, 1929-30. A second edition of volume 1 appeared in 1969). One of the most important critiques of the book was that of Maurice Goguel, "Jésus et le messianisme politique," *Revue historique* 162 (1929) 217-267.

[7] Joel Carmichael, *The Death of Jesus* (New York: Macmillan, 1962).

[8] Samuel George F. Brandon, *Jesus and the Zealots* (Manchester: Manchester University Press, 1967). Cf. review by Jean Daniélou in *Recherches de science religieuse* 56 (1968) 115-118. Brandon pursues his theses in *The Trial of Jesus of Nazareth* (London: Batsford, 1968).

[9] Georges Crespy, "Signification politique de la mort de Jésus," *Lumière et vie*, no. 101 (1971), p. 107.

[10] Cf. Morton Smith, "Zealots and Sicarii: Their Origins and Relations," *Harvard Theological Review* 64 (1971) 1-19. Smith attacks a position widely accepted and defended by historians of note, but we think his arguments are solid. In a case like this, in which confusion is dangerous, everything should be done to avoid it.

[11] The title "The King of the Jews" (Mk 15:26; Mt 27:37; Jn 19:19) was not drawn from the vocabulary of Jewish Messianism. It represents the claim of a political Messiah as defined by a Roman.

[12] He is thus called in Lk 6:15 and Acts 1:13. Mk (3:19) and Mt (10:4) call him *Kananaios*, which shows the root *qana'* or "zeal." Does the surname of Judas Iscariot contain the notion of *sicarius*? Cf. Oscar Cullmann, "Le douzième apôtre," *Revue d'histoire et de philosophie religieuse* 42 (1962) 133-140.

[13] Cf. Martin Hengel, *op. cit.*, p. 33, nn. 52-53. Cf. also Etienne Trocmé, "L'expulsion des marchands du Temple," *New Testament Studies* 15 (1968) 1-22.

[14] On the interpretation of this difficult passage (Lk 22:36), cf. Hengel, *op. cit.*, pp. 17 and 37.

[15] It was usual to take a short sword or dagger (a purely defensive

weapon), when going on a journey; even the Essenes carried one when they traveled. Cf. Flavius Josephus, *De bello judaico* II, 8, 4. On the difference between the pre-Easter mission in Galilee and the sending of the disciples by the risen Christ, cf. Heinz Schür-mann, "Die vorösterlichen Anfänge der Logientradition: Versuch eines formgeschichtlichen Zugangs zum Leben Jesu," in H. Ristow and K. Matthiae (eds.), *Der historische Jesus und der kerygmatische Christus* (Berlin: Evangelische Verlagsanstalt, 1960), pp. 342-370.

[16] It seems impossible, in any event, to follow the interpretation of Brandon in his *Jesus and the Zealots*, pp. 345-349. In Brandon's view, Mark has changed Jesus' words so as to make them more acceptable to Christians living in the Roman Empire; originally, the words would have been those of a typical Zealot, for whom to give God what belongs to Him evidently meant to make His land holy again by forcing the Romans out. But the words cannot be thus removed from their context, in which they are an answer to a question. Brandon's interpretation destroys the coherence of a passage which is among the most solidly constructed of the whole Gospel. See the detailed remarks of Marianus de Jonge in his review in *Vigiliae Christianae* 23 (1969), pp. 228-231.

[17] "Fox" is not an epithet dictated by fear. The fox can indeed be dangerous but it is also contemptible, unlike the lion or the wolf. Cf. Augustin George, "Jésus devant sa mort," *Lumière et vie*, no. 101 (1971), p. 37.

[18] Cf. Maurice Duverger, *Introduction à la politique* (Paris: Gallimard, 1964), p. 29.

[19] Cf. Claus Westermann, *Basic Forms of Prophetic Speech*, translated by Hugh Clayton White (Phila.: Westminster, 1967), pp. 130-136.

[20] Oscar Cullmann, in his *The Christology of the New Testament*, translated by Shirley C. Guthrie and Charles A. M. Hall (rev. ed.; Phila.: Westminster, 1963), is inclined to think that there is no question (in Mark) of a confession by Peter but simply of a reprimand addressed to him because of his false ideas of the Messiah (cf. the discussion on pp. 122-127). Anton Vögtle takes the same view in his "Messiasbekenntnis und Petrusverheissung: Zur Komposition Mt. 16, 13-23 Par.," *Biblische Zeitschrift* 1 (1957), p. 255. But this is to do violence to the text. A prohibition against someone's speaking, even if given in a stern tone, is not at all the same as blaming him for an error. Jean Delorme, in his "Aspects doctrinaux du second évangile," in *De Jésus aux évangiles: Tradition et rédaction dans les évangiles synoptiques (Mélanges Joseph Coppens)* 2 (Louvain: Ephemerides Theologicae Lovanienses, 1967),

p. 92, explains the point much better, we think: "the order to be silent, far from signifying a rejection, suggests rather that we are close here to the mystery of Jesus."

[21] The reservations are especially evident in Lk 22:67-68, but they are already clear in the words "It is you who say it" in Mt 26:64.

[22] Most editions put a break between verses 36 and 37. But, whatever be the source of the various sentences, the apostrophe to Jerusalem seems to be, in Matthew's joining of the sentences, the natural conclusion of the final judgment uttered by Jesus: "For this reason I shall send you prophets. . . . You will find your temple deserted."

[23] Cf. Heinrich Schlier, "Jésus et Pilate d'après l'Evangile selon saint Jean," in his *Le temps de l'Eglise* (Tournai: Casterman, 1961), p. 75.

[24] Cf. Jean Carmagnac, *Recherches sur le "Notre Père"* (Paris: Letouzey et Ané, 1969), pp. 110-117.

NOTES TO CHAPTER 8

[1] *Nouveau Testament: Traduction oecuménique de la Bible* (Paris: Cerf, and Les Bergers et les Mages, 1973), note *t* on Lk 10:42.

NOTES TO CHAPTER 13

[1] Paul-Louis Couchoud, *Le Dieu Jésus* (Paris: Gallimard, 1951), pp. 63-65.

NOTES TO CHAPTER 15

[1] Note, however, that Lk 12:12 is a doublet of Lk 21:15 and that in 12:12 Luke has kept the mention of the Spirit while in 21:15 "Spirit" is replaced by "I." In 12:12 there is a deliberate contrast with the sin against the Spirit of which 12:10 speaks.

[2] The meaning of Jn 3:34 is debated. It may mean: "He whom God has sent speaks the words of God who gives him the Spirit without measure." Or it may mean: "He whom God has sent speaks the words of God and gives the Spirit without measure." Both interpretations presuppose that the Spirit has been given in fulness, but we must note that the words are spoken not by Jesus but seemingly by John the Baptist and really by the evangelist who is bearing witness to the experience of Christians.

[3] It is quite probable that the anointing Peter mentions refers

to Jesus' baptism. Cf. I. de la Potterie, "L'onction du Christ," *Nouvelle revue théologique* 80 (1958), p. 231. It is true, of course, that according to Lk 1:35 Jesus was conceived by the power of the Holy Spirit and that He possessed the Spirit from the very beginning. It is likely, in addition, that the connection between anointing (which recalls Is 61:1) and baptism is a theme proper to Luke and that the early tradition connected the Isaian text rather with the Resurrection; cf. J. Dupont, *Etudes sur les Actes des Apôtres* (Paris: Cerf, 1967), p. 277. But the words "you know" necessarily refer to a public event, which neither the conception nor the Resurrection was.

[4] The Hebrew word represented by the Greek *eudokein* is *rasah, rasôn;* it is not easily translated. The word seems to belong to the language of the court and to signify the favor of the sovereign; cultic texts use it to mean that God accepts a sacrifice, and the prophets came to realize how lovingly God accepts a sacrifice that is worthy (Ps 51:20-21). This is the word God uses in telling the world of the joy He derives from the obedience of His servant (Is 42:1; 49:8). In Jesus, what had been a certainty foretold becomes an experience lived and communicated.

[5] "Son of God," even in the Gospels, does not necessarily have the meaning it has in the Christian creed. It seems clear, however, that for the evangelist the words do have their full meaning here. If "son of God" meant only a more or less special relation to God, the whole episode would lose almost all its point.

NOTES TO CHAPTER 16

[1] Balthasar, *op. cit.*, p. 181.

[2] Albert Vanhoye, S.J., *Situation du Christ: Hébreux I-VI* (Paris: Cerf, 1969), p. 323.

[3] Vanhoye, *op. cit.*, pp. 327-328.